Advance Praise for
We Refuse to Be Enemies

"Rehman and Ruby are each activists in the growing movement of Muslim-Jewish engagement. *We Refuse to Be Enemies* is an epiphany—a profoundly American book."

—Rabbi Burton L. Visotzky, PhD, Appleman Professor of Midrash and Interreligious Studies, Director, Milstein Center for Interreligious Dialogue, Jewish Theological Seminary

"I salute Sabeeha Rehman and Walter Ruby for their important contribution to strengthening Muslim-Jewish relations chronicled in *We Refuse to Be Enemies*. . . . A gripping account of how our two communities stood up for each other in the face of Islamophobia and anti-Semitism, and a prescription for how we can work together going forward to buttress pluralism, democracy, and religious liberty in this country. Not to be missed."

—Dr. Sayyid Syeed, President, Islamic Society of North America

"An essential book for the vital and important emergence of a Muslim-Jewish alliance in the United States. It takes more than a shared disgust with Donald Trump's myriad forms of bigotry to bridge the gap between Jews and Muslims in America. Now this book helps light the path. . . . Rehman and Ruby draw on personal experience, history, theology, and concrete examples of effective partnership to show the hard work that our two communities must continue to do."

—Samuel G. Freedman, award-winning author and professor at Columbia University Graduate School of Journalism

"Today, Pakistan and Israel do not recognize each other. But here are two brilliant writers—one rooted in Pakistan, the other in Israel—who do recognize, understand, and respect each other. Sabeeha Rehman and Walter Ruby, a Muslim and a Jew, are both proud of their faith traditions, while being wise enough to see the deep ties and bridges between them. Their stories and insights give us some hope for the future of the world, including the Middle East, at a time when their current state of affairs isn't too bright."

—Mustafa Akyol, Cato Institute Senior Fellow, opinion writer for the *New York Times*, and author of *Islam without Extremes: A Muslim Case for Liberty*

"This is a unique and remarkably compelling book written as a dialogue between a Muslim woman and a Jewish man. We learn what it takes to understand the many historical issues and experiences of both communities through their lens. They explore challenges as well as the unity among Jews and Muslims in the United States without losing their deep attachments to Pakistan and Israel. A vital contribution for dialogue and peace between Jews and Muslims."

—Mehnaz M. Afridi, PhD, Holocaust, Genocide and Interfaith Education Center at Manhattan College

"A Muslim woman living in an Orthodox Jewish neighborhood; a Jewish man hanging out with Arab Bedouins in Israel. Their stories of transformation and bringing communities together offers hope for America."

—Wajahat Ali, author of *The Domestic Crusaders* and contributing *New York Times* op-ed writer

"Sabeeha Rehman and Walter Ruby's work is at once daring and careful, forgiving and demanding. They share their stories with disarming honesty, having come to their positions through deep listening and personal experience. This book gives a taste of what real Muslim-Jewish dialogue can look like."

—Rabbi Jeffrey Saxe, Temple Rodef Shalom, and Dr. Maqsood Chaudhry, Founder and Trustee, McLean Islamic Center

"In this important book, Walter Ruby and Sabeeha Rehman give us unique insight into their own personal transformation journeys and their years of work on the ground to build authentic Jewish-Muslim relationships in the United States. The authors don't shy away from the difficult issues, but rather show how—through lived experience—they have been able to build lasting relationships that go far beyond the surface. This is a must-read for anyone looking to deepen their own interfaith engagement."

—Dr. Catherine Orsborn, Executive Director, Shoulder to Shoulder Campaign

"Having spent a lifetime building dialogue between members of different religious traditions, I am truly excited for the release of Walter Ruby and Sabeeha Rehman's *We Refuse to Be Enemies*, which focuses on efforts to bring together Jews and Muslims in peaceful coexistence. Given the massive importance of the Jewish-Muslim relationship, I consider Ruby and Rehman's work to be a prerequisite for anyone interested in interfaith dialogue."

—Dr. Akbar Ahmed, Ibn Khaldun Chair of Islamic Studies at the American University's School of International Service, former High Commissioner of Pakistan to the UK and Ireland

WE REFUSE
TO BE
ENEMIES

WE REFUSE
TO BE
ENEMIES

How Muslims and Jews Can Make Peace,
One Friendship at a Time

SABEEHA REHMAN
AND WALTER RUBY

Arcade Publishing • New York

First Edition

Arcade Publishing books may be purchased in bulk at special discounts for sales promotion, corporate gifts, fund-raising, or educational purposes. Special editions can also be created to specifications. For details, contact the Special Sales Department, Arcade Publishing, 307 West 36th Street, 11th Floor, New York, NY 10018 or arcade@skyhorsepublishing.com.

Arcade Publishing® is a registered trademark of Skyhorse Publishing, Inc.®, a Delaware corporation.

Visit our website at www.arcadepub.com.
Visit the authors' sites at sabeeharehman.com and bywalterruby.blogspot.com.

10 9 8 7 6 5 4 3 2 1

Library of Congress Cataloging-in-Publication Data is available on file.
Library of Congress Control Number: 2020951544

Cover design by Erin Seaward-Hiatt
Cover photo: © Jonathan Knowles/Getty Images (ecumenical symbols added)

ISBN: 978-1-951627-33-1
Ebook ISBN: 978-1-951627-63-8

Printed in the United States of America

To my husband, Khalid, my soulmate; and our sons Saqib and Asim, who have brought so much joy in our lives.

—Sabeeha

To my late parents, Stan and Helga, who would have loved to read this book; my son Gene, a compassionate and philosophical soul; and my life partner, Tanya, whose love gives me the strength and inspiration to engage the world each day.

—Walter

CONTENTS

PREFACE

We write these words soon after the inauguration of Joe Biden as president of the United States, an historic event offering hope that our country will return to core values of democracy and mutual understanding and respect between people of diverse racial, ethnic, and religious backgrounds. However, Donald Trump's success in convincing tens of millions of Americans that the 2020 presidential election was stolen from him and the storming of the U.S. Capitol by thousands of his fervid followers as well as the emergence of conspiracy theory–spewing extremists at high levels of the Republican Party, including in the halls of Congress, show that Trumpism—that potent brew of authoritarianism, nativism, mendacity, and fearmongering—is certain to remain a powerful factor in American political and cultural life for years to come. It is also all too clear that anti-Semitism, Islamophobia, and diverse forms of bigotry that Trumped stoked during his term as president are here to stay for the foreseeable future.

When we decided to write *We Refuse to Be Enemies*, our original intent was to chronicle the highly successful and largely unheralded work in which the two of us have been engaged for many years, building vibrant ties of communication, cooperation, friendship, and trust between grassroots American Muslims and Jews. However, as we began writing in earnest during the summer of 2017, we decided that our book should also serve as a manifesto for Muslims and Jews—the largest religious minorities in America—to join forces with like-minded Americans of conscience in a tenacious defense of the core American values of pluralism, inclusivity, and democracy. Safeguarding these values is vital to the safety, human rights, and continuation of a decent life for both our communities.

Consider the cascade of disturbing events that confronted us during those ominous months. Within days of coming to power in January 2017, President Trump had acted on his campaign rhetoric calling for a "complete and total shutdown of Muslims entering the United States" by issuing an executive order banning entry by refugees, immigrants, and travelers from seven majority Muslim countries. Despite multiple court rulings around the nation declaring the so-called Muslim ban to be unconstitutional, the Supreme Court would eventually uphold a later iteration of the ban, preventing virtually all travel from six Muslim and two non-Muslim countries.

Then, in August, we witnessed the shocking march of white supremacists and neo-Nazis in Charlottesville, Virginia, holding aloft tiki torches and chanting "Jews will not replace us," and heard a president of the United States blandly whitewash that evil by declaring that there were "very fine people on both sides." Just over a year later, on October 27, 2018, eleven Jews were savagely murdered while at prayer at the Tree of Life Synagogue in Pittsburgh by a neo-Nazi who blamed American Jews for supposedly enabling Black and Brown immigrants from—what Trump infamously termed—"shithole countries" to flood into the US. It was clear, we realized, that neither Jews nor Muslims were safe in a xenophobic America in which white supremacists, who hate both of our communities, were being validated by the holder of the highest office in the land.

Today, four years on, we are proud of how Muslims and Jews rose to the occasion during the Trump years; repeatedly standing up for each other and fighting bigotry together during multiple moments of crisis. Nevertheless, we cannot afford to let our guard down now. Given the ongoing spread of fear and loathing of the Other in this country, Jews and Muslims must continue to strengthen our alliance and remain active in a coalition of Americans of all faiths and ethnicities committed to upholding the transcendent belief set forth in the Declaration of Independence: that all human beings, regardless of religion, race, or ethnicity, are created equal and deserve an equal chance to realize life, liberty, and the pursuit of happiness. We must reignite the torch of welcome of Lady Liberty and ensure that America becomes again a nation of immigrants where people from countries around the world can realize their own version of the American Dream.

The struggle for a humane, pluralistic, and democratic America continues, and Jews and Muslims must remain at the forefront of that fight. If our communities can join forces as friends and allies, it will serve as a powerful, inspirational example to all Americans that people of diverse backgrounds can indeed come together to build a radiant future. Now is the time for Americans of all faiths, ethnicities, and orientations to step beyond their comfort zones, extend a hand to each other, and declare, "We refuse to be enemies."

WE REFUSE
TO BE
ENEMIES

Part 1

STARTING THE CONVERSATION

Embracing Our Commonalities

CHAPTER 1

WE REFUSE TO BE ENEMIES

We have witnessed humanity at its finest. We have been there in moments when members of our communities have come together, cast aside fear, and embraced each other. We have tasted the joy and felt the promise.

This Is Heaven

"We need two Muslims at this table," a Jewish man stood up and called out.

A Muslim man from another table stood up. "We need a Jew at our table."

I was at an interfaith feast, and the emcee had announced the ground rules: each table had to have an equal number of people from each faith. Voices were calling out for a Jew, a Muslim; men and women were leaving their seats to make room for the Other, crisscrossing one another as they rushed to fill the seats, a Muslim taking the seat vacated by a Jew, a Jew nodding thank-you to the Muslim offering her chair and beaming at the welcoming roar of their tablemates.

Rabbi Roly Matalon took the stage for the invocation.

"This is heaven," he said. "When I hear someone call out, 'We need a Muslim, we need a Jew,' this is heaven."

In that moment, I, a Muslim woman, found my lost paradise—for just an instant. I had witnessed a glimpse of the future I want for my children, my grandchildren, and my country.

Making a Joyful Noise

It was the moment when it all came together—an eclectic concert at which I, a Jewish man, experienced an ecstatic realization of the dream for which I had worked for nearly a decade: Muslim-Jewish friendship and trust taking flight.

The concert, "Together in the City of Angels: A Musical Celebration of Muslim-Jewish Unity," was held at the site of LA's historic first synagogue building, built in 1906, which houses a variety of interfaith activities, including the nation's first women's mosque. It featured Judeo, a raucous band devoted to traditional Jewish klezmer music, and Riad Abdel Gawad, a hypnotic musician specializing in the oud, a lute-like Middle Eastern string instrument. Noor-Malika Chishti of the LA Sufi community articulated the exuberant energy of the celebration: "Not only should Muslims and Jews work together fruitfully, but we also must celebrate together, share our heritages, and make a joyful noise."

It was a joyful noise indeed: an explosion of musical effervescence that reached its climax when the diverse musicians came together in a jam session that brought the audience of four hundred out of their seats to link arms and form a conga line that snaked around the auditorium. In that blessed old synagogue, they created an island of love; a safe sacred space in which Muslims and Jews could step beyond the poison of the past century and embrace each other as friends, allies, and fellow human beings flowing from the same source.

The pure joy shared by so many of us in that magical encounter showed me that Muslim-Jewish outreach wasn't just about talking earnestly, finding commonalities, and forming alliances. Under the right circumstances, Muslims and Jews could truly love one another.

We Couldn't Have Been More Different

The two of us, coauthors of this book, are an American woman and man of about the same age (late sixties/early seventies), but of vastly different life experiences. One of us is a devout Muslim who immigrated to America from a traditional culture; the other an iconoclastic, non-believing American-born Jew shaped by the utopian spirit of the 1960s.

Sabeeha:

I was born in Pakistan. I came to America in 1971 at the age of twenty to join my Pakistani husband, Khalid, who was doing his medical residency in New York. In the ensuing decades I raised a family, participated in the building of a Muslim community in New York, and recently launched a new career as a writer, sharing my love of Islam with my fellow Americans. Growing up in Pakistan, I had never met a Jew and viewed all Jews through the lens of the Israeli-Palestinian conflict.

Walter:

I'm an American-born Jew who spent several of my formative years as an adolescent and young adult living in Israel. I grew up in the suburbs of Pittsburgh and Chicago, with a year in Israel from age eleven to twelve. In those days, I had never met a Muslim and viewed Muslims through my readings of the stridently pro-Zionist novel *Exodus*, published to great acclaim by Leon Uris in 1958.

Sabeeha and Walter:

As young people, we couldn't have been farther apart in our political leanings and cultural orientations, not to mention our tribal loyalties. Yet, after encountering the "Other," each of us experienced a profound change of heart and outlook, moving toward a universalist approach that emphasized the shared humanity of all people, regardless of faith or ethnicity. We became actively engaged in interfaith dialogue, each on our separate tracks, until one afternoon in 2009 when our paths crossed.

Walter:

I was planning the Weekend of Twinning—pairing mosques with synagogues—to hold joint events in cities all over America and Europe. At the time, I was serving as the Muslim-Jewish Program Director for the Foundation for Ethnic Understanding (FFEU), an organization committed to building relations between Muslims and Jews. One of the calls I made was to the American Society for Muslim Advancement (ASMA).

Sabeeha:

And I answered the phone. I was volunteering as the director for interfaith relations. I was floored. I had no idea that there was an organization working specifically to build Muslim-Jewish relationships. A week later, we were sitting around the table in our office.

From that moment on, we often found ourselves in the same space, doing the same work, with the same purpose, be it delivering food packages on the Lower East Side to homeless and hungry New Yorkers from a van operated by Muslims Against Hunger or taking part in a Muslim-Jewish twinning event at Congregation B'nai Jeshurun on the Upper West Side.

A Moment of Crisis

In November 2016, America elected a new president with an exclusionary credo. Abruptly, Islamophobia and anti-Semitism became the new normal, and amid heightened xenophobia, the safety and well-being of both American Muslims and Jews had become very much at risk. In this maelstrom, we knew we had to write this book. It was to be a clarion call for building Muslim-Jewish friendship, affirming our shared moral values and our common humanity.

We recognize that in this hour of crisis, Muslims and Jews cannot afford to let the Israeli-Palestinian conflict divide us. At this pivotal moment in American history, we need to come together as core constituencies of an interfaith alliance to preserve pluralism, religious freedom, and democracy.

Can we make that vision of *heaven* and a *joyful noise* a reality even in these dangerous times? Our experience tells us: *yes, we can*. Indeed, that is the experience we want to share with you: one of initiating heartfelt communication, listening deeply, and in time coming to know each other as individuals, rather than as part of a collective "Other." At first, we came together to learn about each other's faith traditions. Then, as we strengthened fragile ties of friendship and trust, our relationship evolved into a joint commitment to stand up for each other and to defend religious freedom and human and civil rights for Muslims, Jews, and Americans of all backgrounds. We have understood that whatever our differences—and they are considerable—as two individuals and members of two faiths that uphold the values of kindness, compassion, and service, and as fellow Americans who strive to succeed in our own lives and leave a better world for our children and grandchildren, we have much more in common than what separates us.

In this book, the two of us are role-modeling profound and sustained communication and putting the evolution of our friendship under the microscope. We are coming together as a proud Muslim and a proud Jew to explore our differences, celebrate our commonalities, and embrace our shared humanity. In the process, we are appealing to all Jews and Muslims—and ultimately, to people of all faiths and ethnicities—to undertake such personally transformative outreach and join us in that collective bear hug.

Realizing the Promise of America

Through our extended conversation, we have come to understand that we *can* have it both ways—three ways, in fact. We can be wholly Jewish or Muslim, be wholly American, and embrace all of humanity. We can be deeply connected to Israel or Pakistan, be patriotic Americans, and hold the universal truths to be self-evident. In this book, we will share how we made it to our promised land; how we have each evolved from particularistic visions celebrating the warmth and beauty of embracing one's own faith, ethnicity, and culture to a universalistic ethic that affirms the goodness and equality not only of Muslims and Jews, but of all of humanity.

Yet, we remain lovers of our own peoples. A big part of who we are grew out of our formative years, which Sabeeha spent growing up in Pakistan and which American-born Walter spent living in Israel, once as a child on the cusp of adolescence, and later as a young adult. Each of us needed to feel at one with our own, to relish and cherish what is sublime and joyous in our respective traditions, before we could reach beyond our communities and fully embrace the Other.

We humbly offer this account of mutual discovery and inspiration based on lessons drawn, to show how precious is the zone of interfaith togetherness; how easily it can dissolve; and how Muslims, Jews, and people of all faith, ethnic, and racial backgrounds can stand united and fight to preserve it.

Let the record show that neither of us is an imam or rabbi, and neither claims to be a religious scholar, historian, politician, or moral paragon. Rather, we are an everyday Muslim American and American Jew, each of whom has made plenty of mistakes along the way. Yet we've both been on this planet for a fair chunk of time, and over the years we've learned a few things about the complicated relationship between our peoples. Here, as equal citizens of these United States, and on the basis of separation of church/mosque/synagogue and state, we can build a resplendently pluralistic society where people of all faiths and ethnicities can connect with each other while fulfilling their God-given potential.

Yes, our message is about Muslim-Jewish brotherhood and sisterhood, but it is ultimately bigger than our two communities. If Muslims and Jews, long alienated from each other by mutual antagonism over the Middle East conflict, can join together as friends and allies sharing common values, it would inspire Americans of all backgrounds with the conviction that diverse communities *can* unite in pursuit of a just cause and overcome the darkness of fear and bigotry now afoot in the land. We must come together to ensure the country we all love survives as a pluralistic and democratic entity. America can and must be a place where people of all races, religions, beliefs, and orientations celebrate our commonalities and differences, a place where all of us can live together in peace, brotherhood, and mutual embrace. Now is the moment for action.

CHAPTER 2

MUSLIMS AND JEWS BELONG TOGETHER

Coming from such different backgrounds, what led each of us to engage in Muslim-Jewish relationship building?

Sabeeha:

As a Muslim mother, I was driven by my concern for my children's future in the US, later by the necessity to survive in a post–9/11 era, and now in a post–2016 election era. My approach was organic at first, totally unplanned, and later morphed into grassroots activism, totally planned.

Walter:

As an American-born Jew, I was motivated by my desire, in the wake of the collapse of the Oslo peace process of the 1990s between Israelis and Palestinians, to commence an alternative path to peace and reconciliation: bringing together Muslims and Jews in America and around the world. The idea was to prevent the poison of the Israeli-Palestinian conflict from spreading to the many countries in which Muslims and Jews live side by side and to build a global Muslim-Jewish movement for reconciliation and cooperation that eventually would inspire Israelis and Palestinians to renew their own efforts to come together. My work began as a top-down strategy led by faith leaders, which soon led to grassroots initiatives and one-on-one encounters.

What was the impact of our respective efforts? Did we face resistance? Setbacks? What were some of the most inspiring encounters? Did Muslim-Jewish relationship building ultimately work?

Let's find out, and why don't you be the judge?

Sabeeha:

Interfaith Dialogue by the Sidewalk

For me, it started with sidewalk chats, mothers talking to mothers. In the 1970s, I was a stay-at-home mom living in the Willowbrook section of Staten Island, New York. It was only after we moved in that we noticed most of our neighbors were Orthodox Jews. Our new neighborhood was in close proximity to the Young Israel shul (synagogue). My neighbors and I—some Orthodox, some Reform Jews—would be hanging out on the sidewalk, watching our children ride their Big Wheels. How did small talk move into an interfaith conversation? Perhaps when I extended a dinner invitation to Gail and the exchange led to a discussion on dietary restrictions. I remember Gail, a Reform Jew, saying, "I never knew that Muslims don't eat pork either." Within a year, our conversations had graduated to Interfaith 201. If you walked by, you were likely to hear "When does Ramadan start?" or "How long will your sukkah tent be up?" No longer were we gasping at the shock of first revelation, as in "You mean when you fast you can't drink water either?" or "Aren't you cold at night in the sukkah?"

Nothing got the Jewish ladies more excited than talking about arranged marriages. And I loved to enchant them with my arranged marriage story. They would pore over the photos in my red wedding album, swoon over my glittering red dress, wonder at the bride with eyes downcast, and delve into the tradition of separating the wedding couple during the religious ceremony. I would explain that in Islam, sex outside marriage is forbidden. Hence, in some cultures, dating is not permitted, and therefore the only solution to finding a partner is through an arranged marriage. One of the ladies, whose son was marrying a Catholic girl, said, "I wish

I could have arranged my son's marriage to a nice Jewish girl." Speaking of which, when Nancy showed me her white wedding album, it was my turn to be enchanted by the canopy and crushing of the champagne glass.

"Has a groom ever gotten hurt by the shattered glass?" I asked.

We were discovering that we could enjoy one another's differences. As winter approached, we would huddle indoors and exchange notes.

"Does one name a baby after an elder relative?" Nancy was pregnant.

"No. It would be disrespectful to yell at your child calling him by an elder's name. How about you?"

"Only if they are deceased." Nancy explained that it is an honor for a deceased person to have a relative named after him or her.

We would nod with agreeable comments, like "It's all about respect for the family." In their company, I felt at ease expressing my "Muslimness." We didn't always understand one another. One day I complimented my neighbor on her beautiful hairdo and how her hair was always so well-coiffed. She accepted the compliment with a nod. When she left, Gail gave me an education.

"She wears a wig."

"Oh! Is she getting chemo?"

"No! She is Orthodox, and married Orthodox Jewish women cover their hair."

"So instead of wearing a scarf like some Muslim women, they wear a wig?" I asked.

Got it. No, I didn't get it. I had always assumed that the idea behind covering the hair—at least in the Muslim tradition—was for modesty, and, as I said, the wig my neighbor wore enhanced her beauty. But I didn't probe further. I didn't want to come across as questioning tradition.

There would be many more Gails and Nancys—mothers sharing their stories—each opening the door of understanding wider, letting the light in and bringing me closer to my Jewish sisters. It was only a matter of time before you heard me say, "Why, some of my best friends are Jewish!"

From Garden Chats to Grassroots Activism

It wasn't enough to have Jewish friends. As my two boys started school in 1977 and 1980, Khalid and I wanted a platform where we could make our Muslim voices heard. We were feeling the sting of the sound bites on TV—*Arab terrorists*. It had become so predictable that whenever an attack took place, we knew we would be encountering the term *Palestinian terrorists* over and over again. Our two little boys were hearing these high-pitched voices blaring from the TV. *How does it make them feel? What effect is it having on their little hearts?* Our son Saqib was in kindergarten. I shuddered at the thought of him coming home one day and saying, "Mummy, why are the boys in school calling me a terrorist?" Something had to be done to dispel that image before it eroded our children's self-esteem.

Khalid and I were pro-Palestinian. On the geopolitical spectrum, my Jewish friends and I were on opposing sides, but in the social arena, we dined together, shopped together, compared mommy notes, carpooled for soccer games, exchanged books, went to the movies—the usual stuff that friends do. How does one reconcile friendship with politics, or religious commonalities with political division? Maybe you don't have to reconcile these differences. What if you agree to disagree and build on what we have in common? Would that recipe work? And what would it achieve? Well, for one, it would hopefully dispel the image that Muslims are violent. Secondly, it would impress upon Muslims how close their beloved Islam is to the Jewish ethos and how similar our values are. Finally, it would allow us to get to know one another as fellow Americans and build trust.

Why the need for trust building? In my living room conversations, when immigrant Muslims of Pakistani descent gathered over a meal and the talk shifted to current events in the Middle East, one could sense the tension, particularly among the women. Some were homemakers who preferred to socialize among their own—understandable for first-generation immigrants. They had not been exposed to Jews and viewed all Jews through the lens of the Israeli-Palestinian conflict. Men—not social animals to begin with (sorry, guys)—limited their interaction with their Jewish colleagues to 9-to-5 professional relationships. Saying to them, "I know many Jewish families, and they are all really nice people" simply wasn't going to cut it. They would have to experience interaction firsthand. Likewise, I didn't want my Jewish friends to believe that my husband and I were outliers, the "not-like-the-rest-of-them" kind of Muslims.

Well, if you don't make an effort to get to know one another, then how are you going to get to know one another? You are just going to continue to believe what you always believed or what is fed to you. Right? So, where does one begin?

Resistance from within the Muslim Community

There was one person I knew who was a step or two ahead of us. Dr. Faroque Khan, a founding member of the Islamic Center of Long Island (ICLI) and a friend, started holding interfaith dialogues at ICLI. That was the first time I heard the term "interfaith." Fascinated by the concept, Khalid and I decided to attend. People of all faiths had gathered at the mosque to talk and to listen. I recall what a Jewish woman said to me: "Let's just agree that there are things we won't agree on and move on." She had never missed a meeting.

Well, why should we be left behind? If they can do it on Long Island, we can do it on Staten Island. Khalid and I broached the subject with our community members. We got pushback. "What's the point of it? We can't solve the Israeli-Palestinian issue. We need to focus on teaching our children about Islam. Interfaith dialogue will dilute our efforts. It's no use. Thanks to the media, we won't be able to change hearts and minds."

The community support was just not there—at least, not yet. However, there was no stopping Khalid and me from going ahead on our own. It's a free country—thank God! To my surprise and delight, it turned out to be more than a free country. America revealed itself as a nation brimming with people with open hearts and open minds, yearning to learn and get to know the Muslim next door. As a prominent physician in Staten Island and president of the Richmond County Medical Society, Khalid was well known. All he had to do was ask, sometimes not even ask, and faith and civic communities would open their doors, inviting him—and sometimes me as well—to talk about Islam. Khalid and I had to scramble to educate ourselves, reading up and reaching out to seasoned speakers with urgent pleas for "Any advice?" Dr. Khan advised, "If you don't know the answer to a question, just say, 'I don't have the answer, but I can get back to you,' and then take their phone number and call them back." This was before the days of email, so each unanswered question became the springboard for our continuing education and further dialogue/future conversations.

Word of mouth and face-to-face contact are powerful. We were holding interfaith dialogues in places of worship, with professional associations, even on TV. Khalid got himself recruited as a columnist on Islam for the local newspaper, the *Staten Island Advance*. For ten years, he wrote a monthly column and became the go-to Muslim for the media. Not bad, right? We had transitioned from sidewalk chats to grassroots interfaith dialogue. And it was working! People were saying, "We had no idea that Islam gave women all these rights," or "Your values are so similar to ours." A man serving meals at the hospital cafeteria counter said to Khalid, "I read your article about a Muslim father's advice to his son, and now I know what advice to give my son." But despite the work that we and other Muslim pioneers in interfaith relations were engaged in, the balance remained tilted. There were more non-Muslim organizations opening their doors to Muslims than the other way around. It would take a tragedy of immense proportions—9/11—to change that.

Walter:

Turning Point

Meanwhile, as Sabeeha was learning the skills of interfaith engagement, I covered Israeli-Palestinian relations as a journalist and commentator for Israeli and American Jewish newspapers. By the early 2000s, having spent nearly three decades as a journalist, I was feeling bereft as I witnessed the tragic flameout of the Oslo peace accords. I watched with anguish while the prospects for Israeli-Palestinian peace and reconciliation, which had seemed so close to fruition during the 1990s, turned to ashes in the wake of the failed 2000 Camp David summit between President Bill Clinton, Palestinian president Yasir Arafat, and Israeli prime minister Ehud Barak and the subsequent eruption of the Second Intifada. Searching about fitfully for another path to reconciliation, I began exploring whether efforts to build Jewish-Muslim ties in the Diaspora (herein defined as the world beyond Israel-Palestine and Dar-al-Islam, Muslim-majority countries) might prove to be part of the answer. As a reporter, I had covered the blossoming of one of the first successful dialogues between two prominent

Jewish and Muslim communal leaders in America, Rabbi Jerome Davidson of Temple Beth El of Great Neck, Long Island, and Dr. Faroque Khan of the Islamic Center of Long Island (the leader who had inspired Sabeeha and Khalid Rehman with his interfaith efforts), and what I had witnessed influenced me. The experience of living through 9/11 in New York, witnessing firsthand the enormous damage religious zealotry and radicalization can cause if allowed to fester, also drove me to act.

At that bleak moment, I had no idea just how fruitful the path of strengthening Muslim-Jewish relations might turn out to be. Not, that is, until I participated in and reported on the World Congress of Imams and Rabbis in Seville, Spain, in March 2006. The congress was convened by Hommes de Parole, a French interfaith organization created by Alain Michel, a humanitarian visionary. Among the three hundred participants were a delegation from the Chief Rabbinate of Israel and a group of imams from Gaza and the West Bank. There were imams in attendance from places like Pakistan, Bangladesh, and Indonesia who had never met a Jew and prominent rabbis from Europe and North America who had never had a meaningful conversation with a Muslim.

What everyone at the congress imbibed was an infectious spirit of mutual discovery, with many manifesting a deep intellectual excitement about commonalities in the two faiths few had been aware of. These included a web of similarities between *halacha* and *shari'ah*, including injunctions enjoining the giving of charity to succor the poor, hungry, homeless, and others in society most in need; the importance of modesty, performing ablutions, and fasting; and in dietary, circumcision, marriage, and burial customs.

Many of the participants had studied portions of this material years or decades earlier during their theological training. Yet it is one thing to learn about the Other from academic sources taught by a member of your own faith, and very much another to directly explore commonalities and differences in heartfelt discussion with religious leaders from the other faith. Participants basked in a warm atmosphere of ecumenism and the mutual celebration of a common Abrahamic heritage, which was expressed in joint recitation of Jewish and Muslim prayers and nightly jam sessions between Sufi and Jewish mystics strumming ouds and guitars.

I vividly recall one impassioned discussion between an imam from the town of Beit Hanun in the Gaza Strip and a rabbi from Sderot, a small Israeli town hard on the Gaza border, which had been the target of missiles from Gaza that killed and injured several Israelis. As a knot of Muslim and Jewish attendees gathered around them, the rabbi from Sderot spoke about a young woman—a cousin of his—who had been killed by a missile fired from the environs of Beit Hanun. He then added emotionally that despite the death of his beloved cousin and the continuing carnage caused by the missiles, he realized that people on the other side had also suffered greatly from the conflict and that retaliatory violence was not the answer. The rabbi concluded that he deeply desired peace and reconciliation with the people of Beit Hanun and Gaza.

The imam responded by expressing sorrow for the death and destruction in Sderot but explained that Israel's sealing off Gaza from the world was causing devastation for its people, and that this terrible situation was pushing desperate Gazans to sanction violence. The imam pleaded with the rabbi to urge his government to end the blockade and allow food and supplies to cross the border. The rabbi responded that he would see what he could accomplish, and the two men then embraced tearfully.

For me, witnessing that embrace was not only deeply moving but personally transformative. Here were two devout clerics figuratively stepping across the tightly sealed border separating their communities to hug each other and declare that their shared humanity transcended politics and enjoined them to work together for the good of both peoples.

That embrace remains a sacred moment for me today, fourteen years later, even though both the Hamas and Israeli governments effectively ensured that no such cross-border relief effort ever happened. Hamas refused to countenance any change in its rigid policy of non-recognition of Israel's right to exist, and Israel rejected international pleas that it relax its smothering blockade of Gaza. Instead of relief and healing, we have seen horrific cross-border wars between Israel and Gaza in 2009, 2012, and 2014, which killed thousands of Palestinians and a much smaller but significant number of Israelis. We have seen many more deadly clashes in the years since, such as the Israeli army shooting dead nearly two hundred Palestinians, including thirty-two children, who marched to the border fence in 2018.

Nevertheless, despite the terrible bloodletting in and around Gaza that continues to this day and the overall downward trajectory of Israeli-Palestinian relations, the embrace of the imam from Beit Hanun and the rabbi of Sderot, and the collective embrace of imams and rabbis from around the world at the congress in Seville, created for me a new paradigm and a new hope.

After the congress, I understood that the two religions and the millions who devoutly practiced them could be part of the solution to the Israeli-Palestinian conflict and Muslim-Jewish estrangement throughout the world, rather than being an endemic part of the problem. Suddenly anything seemed possible. If we could get Muslims and Jews talking to each other, we could at the very least prevent the violent dynamic of Beit Hanun/Sderot from spreading.

Resistance from within the Jewish Community

The desire to recreate Seville-like moments of mutual embrace would impel me to search for opportunities to bring Jewish and Muslim faith leaders to the table. It wasn't easy. Some in my own American Jewish community were catching the new wind and reaching out to Muslims, but there was plenty of resistance as well.

In the summer of 2006, Rabbi Eric Yoffie, president of the Union for Reform Judaism (URJ), gave a well-received speech at the national convention of the Islamic Society of North America (ISNA), calling for the building of cooperation between the two communities. ISNA and the URJ subsequently collaborated to write a guidebook called *The Children of Abraham* for mosques and synagogues to use in relationship building, and several flagship synagogues and mosques across the country undertook dialogue.

However, after this hopeful beginning, there was little sustained follow-up on the part of URJ, which cited budgetary constraints. Meanwhile, two other major national Jewish organizations, the Anti-Defamation League (ADL) and American Jewish Committee (AJC), insisted that the Jewish community should not talk to either ISNA or the Council on American-Islamic Relations (CAIR), claiming that the latter was fundamentally anti-Israel and the former tainted by alleged murky, decades-old ties with the Muslim Brotherhood, a dubious claim relentlessly pushed by a coterie of Washington-based self-described researchers like Steven Emerson and Daniel Pipes, whose stock in trade, barely disguised under the cover of scholarship, appeared to be anti-Muslim propaganda. The AJC and ADL's opposition to working constructively with ISNA, a policy that continued until 2016, made moving forward on Muslim-Jewish relations even more difficult.

A Very Rocky Start

The glacial pace of outreach to Muslims by the American Jewish establishment left an opening for Rabbi Marc Schneier, founder and president of the Foundation for Ethnic Understanding (FFEU), upon which he decided to act. Now in his early sixties, Schneier is an Orthodox rabbi with a highly unorthodox style, often brash and self-promoting but with a generally liberal political perspective and an enduring commitment to strengthening relations between American Jews and minority communities like African Americans and Hispanics.

In the wake of the devastating riots in 1991 when African American youths attacked Orthodox Jews on the streets in Crown Heights, Brooklyn, and one visiting Torah scholar from Australia was knifed to death, Rabbi Schneier vowed to rebuild the Black-Jewish alliance of the civil rights era in the 1960s, which many leaders in both communities considered all but dead. His outreach effort included leading the way in making the MLK holiday, celebrating the life and legacy of Dr. Martin Luther King Jr., almost obligatory in synagogues across the United States and building ties with Black leaders largely boycotted by mainstream Jewish leaders, such as Jesse Jackson and Al Sharpton. By 2005, Schneier was ready for an even greater challenge: improving Muslim-Jewish relations. After a visit to a Muslim school in Queens that I arranged, the rabbi launched his initiative in November 2006. He invited Imam Omar Abu Namous, then the leading imam at New York's most prominent mosque, the Islamic Cultural Center of New York (ICCNY) on East 96th Street in Manhattan, to visit his New York synagogue. At the very least, the visit by the seventy-two-year-old, Palestine-born-and-bred Abu Namous would create some buzz.

It accomplished that and more. Abu Namous, who later said he had accepted the invitation believing he would be attending a private meeting with Rabbi Schneier, instead walked into the synagogue to find that he was to participate in a public dialogue with the rabbi, attended by hundreds of congregants and representatives of the media, including myself, who covered the event for the *New York Jewish Week*. (The miscommunication may have been due to language issues, as Abu Namous's conversational English appeared to be a little shaky.) After a few desultory questions about similarities and differences in the two faiths, the moderator began pressing Abu Namous to explain why Muslim leaders were not speaking more forthrightly against terrorism.

Abu Namous responded that there were extremists among adherents of Christianity and Judaism as well, mentioning Israel's deputy prime minister, Avigdor Lieberman, as one example. That turned the conversation into a heated debate on Israel and the Palestinians, culminating in an exasperated comment by Abu Namous that, given Israel's massive settlement buildup on the West Bank, he saw no viable two-state solution. He urged instead the creation of a binational Israeli-Palestinian state with full equality for both peoples. That opinion was far more outrageous to mainstream Jewish ears in 2006 than it would become later. Amid groans and catcalls from the congregation, the moderator pleaded with audience members to remain civil and then quickly declared the dialogue closed.

In the Jewish community, there was widespread agreement that the encounter had been a disaster and was not likely to be repeated. Yet, rather than back away, Rabbi Schneier characteristically determined to push forward undeterred, albeit ready to learn from mistakes committed in the first go-round. He made a conciliatory call to Abu Namous to thank him for his visit and urged him to arrange a Muslim-Jewish program to take place at the 96th Street Mosque on Martin Luther King Day 2007, which Schneier promised he would attend together with his good friend Martin Luther King III. Abu Namous may have seen the occasion as an opportunity to clear the ICCNY of the stigma created a few years earlier by his predecessor, Imam Muhammad Gemeaha, who had charged that Zionists, supposedly in command of the nation's air traffic control towers, colluded in the 9/11 attacks. In any event, he invited Schneier to the mosque, with both men agreeing that the Israel-Palestine issue would not be on the agenda.

The second meeting went much better. Speakers on both sides were on their best behavior and promised to move Muslim-Jewish relations forward in fulfillment of the vision of Martin Luther King. Afterward, Schneier was able to point out that he had achieved something tangible: giving a well-received speech at New York's largest and most prestigious mosque to a mixed audience of Muslims, Jews, and Christians.

Two Steps Forward, One Step Back

In 2007, Rabbi Schneier invited me to work in a consulting capacity on a project to create a national summit of imams and rabbis in New York, with the participation of one imam and one rabbi each from thirteen cities across the United States and Canada. I came up with the idea of holding three separate discussions: "Sharing Our Religious and Cultural Commonalities," "Defining an Agenda for Joint Action on the American Scene," and "How American Jews and Muslims Can Act Together As Allies in Times of Crisis."

From the start, there was a warm, upbeat, and mutually curious atmosphere at the summit, held that November, that reminded me a lot of Seville. Most of the rabbis and imams had already dipped their toes into Muslim-Jewish relations locally and were grateful to find a sponsor like FFEU ready to give them a national platform. If any of the participants on either side had doubts whether taking part in a Muslim-Jewish summit would be accepted as kosher or halal by their respective establishments, they received strong positive reinforcement from two heavyweight speakers from their respective communities. These were Dr. Sayyid Syeed, national director of ISNA, and Ronald Lauder, president of the World Jewish Congress (WJC), who was widely seen as a hard-liner on Israel-related issues. At the end of the summit, participants issued a statement calling for the creation of an annual event spotlighting the growth of Muslim-Jewish engagement through myriad local events linking mosques and synagogues in as many cities as possible across North America. This was the genesis of the annual Weekend of Twinning, which would be held for the first time in November 2008.

After the success of the summit, Rabbi Schneier hired me in March 2008 as FFEU's Muslim-Jewish program director.

Sabeeha:

Keep Politics Out of It

As Walter was entering the world of Muslim-Jewish dialogue, I was doing the same in a Muslim-Jewish-Christian context. In both cases, the rules for engagement were similar: (1) Let each group define itself; (2) Enter with an honest intent to listen; (3) Focus on commonalities— our shared heritage and shared values; (4) Stress pluralism as enjoined by the faith; and (5) Keep politics mainly out of it, which in the Muslim-Jewish context means agreeing to disagree respectfully on the Israeli-Palestinian conflict while keeping the focus on working together here at home. The above ground rules had worked for the clergy; they could work for us common folk. Taking cues from their faith leaders, people flocked to the basements and community halls of mosques, synagogues, and churches, curious to encounter the Other: Muslims anxious to be understood, Jews and Christians eager to get to know a Muslim. Calendars of Jews and Christians started getting populated with inter-faith iftar, Eid, Jumma; Muslims were marking Sabbath, Rosh Chodesh, Seder, Yom Kippur, Easter, and Christmas on their calendars. To be sure, only the curious, the eager, and the committed made the time, yet those who came were genuinely wowed by the power of these encounters, and many walked away exchanging emails and phone numbers.

One organization sponsoring these encounters was the American Society for Muslim Advancement (ASMA), headed by Daisy Khan, a New York–based organization which young volunteers were joining in droves, eager to make a difference. I too joined the staff in 2007 as director of interfaith programs, the only volunteer over age thirty. Occasionally, I would hear someone calling me "auntie."

This Is Heaven

Is there anything that bonds and binds people better than breaking bread? That year, 2008, the theme was Interfaith Green Feast—for the scripture of each faith instructs us to protect the environment. My assignment was to bring twenty-five Muslims to the interfaith feast. I had to beg, plead, and cajole to fill my quota. *Jeeesh!* Jews and Christians were knocking down the doors to get in . . . well, enough said.

When leaders of each faith read from the scriptures, if you didn't know who was reading from which holy book, you would think they were all reading from the same book. Check it out.[1] People nodded at one another with the look "*We are all the same.*"

"Tell your name to your tablemates and explain what it means," the emcee announced to the icebreakers.

"My name is Rehman, which means 'mercy,'" Khalid told them as he took a bite of the latke.

"That's also 'mercy' in Hebrew," remarked a Jewish tablemate, relishing the veggie kebab.

"My name is Sarah. Its Qur'anic meaning is 'one who brings joy.'"

"Why, that's a Hebrew name!" Rachel was spooning her potato salad.

Was there an Ishmael and Isaac at the same table? Or a Sarah and Hagar? Figuratively, yes. There we were breaking challah and pita bread together, looking one another in the eye and, more often than not, seeing eye to eye as we shared vignettes and peeled away the layers of mystique of the Other. By the time people parted, they got to know more than just the names of their tablemates; they left with a promise to stay in touch.

In the years to come, we had a Peace Feast, a Music Feast, and a Fall Feast, but the most joyful was the Comedy Feast. Think of it! Muslims, Christians, and Jews laughing at themselves. If we ever make it to heaven, we believe the sounds we hear will be the sounds of laughter.

That is heaven.

Walter:

Our Kumbaya Moment

That same year, in November 2008, I organized the first Weekend of Twinning—based on the premise of one mosque and one synagogue pairing up in cities across the United States and Canada to hold joint events. I tend to consider myself the most disorganized person on

---

1 Qur'an 2:22; Kohelet Rabbah 7:13; and Matthew 6:25–26.

the planet, yet somehow managed to convince leaders of synagogues, mosques, and other venues across North America to put considerable time and resources into organizing local twinning events. The goal was to give grassroots Muslims and Jews across the continent the opportunity to encounter and learn from each other. The specifics of each program were left to local folks.

As the continent-wide events came together, it was a relief to understand the Israeli-Palestinian conflict was not turning out to be an insurmountable barrier to Jewish-Muslim dialogue and cooperation in America. In city after city, Muslim and Jewish leaders seemed to buy into the ground rules: agree to disagree respectfully about Israel-Palestine while building ties of communication and cooperation in their hometowns. I urged "twinners" in various cities to open their sessions with a heartfelt prayer for Israel-Palestinian peace, but then to caution participants that, in the interest of strengthening local ties, there would be no further discussion about the Middle East. In other words, don't try to brush the elephant in the room under the rug, because it is simply too large for that. Yet at the same time, don't let the Palestinian-Israeli issue take over and short-circuit critically needed Muslim-Jewish encounters in our hometowns.

Rabbi Schneier originally set a target of bringing together twenty-five mosques and twenty-five synagogues, but by the time the weekend arrived, there were more than fifty mosques and fifty synagogues involved, not to mention Jewish and Muslim students on campuses. It was a heady time for all involved. Barack Obama had been elected president two weeks before, and the chant of "Yes We Can" seemed to symbolize the exalted feeling of nearly limitless possibilities. If an African American could be elected president of the United States, then could not Muslims and Jews also do what had seemed impossible: reach across the barricades and embrace each other?

Rabbi Alan Brill of New Jersey termed the 2008 Weekend of Twinning "the Kumbaya moment" between American Jews and Muslims, likening it to the late 1950s and early 1960s when synagogues began pairing off with churches because of the efforts of the National Conference of Christians and Jews. I liked that analogy. I also was ecstatic about the overwhelmingly positive media coverage the Weekend of Twinning was receiving in cities across North America. For that brief shining moment, it appeared that Muslim-Jewish brotherhood was truly the "flavor of the weekend" for a media looking for the next big thing after the election and hungry for upbeat "all things are possible" stories.

The Weekend of Twinning kicked off in Los Angeles at the swank Temple Emanu-El of Beverly Hills, which had twinned with the Saudi-built King Fahad Mosque in nearby Culver City. Keynoting the ceremony were Rabbi Schneier and Dr. Muzammil Siddiqui, president of the Fiqh Council of America, the most widely recognized body of Islamic jurisprudence in North America. Dr. Siddiqui is a soft-spoken, gentle, and understated presence but is one of the most esteemed Islamic scholars in North America. The full-throated endorsement he gave that night to Muslim-Jewish engagement echoed far beyond LA. If Muzammil and the Fiqh Council were for it, many Muslims reasoned, it must be *halal*.

In his remarks to an enthusiastic audience of about five hundred, Dr. Siddiqui denounced anti-Semitism as "evil," calling on his fellow American Muslims to do the same, and for Jews to fight Islamophobia. "We have to change ourselves, then we can change others," said Siddiqui. "Muslims and Jews of America can . . . show it is possible to work together. This is the message of the Torah. This is the message of the Qur'an." Rabbi Schneier echoed a similar theme, stating, "Both American Jews and Muslims are children of Abraham and citizens of the same country, and we share a common faith and a common fate."

As Muslim men and women conducted their *isha* (night) prayers in a corner of the temple's social hall, the Jewish group, their shoes removed out of respect for Muslim tradition, observed from the back of the room. Afterward, several of the Muslim visitors walked next door to a small chapel to watch Jews finishing their evening *ma'ariv* prayers. I worried that people at prayer might feel uneasy having their privacy invaded by gawkers, but the evident goodwill on both sides appeared to overcome the awkwardness. After the prayer, intense discussions commenced and continued over an elaborate Middle Eastern feast. Yentas, dressed to the nines in evening gowns, schmoozed with Muslim ladies in chic hijabs and embroidered dresses. It was literally a made-in-Hollywood lovefest, and a home run of an inaugural event.

Reports reaching me from far and wide across North America during the course of the weekend indicated an enthusiastic response almost everywhere. Sandy Vogel, educational director at Beth Tfiloh synagogue in Baltimore, said of the visit of Imam Earl El-Amin to Beth Tfiloh, together with members of his flock at the Muslim Community Cultural Center of Baltimore, "This was one of the best programs we have had in thirty years, with a full house of five hundred people in the audience for Imam El-Amin's speech. The imam talked about how Islam is different than it is presented in the media. A lot of stereotypes were broken down."

In Toronto, there were eight different synagogue-mosque events facilitated by FFEU and the Canadian Association of Jews and Muslims. Samira Kanji, program director at the Noor Mosque, which twinned with Toronto's Temple Emanu-El, remarked, "I think we're all of a mind on the amazing reception that we've seen from our community members to our twinning programs. Clearly, the yearning for reaching out and finding amity is great, sitting so close under the surface that it needed just the tiniest little raindrop of facility to bring such a burst of enthusiasm."

Events at university campuses also resonated in powerful ways. A joint Hillel–Muslim Students Association event at Stony Brook University on Long Island became the locus for a campus-wide expression of outrage at the vicious hate-crime murder of a Hispanic immigrant in a nearby town. At the University of Southern California, students pledged to consult with each other before inviting speakers by either community that might be hurtful to the other side.

So yes, the Weekend of Twinning 2008 was the kumbaya moment for Muslim-Jewish relations, but it was kumbaya as a substantive first step toward deeper engagement, not as a facile, glib, and meaningless exercise. The first Weekend of Twinning powerfully impacted thousands of Jews and Muslims across North America. The question was whether we could sustain the momentum.

Europe and Beyond

Only weeks after that first Weekend of Twinning, Rabbi Schneier informed me that our next big challenge would be a Mission to New York and Washington by thirty European imams and rabbis in the summer of 2009. I was initially resistant, pointing out that we were just getting started in North America. Yet I soon realized that Rabbi Schneier was correct; this was an opportunity to expand our Muslim-Jewish reconciliation efforts to a continent where the two communities were at even more serious loggerheads than in North America, due in large part to Europe's closer proximity to the fierce passions of the Israeli-Palestinian conflict.

When the mission participants from Britain, France, Belgium, Holland, Germany, Switzerland, Italy, Norway, and Russia arrived in New York, the program included a visit to the United Nations to meet high officials, a reception at the 96th Street mosque with New York Muslim and Jewish leaders, a ceremonial visit to Ground Zero, a meeting with Mayor Michael Bloomberg at City Hall, and a Major League Baseball game at Yankee Stadium. In Washington, we had meetings at Capitol Hill with Muslim and Jewish congresspeople, a visit to the Holocaust Museum, and a gala dinner hosted by ISNA.

The high point of the mission came at the very end: a visit to the All-Dulles Area Muslim Society (ADAMS) Center, a mosque located in Sterling, Virginia. The ADAMS Center, headed by Imam Mohamed Magid—a magnetic religious leader originally from Sudan and, until the advent of the Trump administration, the State Department's go-to imam—was a rapidly growing mega-mosque with prayer sites in a number of locations in the area, including, intriguingly, the Northern Virginia Hebrew Congregation. The ADAMS Center espoused a credo and radiated an ambience that seamlessly blended Islam and Americanism.

Imam Magid and his American-born, deeply earnest community outreach specialist, Rizwan Jaka, had arranged a welcoming ceremony that encapsulated that credo—including a group of Muslim Boy and Girl Scouts in uniform, with the girls also clad in hijabs—and led local participants in the Pledge of Allegiance to the US flag. At first I thought that perhaps Magid and Jaka were laying it on a bit thick. Yet, as we were leaving the mosque, I could see that our European visitors were deeply impressed. I remember one French imam exclaiming, "This is exactly what we need in our country," and nearly everyone else on the bus, imams and rabbis alike, expressing vigorous agreement. Suddenly, all of

our visitors were praising the "American model" of equality and pluralism and wondering if it might be replicable in their own countries.

We were able to build on the success of the mission during the Second
Weekend of Twinning in November 2009, during which we had more
than forty twinnings in countries across Europe. Together with North
America, this amounted to about 130 twinnings worldwide. Those
numbers—and the number of countries involved—grew even larger in
subsequent years. Equally significantly, FFEU facilitated gatherings of
European Muslim and Jewish leaders in Brussels in 2010 and Paris in
2012, which were attended by Muslim and Jewish leaders from nearly
every European country. Participants took a united stand for the right
of Europeans of diverse religions to fully practice their respective faiths,
including aspects of Judaism and Islam increasingly under attack by secu-
larist-dominated European governments, such as male circumcision and
kosher and halal slaughtering. They vowed to stand up for each other if
either community was attacked and to fight expressions of Islamophobia
and anti-Semitism within their own communities.

Starting in 2013, FFEU's dynamic European director, Samia Hathroubi,
a young French Muslim woman with a passionate commitment to Jewish-
Muslim solidarity, worked to bring Jews and Muslims together in support
of democracy and in opposition to escalating terrorist attacks in the name
of Islam and the concurrent rise in white ethno-nationalism directed at
both communities. On January 11, 2015, Hathroubi organized a delegation of imams and rabbis from various European countries to take part
in the two million–strong March for National Unity through the center
of Paris in opposition to the deadly terrorist attacks on *Charlie Hebdo*
magazine and the Hyper Kasher market several days earlier. Members of
FFEU's Imams and Rabbis delegation drew loud cheers as they linked
arms and walked silently down the broad avenues of Paris holding banners with slogans affirming Muslim-Jewish solidarity.

In 2012, FFEU also brought a delegation of imams and rabbis to
Washington from Latin America and the following year another one from
Southern Hemisphere countries such as Australia, New Zealand, Singapore,
and South Africa. We had memorable twinning events in Tunisia and
Morocco as well as in Israel-Palestine, organized by our partner agency,

the Interfaith Encounter Association. By that time, FFEU had turned into reality what had once seemed an unattainable fantasy: building a global movement for Muslim-Jewish communication and cooperation.

Sabeeha:
Moving from Public Spaces to Living Rooms, 2013

It was inevitable. In between planning interfaith feasts, team members started socializing.

"What do you think about starting an interfaith book club?" Toni asked me one afternoon as we sipped coffee after watching a movie. I don't remember which movie it was, but it was good—one of those indie movies. Toni was the Jewish member of the interfaith feast planning team.

"I love it."

We had recently been at a book reading by Reza Aslan. Impressed by the talk, Toni suggested *Zealot*, Aslan's controversial book on Jesus Christ. A month later, two ministers, three Muslims, and three Jews gathered in our tiny apartment in Manhattan overlooking the East River (we had moved from Staten Island in 2007). As the lights came on across the river in Queens, we shared an *I had no idea* moment of revelation, as in *I had no idea Jesus was a Jew* or *I didn't know that Jesus in the gospels is different from the historical Jesus.* You can bet this observation engendered spirited discussion, with everyone leaning forward each time one of the ministers weighed in. So taken was the group by Aslan's writing that for the next meeting—it was the Muslim book's turn—they picked another of his books, *No god but God.* Now it was time for the Muslim members to be in the hot seat as they tried to explain the violence over the Shia-Sunni divide. When it was time for the Jewish book, Khalid made a request.

"We would like to read a book that can teach us about Judaism, kind of Judaism 101."

The Jewish members explained that due to the diversity of thought within Judaism, it would be hard to select a book that represents Jewish beliefs that all Jews agree upon. After some back and forth, they picked *Living Judaism: A Complete Guide to Jewish Belief, Tradition, and Practice*, by Wayne Dosick. For the first time, the Muslim and Christian members— and perhaps a secular Jewish member or two as well—understood why meat and dairy are not combined and the story behind why Orthodox Jewish married women wear wigs, but also how divergent are the interpretations of various Jewish denominations.

"Honestly, it gives me comfort to know that we Muslims aren't the only ones who differ over the scripture to the extent that it has divided us into sects, and sects of sects, and subgroups of sects," Khalid said.

If you were a cuckoo bird peeping out of the wall clock, this is what you would have heard:

"So what is the difference between Orthodox, Conservative, and Reform Jews?"

"Is there social mingling across denominations?"

Or on another occasion:

"The priest was compassionate," said the devout Catholic, commenting on *The Power and Glory* by Graham Greene.

"He was not," said the lapsed Catholic.

When intra-faith arguments ensued, the other two pulled back and let them hash it out, often with a draw. Makes one wonder if interfaith dialogue isn't easier than intra-faith. It's been seven years now. We have read memoirs, fiction, academia, short stories. We meet in living rooms over a dinner of pizza and salad, learning, sharing, and inquiring. Inevitably, the discussion on religion segues into personal stories. Do we get defensive? I do. Do we grab the chance to put our best religious foot forward? Khalid does. Do discussions get tense? Sure, they do. But members of the book club are respectful and over the years have become friends. In these meetings, the Israeli-Palestinian issue is off the table. We are learning, we are teaching, and we are getting confused, which some of us believe is the first step in changing hearts and minds.

If you love reading, here is the author's choice: *The Weight of Ink* by Rachel Kadish, *The Cloister: A Novel* by James Carroll, and *Islamic Jesus* by Mustafa Akyol.

Walter:

From Once a Year to All Year Round

By 2013, I had reached an understanding that I needed to pull another rabbit out of the hat to give new impetus to Muslim-Jewish coalition building. As a one-man organizing band, I was unable to continue expanding the number of participating congregations and organizations in the Weekend of Twinning every year. I found myself bending under the weight of the grueling 24-7, ten-months-a-year effort needed to make the annual event—now rebranded as the Season of Twinning and taking place throughout November and December—bigger and better every year. Another problem was that many mosques, synagogues, and other conveners of twinnings faithfully held their twinning events every November but did next to nothing concerning Muslim-Jewish relations during the remainder of the year. Yes, more congregations and organizations were beginning to accept the premise that nurturing interfaith relations was a good idea, but in most cases the cause remained well down their list of priorities. I realized it was necessary to create grassroots bodies that would focus full-time on strengthening Muslim-Jewish relations as their raison d'être. Their emphasis would be on educating our communities about each other, holding festive and social service events, and standing up for each other when either community was under attack.

In short, we needed to create a new kind of animal, which I labeled the Muslim-Jewish Solidarity Committee. The challenge was to find enough people in various major metropolitan areas who would be willing to create and sustain such volunteer bodies without getting paid to do so. In late 2013, I pitched this idea to my network of activists and early the following year hit the road to major cities to encourage them to follow through.

Muslim-Jewish solidarity committees (also referred to in some cities as "forums") were created in New York, Northern and Central New Jersey, Washington, DC, Detroit, and Los Angeles, together with the previously existing Canadian Association of Jews and Muslims in Toronto. Each was loosely affiliated with FFEU, but they were independent in their operations and empowered to set their own agendas. As creator of the concept, it has been wonderful to watch each of the committees form its own unique personality and set of priorities.

Sabeeha:
And I ended up serving on the board of the New York Muslim-Jewish Solidarity Committee. It's all about grassroots activities—be it a walk

through an ethnic neighborhood sampling food, interfaith music and dance, calligraphy, scriptural reasoning, Seder in a mosque or iftar in a synagogue. We are connecting people in intimate settings. All it takes is one committed leader and magic happens. Michelle Koch, the executive director, a mother of a gorgeous four-year-old boy, waves her magic wand, churning out event after event, filling my calendar to the brim. I just show up, but she is the force.

From Advocates to Friends: One Woman at a Time

"We Will Wage Peace." That was Sheryl Olitzky, rousing the assembly of four hundred-plus Muslim and Jewish women at the 2016 conference of the Sisterhood of Salaam Shalom. If you have any doubts about women waging peace, remember the movie *Pray the Devil Back to Hell?* Women in Liberia, sick of the civil war, banded together—Muslim and Christian—and dragged their husbands to the peace table, locking them inside with a threat: make peace or we will strip ourselves in public. Peace happened. This time around, though, in 2016, the agenda was not about ending a civil war but rather preventing one. An exaggeration? Let's face it. If our nation does not come together as one nation under God, and if we continue to look upon one another as the Other, we might well be in a cold civil war. A very cold one.

Long before the 2016 election, Sheryl Olitzky had a vision. If you haven't already gathered, Sheryl is Jewish. She reached out to Atiya Aftab, a Muslim. Together they launched the Sisterhood of Salaam Shalom. The name says it all. Its mission is to grow relationships between Muslim and Jewish women to build bridges and fight hate, negative stereotyping, and prejudice—and change the world, one Muslim and one Jewish woman at a time. The movement has taken off, and today it has more than 150 chapters nationwide.

Months earlier, Sheryl had invited me to the conference and connected me with Caren Singer. She suggested that the two of us start a chapter in Manhattan. Chapters have to have a 50/50 composition of Muslim and Jewish women, with a maximum of sixteen to twenty members. Keeping the numbers small helps cultivate relationships. The members engage in activities that enhance awareness and foster fellowship.

The Israeli-Palestinian topic is to be avoided until the chapter is on strong footing, usually after eighteen to twenty-four months.

Caren asked if we could meet over coffee. I walked into the coffee shop having no idea what Caren looked like. I presumed I was somehow more recognizable as "the Muslim in a coffee shop"—even though I do not wear the hijab—than Caren would be as a Jewish woman in NYC.

A petite, red-haired woman in the back waved. Ah, that must be Caren!

"You are the first Muslim person I have met."

Why was she yearning to know a Muslim? What is driving any of these Jewish women to join the sisterhood?

"We can change hearts and minds by getting to know the person as a person. We have to have respect for sameness and respect for differences . . . and respect cannot be legislated," Caren said.

I saw in her the drive to stand up for the Other. In her presence, I felt myself shrink. I was joining the sisterhood to protect my Muslim people, but Caren was looking out for me.

The Manhattan chapter got going, meeting every month in living rooms. The coleaders define the topic of discussion, and over a potluck vegetarian meal (with no alcohol), a Muslim woman and a Jewish woman lead the discussion.

"I want to know about your faith, but I also want to know *you*," said the coleader one evening.

It thus came to be that at every session, one Muslim and one Jewish woman would tell their story. The first to share was a woman in her eighties who was the wife of the consul general of Pakistan to the United States in the 1950s. Her listeners were enthralled as she narrated her memories of accompanying Pakistani president Ayub and President Kennedy to Mount Vernon, George Washington's home. Soon we were looking up black-and-white videos on YouTube of the news coverage of the ticker-tape parade in New York honoring President Ayub, our voices rising in excitement at seeing one of our members alongside the glamorous JFK and Jackie. The dignified Pakistani lady also made her listeners laugh when she spoke about the joys—and challenges—of climbing an apple tree in a sari in upstate New York.

Caren has become a fixture in my life. We join one another for events, give talks, and volunteer together, such as serving lunch on Christmas Day. Caren has plugged me into Jewish organizations, organized talks for me, and helped me expand my network. Just a year ago, I was the first Muslim she had met; now she can't keep up with her rapidly expanding Muslim e-rolodex. One day during a lecture Caren and I were giving at the Center for Learning, an attendee asked pointedly, "Why aren't the moderate Muslims speaking out?" Before I could open my mouth, Caren spoke up. "Until recently, I used to believe that too, but let me tell you . . ." and she went on to make the case, citing several examples, that prominent Muslims were in fact unequivocally and consistently denouncing terrorism. Caren is just one instance of how my friends are becoming defenders of my faith.

One afternoon, Khalid and I were having lunch with Toni at Kati Roll by Bryant Park. We had just come back from visiting an exhibit on Jerusalem at the New York Public Library.

"I asked my sister to join us today, but she canceled because of the rain," Toni said. "I told her that two of my friends would be joining us. A few years ago, I would have said, 'Two of my Muslim friends will be joining us.' But now, that seems irrelevant. You two are just friends."

Just friends!

Now that's a place we would all like to be.

Moving the Mountain Isn't Easy

Walter:
The LGBTQ Challenge

Obviously, our work in strengthening Muslim-Jewish relations is not all hearts, flowers, and kumbaya. Coalition-building across religious and cultural lines sometimes unearths serious cultural dissonance. For example, the evident disapproval of homosexuality by many in the mainstream Muslim community made it difficult for me to respond positively to requests from several gay synagogues that we help them find Muslim partners with whom to participate in the Weekend of Twinning. One such synagogue in San Francisco did take part one year as a partner of a

Muslim center without explicitly identifying themselves as gay, and after the event, both congregations sent us glowing reports about how well the event had gone.

However, the following year, as the two congregations were planning a second get-together, the president of the Muslim center called the rabbi and asked him point blank if his congregation was a gay synagogue. When the rabbi confirmed it, the Muslim leader told him regretfully that, despite all the goodwill engendered the year before, his side was unwilling to continue the relationship, because Islam considers homosexuality as morally wrong.

That situation caused me pain, but I decided against calling the president of the Muslim center and urging him to reconsider. First, I knew it wouldn't have worked, and second, I believe Muslims and Jews each have a right to their religious convictions, whether on gay rights or Israel-Palestine. It is one thing to assert, as I absolutely do, that it is morally wrong, indeed illegal, to discriminate against anyone on the basis of sexual orientation. But as a Jew committed to strengthening relations between the largest possible number of Muslims and Jews, it wasn't appropriate for me to lecture a Muslim leader that he was morally bound to twin his mosque with a gay synagogue.

The Hijab

On another gender-related issue, my sustained encounters with smart, assertive Muslim women illuminated for me why so many choose to don the hijab. While in some Muslim countries putting on hijab or the more restricting black-shrouded niqab is enforced by strong social pressure or even religious police, I came to understand over time—after no-holds-barred discussions with many articulate and thoughtful Muslim women in the US and other Western countries—that for these women, the decision to cover their hair was freely chosen to publicly affirm their faith and assert their right not to be viewed as sex symbols but as full human beings.

On an intuitive level, I could readily comprehend why some women would choose to make a public statement that they are not willing to be sexualized for my or any man's viewing pleasure. And over time, I was deeply impressed that so many Muslim women of diverse ethnicities and

social circumstances willingly chose to wear the hijab in a period of rising anti-Muslim bigotry, thereby increasing their risk of being shunned,
ridiculed, or verbally abused by passersby on the street or even physically
attacked by assailants intent on ripping their hijabs off their heads. In
their place, would I have that kind of courage?

The Christian Question

One question I often felt challenged to answer convincingly was why
FFEU chose to limit its work to bringing Muslims and Jews together
instead of focusing on a broader Abrahamic initiative involving
Christians too, or on building an interfaith movement involving all religions. Whenever I tried to respond, especially when asked by Christians,
I invariably gave a rambling, not always coherent explanation reflecting
my own ambiguity on the subject, emphasizing that FFEU did not seek
to be exclusivist and was happy to affiliate its Muslim-Jewish coalition-
building efforts with broader interfaith initiatives involving Christians.
Nevertheless, FFEU was committed to the premise that direct, sustained, and unfiltered Muslim-Jewish interaction is needed because
the estrangement between our two communities is so severe and so
dangerous.

After hearing me out, the majority of Christian interlocutors would
tell me they found my rationale convincing. Though reassuring, that
didn't prevent my feeling awkward and somewhat guilty the next time a
kind and compassionate Christian asked the same question.

Sabeeha:

Preaching to the Choir

Excuse the cliché. It was the summer of 2017, and Khalid and I were listening to an interfaith speaker at the Chautauqua Institution who made the
point: "If you want to fight bigotry, then tell your stories, because stories
have the power to move." During Q&A, I walked over to the microphone.

"My husband and I have been going from city to city, telling our
Muslim stories. However, the only communities that have invited us are
those who are open-minded. How do we reach the people we really
need to touch?"

"These people will not invite you," the speaker replied. "But they will invite me. Tell us your stories, and we will relate your stories to them. One other thing: Don't overestimate the open-mindedness of all your audiences. The skeptics are present, but they came and they listened, and that is a start. So, keep telling your stories."

Postscript: One evening after an interfaith meeting, I was walking home with one of the Jewish members. "Sabeeha, I never told you this, but the first time we met was at your book reading for our women's group two years ago. I and several other women had decided that we would come, hear what you have to say, but we would *not* buy your book. After your talk, I was the first to get in line, and all those women lined up behind me and got your book." She is now an active member of an interfaith dialogue group and regularly attends iftars during Ramadan. *The power of stories at work!*

WANTED: *Muslims*

Muslim-Jewish relations haven't always been a walk in Central Park. At times, the walkways have opened up to the stunning beauty of spring, with flowers budding with the promise of color, fragrance, and beauty; sometimes the path has hit a boulder.

"Why is it so hard to recruit Muslim women in the sisterhood?" Caren asked me when we first met over coffee.

I didn't have an answer. I would later learn that many chapters were facing this challenge. The Jewish women were on a waiting list, and the Muslim slots were hard to fill. Some chapters couldn't get off the ground because there wasn't a critical mass of Muslim members.

Then there is the issue of opening our doors. There are more synagogues and churches opening their doors to Muslims—to join services, give lectures, read from the Qur'an—than there are mosques welcoming the Other.

How do we explain that?

Is it apathy? I hope not.

Are Muslims small in numbers? We don't think so.

Is there a trust issue? Perhaps.

Is it insecurity? Probably.

Or is it that Muslims in America—particularly immigrants—are at an early stage in their trajectory and have yet to mature in the realm of activism? Immigrants are focused on settling down, while the next generation is shuttling between PTA meetings, being baseball and ballet moms, and studying for the Medical College Admission Test. Give them another ten years.

Readers, please challenge this assumption, because our sample size is too small to know for sure. Either way, it is telling. We have work to do. But we can dream that one day, leaders of all mosques, synagogues, and churches in America will embody Abraham's tent and make room in their holy space for all children of God.

Walter:
WANTED: *Jews*
Sabeeha is understandably chagrined that Muslims are often slower to get involved in Muslim-Jewish reconciliation efforts than are Jews. But believe me, that is not always the case. During my ten years of work at FFEU, I found that in many of the cities where we worked, including New York, Washington, Los Angeles, San Francisco, Atlanta, St. Louis, and Detroit, people from both communities were equally interested to get involved. However, in other cities, most notably in Chicago, the Muslim community was resistant to taking the plunge, while it was the Jewish side that held back in other cities, especially Boston.

At the beginning, it was hard to divine why the vibes were right for strengthening Muslim-Jewish relations in one city and not another. Over time, I was often able to discern reasons, but not necessarily to come up with solutions.

In the case of Chicago, it appeared that the main Muslim umbrella organization—the Council of Islamic Organizations of Greater Chicago (CIOGC)—was resistant to promoting twinnings because some of the key leaders were Palestinians and they objected to forming alliances with a Jewish community that strongly supported Israel. That was a reality in cities around the country: South Asian or African American Muslims tended to be more willing to build ties with the Jewish community despite differences on Israel-Palestine than were Arab Americans and especially Palestinian Americans. There were exceptions, but more often than not, this turned out to be the case.

I consider that unfortunate but understandable and certainly respect the Palestinian community in Chicago and across the country. I understand the trauma of being children and grandchildren of people who were uprooted from their homeland, which obviously has a real impact in shaping those attitudes.

As for Boston, a liberal city where one might have expected the Jewish community to support engagement with Muslims, a wealthy and influential donor to Jewish causes led a faction that insisted that the Islamic Society of Boston (ISB)—by far the largest mosque in the metro area—was linked to the Muslim Brotherhood and therefore not an acceptable partner, despite the ISB's express interest in working more closely with the Jewish community. Because of the donor's outsize influence, leaders of the Boston Jewish establishment were unwilling to cross him, even though several told me in off-the-record comments that his claims concerning the ISB were suspect and that his overall anti-Muslim advocacy was misguided and counterproductive. So, efforts to improve Muslim-Jewish relations in Boston moved at a snail's pace.

In some cities, lethargy, mutual suspicion, and disinclination to rock the boat held things back on both sides, but overall my decade of work in bringing together Jews and Muslims around the continent went a hundred times better than I would have imagined possible when I started out in 2007–2008. For me, the glass is much more than half full. Hey, you can't win 'em all.

Forging a New Path

Walter:

Soon after the 2016 election, I resigned from FFEU after nearly a decade of fruitful, life-transforming work, intent on forging my own path forward. I remain grateful to Rabbi Schneier for giving me the privilege of being present at the creation of a new paradigm for Muslim-Jewish relations and allowing me to spend the next decade in grassroots coalition-building. Thankfully, the refusal by some Jewish organizations to engage the Muslim community is changing dramatically. Since late 2016, both the Anti-Defamation League and the American Jewish Committee have at long last begun working constructively with mainstream Muslim organizations like ISNA and MPAC. Indeed, AJC has joined with ISNA to create the Muslim-Jewish Advisory Council, a group of Muslim and Jewish business, organizational, and political leaders who have vowed to work together, with special emphasis on the issue of fighting hate crimes. A series of hate crimes against both communities in the early months of 2017 and President Trump's shocking whitewashing of white supremacist and neo-Nazi marchers in Charlottesville, Virginia, that August graphically signaled the dangers confronting members of our two minority faith communities and clearly showed the advantages of standing together.

Necessity, as they say, is the mother of invention, and if the shock of living in Trump World propelled Muslim-Jewish coalition-building efforts, then so be it. Certainly, this long-desired forward motion by the establishment organizations would not have happened if Rabbi Schneier and FFEU had not stepped forward a decade ago and "koshered" Muslim-Jewish relations. It would not have happened if pioneers had not created a functioning network for Muslim-Jewish relations through the Weekend of Twinning and many other events.

For my part, I have transitioned to the role of Executive Director of Jews, Muslims and Allies Acting Together (JAMAAT), a Washington-area grassroots Jewish-Muslim organization. I also serve as coordinator of the Washington chapter of Project Rozana, an international NGO that helps bring desperately sick Palestinian children to Israeli hospitals for lifesaving treatment and to improve the quality of health care in the West Bank, Gaza, and East Jerusalem. By all means, I intend to stay fully engaged. The pioneering stage of Muslim-Jewish relations is over, but there are enormous challenges ahead of us in standing together to protect our communities against the ongoing rise of Islamophobia and anti-Semitism in the United States and transforming the network we have created into a global Muslim-Jewish movement.

Sabeeha and Walter:
Shared Principles

As proud and satisfied as both of us are to have taken part in the sacred work of Muslim-Jewish alliance building that begins with heartfelt communication, leading to reconciliation and cooperation, we are aware that none of the successes would have been possible were it not for the shared core principles that animate both Islam and Judaism. In the following three chapters, let us examine how each of our faiths venerates these sacred principles and how we can live them together as a common creed.

CHAPTER 3

IF YOU SAVE ONE LIFE,
IT IS AS THOUGH YOU
SAVE THE WORLD

Our first shared principle is that life is sacred. Every human soul is divine, and if we are able to save even one life, we save the world.

> *Whoever destroys a single life is considered by Scripture to have destroyed the whole world, and whoever saves a single life is considered by Scripture to have saved the whole world.*
> Mishnah Sanhedrin 4:5; Yerushalmi Talmud 4:9

> *If anyone slays a human being . . . unless it be for murder or for spreading corruption on earth—it shall be as though he had slain all mankind; whereas, if anyone saves a life, it shall be as though he had saved lives of all mankind.*
> Qur'an: Surah Al-Mai'dah 5:32

Walter:
Muslim Saves Jews in Subway Attack, December 2017
I recall first hearing "If you save one life" uttered in an Islamic context when I attended a Muslim community event in New York City in late

2007 to honor Hassan Askari, the so-called "Muslim subway hero." A Bangladeshi-born student in his twenties, Askari jumped into the fray to prevent anti-Semitic skinhead thugs from beating up several Jewish passengers on the New York City subway, suffering two black eyes in the process. This was one of the first Muslim events I had ever taken part in, and my mouth fell open in astonishment to hear a speaker say that in bravely coming forward and risking his own neck to protect Jews from attack, Askari was acting on the Qur'anic precept that if you save one life, it is as if you save the world. I had heard the same precept cited many times as coming from the Talmud, yet until then I had no idea it was also an important Islamic precept.

That moment powerfully humanized Islam for me. Before, I had formed friendships with Arabs and Muslims in both Israel/Palestine and America but had a somewhat vexed relationship with Islam itself, considering the religion to be militant, medieval, and inflexible. To be sure, I have a similar negative take on aspects of Judaism, especially as expressed in the Orthodox version. Yet I had always felt inspired by the Hebrew Prophets' thirst for universal justice and the centrality of "If you save one life, you save the world," which led me to the conviction that, at its core, Judaism is about mercy, compassion, justice, and the preciousness of each individual life. Hearing that Islam highlighted the same precept led me to understand in a flash that at its core, Islam must be about the same universal concepts.

Sabeeha:

Together We Remember

I recall first hearing "Whoever kills a soul . . ." in a Jewish context when our group of Muslim families hosted Holocaust Remembrance Day in 2017.

That evening, a group of Muslims congregated with Jews from Base Hillel (a pluralistic home-centered outreach program) in the community room of an apartment building on the Upper East Side of Manhattan to honor victims of the Holocaust. There they were, more than twenty-five people, and they just kept coming as Emaan and Zaki, the hosts, brought out more and more chairs, worrying whether they had enough food (they did, and more). The people gathered in a circle. Rabbi Avram Mlotek, cofounder of Base Hillel and himself the grandson of a Holocaust survivor, shared "Moments of Faith," a song composed during the Holocaust.

Laila Al-Askari spoke on behalf of the Muslims in the room. "The world failed the Jewish community. It is our responsibility to make sure that this never happens again." She quoted the Qur'an: "If you kill one person, it is as though you have killed all of humanity . . . and if you save a life, it is as though you have saved all of humanity."

"That is similar to our scripture," a young Jewish man spoke up, and then quoted: "Whoever kills a soul . . ."

I had no idea that the Jewish scripture contained the same injunction and in almost the same words. God was simply reissuing the same edict centuries later, almost like a copy-and-paste.

"Say that again," I asked the young man.

Picture the Aha! moment in the group: young Muslim and Jewish men and women, their jaws yielding to the force of gravity, and eyes open in wonder.

"You have the same text?" Jews and Muslims were asking each other in astonishment.

But why are we surprised? After all, it's the same source—same God, imparting the same message to His Prophets.

Sabeeha and Walter:

We Are Honor-Bound

Our joint advocacy for strengthening Muslim-Jewish relations in the United States and around the world, and our common embrace of the equality of people of all faiths and ethnicities, have everything to do with the fact that the holy books of Judaism and Islam advocate the same compelling moral precept: that every human life is sacred. This precept makes unmistakably clear that all adherents of our respective faiths—including the two of us—are honor-bound to do everything within our power to preserve and protect life.

This affirmation of the inviolability of every individual life, no matter how humble, originates in the belief that humanity began as one individual, Adam, who was created by God in his own image. Grotesquely, only a generation later, Cain, one of the sons of Adam and Eve, killed his brother, Abel, in a fit of jealousy. When pressed by God as to his murdered brother's whereabouts, Cain replied contemptuously, "Am I my brother's keeper?" (Genesis). Wrong answer, especially to an all-knowing God! In any case, as the Talmudic and Qur'anic precepts make clear, our faiths teach that each of us *does* have a responsibility to be our brothers' and sisters' keepers. If we live by that credo, we will not only avoid the temptation to lash out and, God forbid, kill each other, but also can realize the millennial dream of ending the cruel cycle of bloodshed and war that has stalked the world since Cain slew Abel.

To our minds, there is a sense of wonder and inspiration and a cause for deep satisfaction and pride that "If you save one life" is at the heart of both our faith traditions. That is wonderful news. The not-so-good news is that only a tiny percentage of Jews and Muslims are aware this precept is prominently featured in the scriptures of the Other. That mutual ignorance about each other's core beliefs needs to change if Jews and Muslims are to cease demonizing each other and get beyond a century of acute conflict.

The two of us won't pretend that there aren't sharply divergent narratives over our shared history, going back to Abraham and his sons, the Prophet Muhammad's relationship with the Jewish tribes of Arabia, and continuing right up to the modern-day Israeli-Palestinian conflict. We will dialogue frankly and at length on these issues. Yet here, at the very beginning, we want to proudly hold our joint credo aloft and celebrate that both of our faiths affirm the preservation of life at their core. For us that message is a clarion call that is universal, to do all within our power to preserve life, regardless of faith, ethnicity, race, gender, or other qualities. On that basis, we come together.

CHAPTER 4

WELCOME THE STRANGER

Our second shared principle is that we have an obligation to protect the stranger, for we ourselves have been immigrants and marginalized strangers many times and in many places throughout history, going all the way back to when the ancient Hebrews were slaves in the land of Egypt and when the Prophet Muhammad made his hijra from Mecca to Medina.

> *Those who migrate for the sake of God shall find many places for refuge in the land in great abundance.*
>
> Qur'an 4:100

> *Those who have forsaken the domain of evil and those who have sheltered [them]. . . . God is well pleased with them.*
>
> Qur'an 9:100

> *When strangers sojourn with you in your land, you shall not do them wrong. The strangers who sojourn with you shall be to you as the natives among you, and you shall love them as yourself; for you were strangers in the land of Egypt.*
>
> Leviticus 19:33–34

It is the 1940s. Two women risk their lives as they leave their homeland to seek refuge in a safe haven. Helga, a German Jew, escapes from

Hitler's Germany, making her way through Belgium, France, Portugal, and finally to America. Farrukh, an Indian Muslim, leaves her home in the newly partitioned India and takes a harrowing train ride to Pakistan.

They almost didn't make it. Had they perished, we would not be writing this book. These two women were our mothers.

Our mothers were refugees. Both were once strangers in their adopted lands. One made a home in the newborn country of Pakistan, the other in America. By emigrating from India and Germany under conditions of great peril, both managed to survive and thrive. Both were welcomed in their new countries, and both realized their dreams. Farrukh loved Pakistan with a passion. Helga became fully Americanized and loved America deeply. (We take you on their journeys in chapter 7.)

Sabeeha:

A Challenge to the American Dream:
An Unwelcome Stranger, January 2017

First they came for the Mexicans: Put up a wall, keep 'em out. I wasn't a Mexican, neither was my friend Caren, but we came out to speak out, joined the fight, held up those posters, and stood up for the Mexicans.

Then they came for the women: *Grab 'em, humiliate 'em, control their bodies.* I marched and raised the posters up high. But it wasn't only women who marched alongside us—it was my husband, Khalid, Caren's husband, Harold, and hundreds and thousands of the men who joined us in the Women's March of 2017 in New York City. Walter and thousands of other men marched alongside their sisters in the Washington Women's March.

Then they came for the Muslims and refugees: *Ban their entry.* Cathy and Joseph were not Muslims, neither were Singh and Amrita, nor did they have any link to refugees other than humanitarian, but they and thousands came to speak out, took to the streets chanting: "No hate, no fear, Muslims are welcome here. Refugees are welcome here."

Next they will come for *me.* I have no illusions about it. Will anyone stand by me, behind me, with me, for me? You bet. Not in thousands, but in millions.

Honestly, I didn't think it would happen—the travel ban, that is. As an American, I was embarrassed. As a Muslim, I feared where this would take us. No sooner was it announced than I started getting WhatsApp messages from family in Pakistan. Even though Pakistan was not on the list, they were worried about how they would be treated at US airports. My sister-in-law was planning to come to be with her daughter for the birth of her grandchild. Will Pakistan be added to the list?

My cousin's daughter was enrolled in college in the United States and was planning to go to Pakistan during spring break. Should she cancel her visit home? My son Saqib, a natural-born American citizen, was planning to take Laila, his thirteen-year-old daughter, to Pakistan for a family wedding. It was to be her first visit. What if on reentry the immigration officials treated him or my granddaughter the way they detained boxing legend Muhammad Ali's son, questioning him about his religion? Should he cancel the trip with Laila? They decided to go and had a wonderful time. During the long hours on their return flight, I sat on my prayer rug at home in New York, praying that all my imagined worst-case scenarios were just imaginary. Only when I got a text from Saqib, *In the car on my way home*, did I finally exhale.

My sister in Pakistan called with happy tidings—my niece was getting married—and asked me to come for the wedding. I was definitely going, no question about that. So I went through my "traveling while Muslim" checklist. No shalwar kameez—Pakistani outfit—while traveling; no Arabic-sounding words to be uttered, no matter what, not even *InshAllah* or, if I happen to sneeze, *Alhamdulillah*—just let someone bless me (that was pre-COVID). What about the Qur'an and Prayer Time apps on my iPhone? Delete? That it should come to that! I drew the line—the apps stayed.

I wept, not with sorrow over the executive orders but with gratitude at how my fellow Americans were standing up against it. On January 27, 2017, the cold and snowy day when the first travel ban was suddenly imposed, I stood in Foley Square in protest of the Muslim ban, where there were as many people of other faiths as there were Muslims. They were giving interviews to the press, raising their voices, and holding banners proclaiming JEWISH NEW YORKERS SUPPORT OUR MUSLIM NEIGHBORS. We held Jumma (Friday) prayers in the square, the courthouse beyond looking like a temple, and as we sat on the blue tarp over the cold concrete listening to Imam Khalid Latif, the Muslim chaplain at New York University, give the sermon, I felt snowflakes brushing my cheek. Others stood forming a shield around us. In that moment, I didn't feel alone.

We all know what happened in the days that followed. Detentions at airports, travelers off-loaded from planes . . .

Americans got moving. They descended on JFK, on Logan and LAX. Cab drivers at JFK went on a one-hour strike; pro bono lawyers took seats on the hard floor, their laptops in their laps; Jews on the Sabbath joined the protest. On this cold night, people spilled out into the streets and onto the rooftop garages. I had never seen anything like it. Politicians took notice. Courts were petitioned. And it worked. You all know what happened.

I knew it wasn't over. It had just begun. But I saw that pushback works. If I had been disillusioned about the power of the people, my faith in democracy was restored. But I learned something else. I have true friends—foul-weather friends. I received emails from people I knew and people I didn't know. Why would people I don't know write me? Because they had read my book, looked me up, and took the time to write a warm letter of support. I don't even know what they look like, but I knew that they were praying for me and sending me their positive energy. They said they were weeping as they wrote these letters. I wept with them.

The next morning my Jewish and Christian friends organized a call to urgently discuss "How can we help Muslims?" As we adjourned, one of them asked, "Do you think the officials at the airport will refuse to carry out the executive order?"

"I suppose not. They are afraid for their jobs."

"You know what this reminds me of? '*I was only doing my job.*'"

This Is How the Holocaust Started

On a cold February morning in 2017, in the warmth of the sanctuary of the Church of St. Francis Xavier in New York City, Khalid and I found ourselves shoulder to shoulder with faith leaders who had gathered to offer words of solidarity for Muslims as they invoked the scriptures. Standing behind flickering candles, Rabbi Perry Berkowitz, president of American Jewish Heritage Organization, spoke.

"I taught the origins of Holocaust together with Elie Wiesel. . . . Let me tell you how the Holocaust started."

He went through it step by step. First, they discredited the Jews, then they labeled them, then they demonized them, then they took away their rights . . . isolated them . . . detained them . . . dehumanized them . . . and by the time the Holocaust occurred, no one cared what happened to them.

I shuddered. *OMG! This is what is starting to happen to us.*

He continued. "If you don't push back NOW, it will drown you."

Push back. We have teachers, we have allies, and we have ambassadors. We are not alone.

And push back we did. But we could not have done it alone. We needed our fellow Americans to stand with us—Jews, Christians, Hindus, Buddhists, atheists . . . anyone and everyone who subscribed to the American ethos of welcoming the stranger. And stand by us they did. Their support did not go unnoticed by our Muslim community.

Welcoming the Stranger in a Moment of Peril

"I have never been inside a mosque," Rabbi Beni Wajnberg said to Khalid at Temple Shaaray Tefila on the Upper East Side of New York City.

They had met when the synagogue had convened a gathering the day after the 2016 presidential election to offer comfort and support. Stunned by the election outcome and knowing how much the support from people of another faith would mean to us, we had elected to go to our neighborhood synagogue.

Khalid called the Islamic Cultural Center of New York on 96th Street and made an appointment for the rabbi to meet the imam after Jumma Friday prayers.

"Should I remove my kippah [yarmulke]?" the rabbi asked as they entered the mosque.

"Keep it on."

Khalid noticed that many non-Muslim members of the community were filing into the mosque. Show of support! The rabbi was very noticeable as a Jewish person. He sat down on the prayer rug beside Khalid, listened to the imam's sermon, and stood shoulder to shoulder with the congregation in prayer. As soon as the prayer was over, people started walking up to the rabbi.

"Thank you for coming," they said as they shook his hand.

"Welcome to our mosque . . .Thank you for coming."

A distinguished-looking elderly man, dressed in a white shalwar kameez, walked up to the rabbi.

"I would like to give you a gift, but I have nothing on me." He then held out his hand and showed the rabbi his prayer beads. "This is my *tasbeeh*. It is a family heirloom, which I treasure. I would like you to have it." He placed the prayer beads in the rabbi's hands. The rabbi's eyes teared up.

In those dark days, we witnessed many silver linings. We witnessed the best of America. Wasn't it Martin Luther King who said, "Only in the darkness can you see the stars"? Here in America, the stars had clustered, shining their lights upon people of all faiths who were standing together.

Walter:

We've Seen This Movie Before

We American Jews found ourselves in an anomalous position after the 2016 presidential election, the rapid implementation of brutal anti-immigrant policies, and the explosive growth of white nationalism. On one hand, we were not directly threatened because, since the beginning of the twenty-first century, there have been very few Jewish immigrants coming to the United States. On the other hand, despite our relative security, Jews simply could not keep quiet about the Trump administration's racist and xenophobic immigration policy, nor can we today simply look away from the threat posed by the resurgence of white nationalism unleashed during the Trump years. All of this offends us profoundly to our psychic core, defiling the Judaic principle of "welcome the stranger" and the American ethic of openness and diversity.

We Jews simply can't feel safe and comfortable living in a closed and bigoted country intent on preserving a white, Christian identity. We can't sit idly by and watch America be transformed into a place where a Sabeeha Rehman has to fear that sooner or later they may come for her. We can't allow that to happen because one in every three Jews in the world was murdered during the darkest days in history. After the Holocaust, Pastor Martin Niemöller wrote, "First they came . . ." in which he ruefully lamented his own failure to speak up in time. We won't be able to live with ourselves if we don't stand up this time and fight back against this obscenity.

We remember all too well that America's rejection of diversity and openness during the 1930s and 1940s had tragic consequences for hundreds of thousands of Jewish refugees searching for a haven from Nazi persecution. Indeed, my mother and so many other Jews, desperately seeking to escape Europe and reach safety in America, were subject to the same cruelties and rank bigotry besetting Muslims, Latinos, and other refugees seeking to arrive here today.

Just as modern-day Muslim refugees fleeing violence and terrorism were falsely stigmatized by the president and supporters of his America First ideology as potential terrorists and purveyors of an alien culture, Jews were scapegoated by the "America First" crowd of the 1940s as un-American interlopers who threatened to dilute the country's supposed "Christian character." Like the desperate Jews in the 1930s and 1940s, refugees today are fleeing life-threatening violence and persecution in countries like Syria, Afghanistan, and Yemen. Tragically and unforgivably, on June 26, 2018, the US Supreme Court ruled 5–4 to uphold the Trump administration's travel ban, literally condemning to death innocent human beings at risk of their lives, with nowhere to go. What could be more un-American than turning our backs on people in desperate need of succor?

One lovely early summer evening, three weeks before that fateful ruling, I addressed a small group of protesters on the sidewalk in front of the Supreme Court and told my mother's story. I said that whenever I hear demagogic politicians refer sneeringly to desperate refugees, who are enduring terrible hardships to cross the Rio Grande as "illegals" who are "infesting" America, I want to shout back, "Excuse me. My mother was 'an illegal' too. And she didn't infest America, she helped uplift it." Helga Ringel went on to live a happy and productive life in America until her passing in 2005: working in advertising, raising three children, and contributing to the cause of good government. Yet in 1940–41, she was like a hunted animal, running from country to country, port to port, desperately seeking a way out of Nazi-controlled Europe. And she was literally a nobody to US officials at the embassy in Lisbon and the State Department in Washington, DC, who cared more about upholding a strict quota on Jewish refugees than in saving her life and those of countless other Jews, many of whom ended up being liquidated in Auschwitz and other camps. Tragically, the US government today is exhibiting the same indifference to and contempt for desperate refugees fleeing for their lives.

. . . For You Were Once a Stranger in This Land

The commandment to "welcome the stranger" and be charitable to the wayfarer, to offer them hospitality, kindness, and respect, is clearly a core principle in both Judaism and Islam. "Welcome the stranger" is repeated thirty-five times in the Torah, more than any other commandment. The term for migration in Islam is *hijra*, the same root as *hegira*, which refers to the migration of the Prophet Muhammad and his followers from Mecca to Yathrib (later renamed by him to Medina) in 622 CE to escape persecution for their beliefs. The world Muslim community would not exist today if the people of Medina had not given him refuge. Within the shelter of a welcoming community, the faith flourished, and a Muslim community was born. So meaningful was this episode that the date of the Prophet's migration marks the beginning of the Muslim calendar— the Hijra calendar.

In both of our intertwined faiths, the reasons given for this commandment go back to our roots, to the times when each of our peoples experienced homelessness and vulnerability. The most towering figures of our respective faiths—Abraham, Moses, and Muhammad—were all refugees. As Zeki Saritoprak of John Carroll University notes in an article entitled "Prophet Muhammad's Migration and Its Implications in Our Modern Society," the Qur'an identifies the first refugee as Adam, the first human being, who migrated from heaven to Earth. The Islamic tradition considers all human beings—all descendants of Adam and Eve—to be immigrants. The primordial fatherland of humanity is heaven, while the Earth is a place for temporary relocation. Saritoprak writes, "This view seems to be dominant in the sayings of the Prophet as well. He likens himself to a traveler who stays for a short time to rest under the shade of a tree and then continues on his journey."

Our common Patriarch, Abraham/Ibrahim, made the fraught decision to abandon his ancestral home in the city of Ur in southern Mesopotamia with its obeisance to clay idols and, following the command of his God, journeyed to the far-off Land of Canaan, where God had promised to bless him and make his descendants into a great nation. During the ensuing years, as he struggled to fulfill his destiny in Canaan through times of famine and plenty, Abraham received hospitality and provided it. Generations later, the Children of Israel became slaves in Egypt and endured four centuries of oppression before Moses liberated them. They managed to escape the Egyptian army after God offered a path through the Red Sea, the first steps on a forty-year passage through the desert on the way to their homeland.

Likewise, the first Muslim migration took place in seventh-century Arabia, when, to escape persecution, eighty-three men and eleven women left their homes in Mecca and sought refuge with King Negus in Abyssinia. When the Prophet Muhammad's life was threatened, he and his followers quietly left town in the darkness of night, hiding in a cave, and made their way to Medina. The people of Medina welcomed him, and he was able to preach his message and establish the first Muslim community. Honoring that history, today Muslim countries top the list of countries of refuge: Turkey provides refuge to 3.5 million refugees, followed by Pakistan and Uganda with 1.4 million each, Lebanon 1 million, and Iran 975,400 (UNHCR 2018).

During the Passover Seder each year, Jews remember their history as strangers in Egypt. Yet, as searing as that experience was, it was only one of many times in history that the Jews became strangers in strange lands. From the destruction of the First Temple in Jerusalem in 70 CE until the creation of the State of Israel in 1948, the dominant image was of the Wandering Jew passing from the Middle East and North Africa to Western, Central, and Eastern Europe and later to the Americas. In all of those places, the Jews were strangers; in many of them, during most of the two-thousand-year history of the Jewish Diaspora, they suffered discrimination and abuse. They were forced to live in ghettos and frequently were victims of murderous pogroms by native populations who were conditioned by princes of the Church to believe that "the eternal Jew," regardless of where or when each member of the tribe lived, was collectively guilty of deicide: the crucifixion of Jesus Christ. So much of the passion of American Jews for "welcoming the stranger" is directly related to that fraught and tragic history. Jews truly understand in their bone marrow what it is to be persecuted, homeless, and despised, and though they are more secure today, they can't turn away when others are mistreated or turn a blind eye at the border.

Jews were present in America in relatively small numbers from its inception. In 1790 President George Washington wrote a letter to members of the Touro Synagogue in Newport, Rhode Island, assuring them that the government of the United States would give "to bigotry no sanction, to persecution no assistance." Millions of Jews flooded into America between 1880 and 1920, escaping oppression and violence in the Russian Empire and other parts of Europe. As they sailed into New York Harbor, unsure of what would come next, they glimpsed the Statue of Liberty holding her torch of welcome and instantly bonded with their new country. It is not surprising that it was a Jewish poet, Emma Lazarus, who wrote "The New Colossus," the definitive tribute to the recently built Statue of Liberty and its meaning, not only for Jews but for refugees from around the world then pouring into America, including early Muslim immigrants from Syria and Lebanon. Listen again to the poem's immortal lines:

> Give me your tired, your poor, your huddled masses yearning to breathe free,
> The wretched refuse of your teeming shore.
> Send these, the homeless, tempest-tost to me,
> I lift my lamp beside the golden door!

The celebration of immigration is in the DNA of American Jewry, including the refugee processing center of Ellis Island, as well as the nearby Statue of Liberty. But what is often overlooked amid all that hagiography is that in 1924, Congress voted for tough new immigration regulations that cut the flow of Jews and all other non–Northern Europeans to a trickle for the ensuing forty years. During the late 1930s, as Nazi Germany intensified its savage persecution of German Jews and prepared to conquer the rest of Europe and liquidate millions of Jews, America refused to relax its strict anti-Jewish quotas and left millions of helpless European Jews to their fate.

The fifty-year period between 1965 and 2015, when immigration laws were substantially relaxed, was for the American Muslim community what 1880–1920 was for the Jewish community. Millions of people migrated to America from across the Muslim world, from Indonesia, Bangladesh, Pakistan, Afghanistan, and Iran to the Arab lands—Palestine, Syria, Iraq, and Egypt—including people like Steve Jobs's father, from Syria—and from countries across Africa. From the start, the Trump administration was bitterly hostile to immigration, both legal and illegal, but especially venomous to two groups: Hispanics and Muslims. On December 7, 2015, then-candidate Donald Trump called for a "total and complete shutdown of Muslims entering the United States," and he followed that up as president with a modified travel ban that the Supreme Court upheld in June 2018. That act bans travel and immigration to the United States by citizens of seven countries, five of them Muslim, including Syria, Iran, Yemen, Libya, and Somalia, together with North Korea and Venezuela, two countries likely added to the mix as a fig leaf to show that the premise of the ban is not bigotry against Muslims but security for American citizens. This clearly spurious claim was nevertheless accepted by the Supreme Court in one of its most morally squalid rulings since *Plessy v. Ferguson* and *Dred Scott*. Not surprisingly, but significantly, the three Jewish members of the Court all voted against the travel ban.

Trump's overt message—that the United States would no longer serve as a place of refuge for desperate people fleeing from violence and oppression, and indeed, had no concern whatsoever as to whether residents of such "shithole" countries, as Trump called them, live or die—is antithetical to the ethos and fundamental values of a polyglot nation, all of whose ancestors, except Native Americans, emigrated here from somewhere else.

Reversing the Trump administration's attack on immigrants and refugees and returning America to its historic place as a refuge for people the world over fleeing violence and oppression is a priority for both the American Jewish and American Muslim communities. We must stand up together for the rights of refugees from Muslim and non-Muslim countries alike to reach America, while reaching out a hand of compassion and support to poor and unemployed refugees who are already here. There is no issue on which Jewish, Muslim, and American values come together as compellingly as on the issue of "welcoming the stranger."

For those huddled masses, let us wade into the water and call out: "Take my hand, and I will lead you to the shore. Take my hand, and I will bring you into the welcoming arms of America. Take my hand."

CHAPTER 5

ISLAH AND *TIKKUN OLAM*

Our Common Moral Imperative to Help Those Most in Need

Our third shared principle is that our respective faiths enjoin each and every one of us to repair the world, to reach out a hand of compassion and support to those in society who are most in need.

Islah is an Arabic word that conveys the idea of improving, purifying, reconciling, repairing, and reforming.[2] This concept is revealed in the Qur'anic verse:

> *Make peace between your two brethren, and remain conscious of God so that you might be graced with His mercy.*
>
> Qur'an 49:10

Tikkun olam (Hebrew for "repairing the world") has come to connote social action and the pursuit of social justice. Concern for the poor, hungry, and oppressed is a cornerstone of Judaism going back to the time of the Hebrew Prophets.

---

2 Charlene Tan, *Reforms in Islamic Education: International Perspectives* (New York: Bloomsbury Academic, 2014), 4.

The Prophet Isaiah said:

If you banish lawlessness from your midst, the menacing hand and evil speech, and you offer your compassion to the hungry and satisfy the famished creature—then shall your light shine in darkness, and your gloom shall be like noonday.

Isaiah 58:10–11

Why *Islah* and *Tikkun Olam* Can Bring Us Together

It seems to us that, first and foremost, *tikkun olam* and *islah* are calls to action to express and share with the world the common moral imperative in both Judaism and Islam to help those most in need. This imperative is built into the fabric of the two faiths. Yet few Jews understand that this is at the core of Islam, and few Muslims are aware of the same principle in Judaism. Once we discover that, we not only appreciate each other in a more positive manner but come together to undertake good works of public service.

In the Qur'an, God repeatedly instructs the believers to "establish prayer and give zakat (charity)," making charity equivalent to worship of God. It is reported in a hadith that the Prophet Muhammad said, "Feed the hungry, visit the sick, and set free the captives." Islam advocates feeding the hungry, regardless of race, religion, or background. It is such an important part of the religion that the Prophet Muhammad said a person is not really a Muslim if he goes to bed satiated while his neighbor goes hungry. The third of the Five Pillars of Islam is *zakat*, which means purifying your wealth. The zakat is an amount of money that every financially able Muslim adult must pay annually to help the poor, the wayfarer, and the orphans.

In Judaism, there are myriad texts enjoining individuals to help the less fortunate, including Psalm 82:3–4, which says, "Defend the poor and the orphan; deal justly with the poor and the destitute. Rescue the weak and the needy; deliver them from the hand of the wicked."

The Prophet Isaiah asks: "Is it not to share your bread with the hungry, and bring the homeless poor into your house; when you see the naked to cover him?"

Giving expression to these concepts affords us an opportunity to come out of our comfort zones and improve conditions for people in need.

Those of us involved in Muslim-Jewish relations have focused on creating opportunities for Jews and Muslims to join with each other to carry out acts of kindness and mercy together, something that not only provides us with the opportunity to repair the world together but strengthens ties of friendship and trust. As a result, over the past decade, Muslims and Jews across North America and around the globe have undertaken numerous joint activities focused on reforming and repairing the world together, including feeding the hungry, visiting the sick, sprucing up parks and derelict lots, holding health fairs, and working together against bigotry.

As Zamir Hassan, president of the Muslims Against Hunger, puts it: "It is one thing for Muslims and Jews to discuss with each other what our holy books say about the righteousness of feeding the hungry. Yet coming together to actually feed hungry people, to stand side by side in a homeless shelter, putting on serving aprons and ladling out hot and nourishing food to people in need of sustenance, is on a whole different level. Feeding hungry people together allows Muslim and Jewish servers to personally fulfill the respective commandments of their holy books while sharing that experience with each other. In the process, they have the chance to communicate with each other in a genuine and personal way."

Walter:

Muslim Doctors Without Any Borders

As I got to know Muslim communities in cities across America, I was deeply impressed by the inspiring way American Muslims stay connected to the broader community and take responsibility for helping others through charitable acts. Both the Christian community and my own Jewish one could learn much from their example.

Muslim doctors, nurses, and dentists volunteer their services one Sunday a month to offer health screenings to people of all backgrounds without medical insurance. Mosques and Muslim communities in New York, Maryland, northern Virginia, Houston, Detroit, Los Angeles, and elsewhere have set up full-service medical and dental clinics to serve the larger community. Among my proudest moments during my ten years of working in Muslim-Jewish relations was encouraging Jewish doctors and dentists to join with their Muslim counterparts in joint health fairs, at which folks without insurance from diverse backgrounds receive medical services for a variety of ailments. One such event was the Queens Muslim-Jewish Health Fair of June 2010, which FFEU cosponsored with Imam Shamsi Ali's Jamaica Muslim Center and the Bukharian (Central Asian) Jewish community of Queens. The events brought together several score Muslim and Jewish doctors, nurses, and assorted medical personnel from across New York City on a beautiful Sunday afternoon to offer free services to several hundred Queens residents of diverse backgrounds, most without health insurance, including blood tests, eye exams, and other procedures.

The success of the event was really about piggybacking, getting Jewish doctors to take part in a long-standing Muslim event. I was subsequently able to bring Jewish doctors and dentists to Muslim health fairs in Houston and in northern Virginia, where they served recently arrived Syrian refugees. In other locales, I was unsuccessful in convincing Jewish doctors to volunteer because of concerns that they might be sued by someone to whom they provided health screenings. While such fears are understandable, similar worries do not prevent thousands of Muslim medical personnel from regularly providing health screenings and hands-on medical and dental care to uninsured people. For them, their religiously motivated commitment to healing people in need supersedes fears of being sued.

The extent to which the Muslim community acts upon its spiritual and moral commitment to help people in need is a major untold story, one that contrasts markedly with the negative stereotyping to which Muslims are too often subjected by the media. Whenever I have suggested to Muslim colleagues that there should be a PR blitz on this theme, they tend to shrug and say that *sadaqah* and *islah* are core concepts of Islam that Muslims uphold quietly in their own lives, not something to boast about in a self-promotional way.

Sabeeha:

Power of Sisterhood

"I am afraid I will get deported," she said.

The eight of us were at a meeting of the Sisterhood of Salaam Shalom, sitting in the living room of a Jewish member, surrounded by plants reaching up to the ceiling. We sat around the coffee table, listening to each of us tell a story of an object that means something to us. A young, petite Turkish woman in a hijab held up a bracelet. "My father made this for me when he was in prison."

We leaned in.

Teary-eyed, we listened to her story. To keep his daughter safe, he had encouraged her to move to the US and pursue her career as a doctor. Now, she was afraid to go back. But once her passport expired, she would be at risk of deportation.

Instantly, the ladies whipped out their phones, scrolling through their contacts: "Contact HIAS. Here is the number."

"I will connect you with a lawyer. Pro bono."

"Call . . . Look up . . . Contact . . ."

Within minutes, we had a plan.

Despite her protests, the ladies launched crowdfunding.

Within a week, her case had been taken up by the court, and she was given five years to stay in the US and then report for her asylum case to be heard.

Bingo!

She is now well on her way, safe, and on a career path.

That is impact! The power of sisterhood.

Sadaqah/Tzedakah

That's "charity" in Arabic and Hebrew. Isn't it amazing how similar the terms are! On Christmas Day, the Sisterhood of Salaam Shalom takes over the responsibility of serving meals in churches across America, allowing their Christian fellow Americans to take the day off. Downstairs in the hall of Church of St. Francis Xavier, Muslim and Jewish women (and men), capped, gowned, and gloved, take their assignments and fan out. Some at serving stations, some rinsing dishes, others spreading out to talk to the seated guests as they savor their Christmas meal. I stood at the assembly line with Caren Singer and Harold, receiving empty dishes, scraping them clean, and handing them to the "rinsers." For two hours, that was all we did, loving every minute of it. A charitable act makes one feel good, but when you do it together, it becomes an act of joy; if you are of different faiths, it makes you wonder if you are really that different. For me, these were moments when the playing field felt smooth and even.

It's Child's Play

During the spring, if you walk by Ruppert Park in upper Manhattan, you will hear the laughter of children, not playing but getting their hands dirty planting flowers, teenagers planting shrubs, mommies and daddies doing the heavy cleaning. During the fall, you will find them raking leaves and planting bulbs as the borough president raises her bullhorn to say a huge "Thank you!" The Muslim Volunteers for New York (MV4NY) are a ubiquitous presence wherever there is room for *islah*, be it a food drive for Meals on Wheels, a book drive for disadvantaged schools, toys for tots, or Valentine's Day gifts for seniors. What I cherish about this organization is that their leaders, Sahar Hussein and Mubeen Siddiqui, are getting children involved in repairing and beautifying the world.

Take My Hand

At an interfaith Seder in the Mid-Manhattan Mosque, a Jewish woman introduced me to a Pakistani refugee.

Wait, what? How come she knows a Pakistani refugee?

"HIAS brought him over from the island of Nauru in the South Pacific, where he had escaped to, fleeing from Shia-Sunni violence in Pakistan. Our synagogue has sponsored him, and we are helping him settle." (HIAS, the Hebrew Immigrant Aid Society, has been working to welcome and resettle refugees in America since 1881.)

Jews rehabilitating Muslim refugees—displaced, persecuted, with broken hearts and empty hands. The Muslim community should be doing this work too. Maybe they are and I am just not aware of it. I am embarrassed. I have nothing to add. I later learned that Muslims were indeed involved; I just wasn't paying attention. Khalid and I have gotten to know this young refugee and have introduced him to the Islamic Center of New York University.

Back at my computer, I WhatsApp-ed and Facebook-ed what Jews in America were doing for the huddled masses of Muslims—for humanity in need. I beamed this across the oceans into the heartland of Pakistan. Spread the good feeling.

Sabeeha and Walter:

For each of us, discovering that the other's faith—like ours—mandates lending a helping hand to people in need is a wonderful by-product of what happens when Muslims and Jews do *tikkun olam* and *islah* together. We know that charity is also a fundamental tenet of Christianity. And we realize that if we have come to appreciate this about each other's faiths, so too have untold thousands of our coreligionists who have gotten involved in interfaith relationship-building.

Once Jews and Muslims feed the hungry or heal the sick together, it becomes next to impossible to demonize people of the other faith we served alongside. It also becomes harder to bad-mouth the religion that motivated them to help the needy. Yes, we are healing people in need, but we are healing ourselves as well; opening our minds and un-hardening our hearts toward each other.

So let's roll up our sleeves and go out together to repair the world. God knows there is a huge amount to be done.

CHAPTER 6

STANDING UP FOR
EACH OTHER

Minority Communities Fighting Bigotry Together

Sabeeha:

Today I Am a Muslim

On a bright sunny Sunday in February 2017, soon after the travel ban was announced, Khalid and I stood in Times Square among thousands, many waving posters that said TODAY I AM A MUSLIM TOO. Except that most of those gathered were not Muslims. FFEU, which is first and foremost a Jewish organization, was the originator and principal organizer of this event. I walked through the crowd, rubbing shoulders and arms, stopping in front of people, hoping to lock a gaze, so that I could say "Thank you." I stopped in front of a lady in a wheelchair. She must have been in her nineties; she could barely lift her head. Think of what it took for her to be there. Someone must have helped her get into her heavy coat and woollies, put her in a wheelchair, wheeled her out of her apartment into the elevator, hailed a cab, lifted her out of her wheelchair into the car, folded her chair into the trunk, got her to Times Square, got her out, and wheeled her over the bumpy sidewalk, around the railings, into the square. There she sat, joining the protest against the Muslim travel ban, with her head bent, protesting loudly by her silent presence. I lowered myself, hoping to meet her gaze. I wanted to tell her how much I appreciated what she had done. She probably could not hear me. My voice was lost in the sounds of love in the square.

This was a Sunday. All these people from across the East Coast could have been anywhere on their day off, but they gave up their day to speak up for their fellow citizens, Muslim Americans. Dignitary after dignitary took the microphone, but it was the people on the streets, who stood there for hours, that spoke the loudest to me. My non-Muslim friends from across the nation who were following the news coverage were texting me love notes, "Today I am a Muslim," with arrows piercing pink hearts.

And then, only a few days later, the tables were turned, and it was the Muslims' turn to stand up for the rights of their fellow Americans.

Today I Am a Jew

It was another cold morning during that eventful month of February 2017, only a month into the new administration, when America woke up to the news of twelve bomb threats made to Jewish community centers across America. What happened next—desecration of Jewish cemeteries in Philadelphia and St. Louis—shouldn't happen in a civilized country. That Jewish cemeteries—any cemetery for that matter—would be desecrated left me shocked and disoriented. "What would make anyone do this?" I kept asking Khalid. I'd walk away from the TV, then walk back in. "Where is this coming from? Is this how people feel about Jews?" I couldn't comprehend what I was reading, hearing, watching. "What has happened to the moral psyche of our nation? Why desecrate a cemetery?"

Because the dead can't resist.

Because the dead can't cry out.

Because the dead are dead.

I pictured them in the act. In the stealth of the night, creeping into the cemetery, using their hands and feet to knock the headstones over the sleeping dead, and scurrying away under the cover of darkness. I shuddered. As I grappled with *How can I help? What can I do? Who do I call?,* a movement had already started, and the speed was like lightning. It wasn't about all the Muslim organizations condemning the act—which they did—or the Council on American-Islamic Relations putting out a reward for information leading to the perpetrators—which it did. It was the swift crowdfunding.

At 2:00 p.m. on February 21, 2017, two Muslim activists, Tarek El-Messidi, a social entrepreneur, and Linda Sarsour, former executive director of the Arab American Association of New York—whom some Jews take issue with for her pro-Palestinian advocacy—launched a fundraiser, Muslims Unite to Repair Jewish Cemetery, hashtag #RestInPeace. Their goal: to raise $20,000 in twenty-eight days. They met their goal in three hours. Within twenty-four hours, they had raised over $92,000, and by the time the clock stopped, the contributions totaled $162,468. Additional funds would go to other vandalized Jewish cemeteries around the nation—to repair our world, literally and figuratively.

And the perpetrators thought they could walk over the dead.

Even the dead have power. Because there are people with a heart watching over them. Because humanity among the living still exists, even if there are heartfelt disagreements on Middle East issues.

Don't you trample over my dead. *Islah* and *tikkun olam* still exist.

We were seeing that all efforts to isolate and hurt specific groups were having the unintended consequence of bringing diverse communities together as never before. People standing up for people. People opening their arms and wallets to embrace people they had never met, had never known. That day, a post lit up my Facebook. Nadeem Ali Khan, a young Muslim from a village in India, moved by the desecration of the cemetery, posted this message on his page:

"Yesterday you guys put up signs in New York City saying, 'You are all Muslims,' today this Indian Muslim is saying, 'Today I am a Jew too.'"

That's right!

TODAY I AM A JEW.

Jews Stand Up for Muslims

It caught everyone's attention: a February 2016 blog post on the Sisterhood of Salaam Shalom's Facebook page, "The Night I Prayed behind Bars." Rabbi Jesse Olitzky and 250 of his rabbinical colleagues had traveled from New Jersey to the Trump International Hotel at Columbus Circle, New York City, to protest the president's anti-Muslim, anti-immigrant, and anti-refugee agenda. That cold Friday evening, Rabbi Olitzky and eighteen other demonstrators marked the Jewish Sabbath by getting arrested after they sat down in the middle of the street, sang "The Song of The Sea"—words that the Israelites sang when crossing the parted Red Sea during the Exodus from Egypt—and refused a police order to vacate the street. The rabbis spent the night in a holding cell in New York City's 33rd Precinct.

Why would a group of rabbis subject themselves to a night in jail to protest a ban on Muslims? Because, according to Rabbi Olitzky, "We know all too well what happens when one faith doesn't stand up for another."

How could anyone not be moved? Khalid and I felt ready to go to jail for Rabbi Olitzky and his colleagues.

P.S.: In case you haven't made the connection, he is Sheryl Olitzky's son.

Muslims Stand Up for Jews

On Saturday afternoon, October 27, 2018, I was at the Yorkville Library at the Writers Circle, sharing an op-ed I had written on the would-be pipe-bomber, Cesar Sayoc. Walking home, Sayoc was still on my mind—he had mailed pipe bombs to critics of Trump, including Barack Obama and Hillary Clinton. *What if the bombs had gone off? We would be burying dead bodies and consoling families.*

I sent a quick text to Khalid: "On my way."

Khalid was waiting by the door. "Did you hear?" he asked.

His stricken look told me that something awful had happened; something worse than another pipe bomb intercepted.

"A gunman has shot and killed worshippers in a synagogue in Pittsburgh," he said.

Shock is hard to absorb. Shock is hard to describe. When you are told that a gunman attacked a synagogue and killed worshippers while shouting "Kill the Jews," the emotional impact is staggering.

Hate. Hatred of Jews. Hate turned to violence. Violence intended to exterminate. Hate so intense that it can drive a man to attack a house of worship and kill people at prayer.

Madness out of control! People are dead.

My son was shaken up. One of the victims was his best friend's mentor. As I listened to his shocked account of the sudden loss of a man who had meant so much to his close friend, I pondered: Did the victims imagine this would be their last prayer? Had any of them ever thought their lives might end with a bullet? As the news unfolded, all we could think of was their last moments: the shock of being fired upon, the pain inflicted, the sound of screams, desperate thoughts as they took their last breath. What did it do to the victims' families when they heard the news: *I hope it's not Mom; maybe Dad was late for services this morning.* Frantic calls to the synagogue, and hearing the crushing news that it *was* Mom, it *was* Dad; Mom is dead, Dad is gone. *Where did the bullet hit? Was it instant death? Did she suffer? When can I see the body?* How did they break the news to their children, that Grandpa was shot and killed? What did they say when they asked, "Mom, why did the shooter kill Grandpa?" "Dad, why did he hate the Jews?"

Where does one turn for comfort? How does one not lose faith? Faith leaders reached out, offering comfort. I received an email from Imam Feisal Abdul Rauf, president of Cordoba House, invoking the Qur'an: "The Qur'an commands that we restrain each other to protect 'monasteries, churches, synagogues and mosques in which God's Name is oft-remembered.' (Qur'an 22:40)." At the vigil on the doorsteps of Temple Emanu-El, Khalid and I sought comfort in the reading of Psalm 121, "The Lord will watch over you." I poured my heart out on my blog, "The Last Prayer." My friend Rabbi Frank Tamburello of the Makor Center for Spiritual Judaism posted a comment: "Thank you for this, my dear friend Sabeeha. I will be reading this at our Shabbat service this evening. Psalm 133 says: Behold how good and how pleasant it is when brothers and sisters live together in peace and in unity."

The American Jewish Committee (AJC) launched a campaign to #ShowUpForShabbat, calling on Jews and non-Jews to fill the synagogues that coming Friday evening or Saturday morning for a show of support. Khalid and I decided to go to our neighborhood synagogue, Temple Shaaray Tefila. I wrote to Rabbi Joel Mosbacher, inviting ourselves to Friday services. But then Rabbi Tamburello invited us to come to *his* synagogue for Friday services. So, Khalid and I decided to split up: he would go to the Makor Center and I to Shaaray Tefila. For Saturday services, I emailed my friends Toni and Jenny, inviting myself to Sabbath services at their synagogue, B'nai Jeshurun—affectionately known as BJ. When Rabbi Leah Berkowitz, president of American Jewish Heritage Organization, invited us for Friday services at the East Side Synagogue, having already booked myself, I had to regretfully decline.

"May they never need us, as we need them now," said Rabbi Mosbacher, as he acknowledged the presence of non-Jews that evening. The place was packed, families with children—lots and lots of children. I knew no one other than the rabbi. I took an aisle seat near the front. A woman walked up to me and said, "I have not seen you before, and I just want to say, Welcome. We are happy to have you with us." She took me around and introduced me to a few people. As the rabbi led the service in song, Sunday school students gathered under the canopy swaying to the music. I felt the power of community as the congregants sang, hugged each other, mourned their collective loss, and celebrated life. The rabbi called upon leaders of other faiths to come up to the *bimah*—the raised platform in the front of the synagogue—and join him in song and prayer. As I joined them, a gentleman standing next to me asked, "What organization are you representing?"

I was not representing any organization. I had just come.

"I live in the neighborhood," was all I could muster.

Later, Khalid told me that Rabbi Tamburello read my blog post "The Last Prayer" to the congregation. He then asked Khalid to come up to the bimah and read a verse of the Qur'an—the same verse quoted by Imam Feisal. For the rabbi to make the time to share a message from a Muslim (not a short message) and to have his congregation listen to Qur'anic verses during Sabbath services was to proclaim that we are stronger when we hear each other's thoughts and voices, when we stand up for one another.

On Saturday morning, as I walked into the sanctuary of BJ, Jenny and Toni waved to me from the front rows. Thankfully, they had saved me a seat. Rabbi Matalon came to the bimah and commenced a Call to Action. I took out my notebook and scribbled. "First, secure yourself."

The rabbi had heeded his own advice: security guards were checking all bags. "We realize that our country is at risk. Not just Jews . . . the whole country is at risk. Therefore, we form partnerships and alliances with groups that are also at risk. We have many allies here. I see Sabeeha and Khalid, who are members of the Muslim community. They've been here many times at BJ, because they believe in the power of these alliances, because they know that when they are at risk, we are at risk, and vice versa." I wish I could recall what else he said, but at that point Jenny gently cautioned me about taking notes during Sabbath. So, all I can remember is the core of his message—we have a moral obligation to *stand up for each other*—and how it made me feel: *We are in this together.*

"Don't you feel that you need to distance yourself from this attack?" A reporter for WNYC, New York's public radio station, had picked up my Twitter feed on #ShowUpForShabbat. She wanted to know what compelled me to show up for Shabbat, when many people had gone numb and were distancing themselves from horrific reports saturating the media. "I cannot distance myself," I said. "These are my friends, my Jewish sisters and brothers, my cousins in faith, and they are hurting. Besides, they were there for us when the travel ban went into effect, so now it's our turn to stand up for them."

Two Muslim organizations began a crowdfunding program to raise $25,000 for the families of the victims in Pittsburgh and for the two African American men killed by a white supremacist in Jeffersonville, Kentucky. They reached the goal in six hours; by the time the campaign closed, they had raised a staggering $238,000. It was a stunning example of the power of standing up for one another in an hour of crisis and grief.

Walter:

No Longer Safe to Be a Jew in America

News of the domestic terrorist attack at the Tree of Life Synagogue in Squirrel Hill, Pittsburgh—located two blocks from the synagogue where I studied Hebrew and attended services as an eleven-year-old—struck me viscerally with a sense of horror and dread, yet at the same time I wasn't really surprised. Amid the anti-Semitic invective on the internet, cemetery desecrations, and marching Nazis in Charlottesville, I had feared something like this was bound to happen somewhere in America, though not necessarily in my former hometown.

My second thought was that American Jews' assumption that they were safe in their own country—which most had believed ever since Washington upheld religious liberty for Jews during his visit to the Touro Synagogue in 1790—was no longer the case. For the first time in my life, I ceased to feel safe as a Jew in America. A homegrown Nazi sympathizer who believed Jews were scheming to infuse this land with dark-skinned foreigners had stormed into a synagogue and murdered elderly Jews at prayer, and other neo-Nazis certainly held the same beliefs. Some of the victims were old enough to have grown up aware that Hitler was mass-murdering Jews in Europe. Now, in their last seconds of life, they had confronted at home in Squirrel Hill—in their very own synagogue—the specter of Nazism reborn and intent on killing Jews.

So yes, the massacre at the Tree of Life meant Jews are no longer safe here. But then, *no one* is safe in an America gone to political extremism and white nationalism. Neither Jews, Muslims, nor any minority faith is safe in an America that promotes fundamentalist Christianity as the all-but-official creed. The solution to the present crisis has to be to *stand up for each other*, as Sabeeha has elucidated. For Jews, Muslims, and all Americans of conscience, the best possible response is to publicly affirm our determination to be there for whichever community is under attack.

Four evenings after Pittsburgh, my wife, Tanya, and I attended a deeply healing "Service of Comfort, Community, and Solidarity for the Tree of Life," held at Temple Rodef Shalom in Falls Church, Virginia. There was an enormous turnout at the synagogue, not only of Jews but also of several hundred Muslims and smaller numbers of Christians, Sikhs, Baha'is, Hindus, and Buddhists, people of all faiths and no faith. For five years, Temple Rodef Shalom has been engaged in a series of twinning events with nearby McLean Islamic Center, and the warmth and ease of that relationship came through vividly during the memorial ceremony.

Surrounded by Muslims on all sides, I felt a sense of well-being. At one point, I turned to a Muslim man with two small children sitting next to me and asked why he had decided to bring his family to the synagogue. The man replied, "The natural thing was to come here and respond to what happened. I can't sit at home when my neighbors have been attacked. We are all in this together." Moved, I reached out to shake his hand and then spontaneously embraced him.

The service, led by Rabbi Amy Schwartzman and Rabbi Jeff Saxe, included the *Mi Sheberiach* prayer for the injured and a heartrending mourners' Kaddish for the dead. Yet the event was also universalist, as people of all backgrounds swayed together to the soulful music during the service. There seemed to be a collective consciousness in the room, trying through prayer and fellowship to will America out of its darkness to a place of hope and inspiration. I left uplifted and inspired by the mutual embrace of so many diverse people who were saying by their presence, "We will not meekly surrender our freedoms. We will not allow America to become a dark and hateful country. We will ensure that love and justice and decency ultimately prevail."

That week, there were hundreds of similar services happening all around America. If Jews felt alone and scared, they had only to open their eyes, ears, and hearts to feel the love and support of millions of their fellow Americans. It is my belief that the salvation of America will come from the same vision that has undergirded Muslim-Jewish relations for the past ten years: a willingness to put our names, our reputations, and our bodies on the line in order to *stand up for each other*.

How SUFO Became Our Credo

When FFEU began its work in Muslim-Jewish relations back in 2007, it was clear that Standing Up for Each Other (or SUFO, as we came to abbreviate it), had to be one of our guiding principles. As Rabbi Schneier said, "It is very important for Muslims and Jews to dialogue and get to know each other. Yet, unless we are willing to be there for the other side when they are attacked, the whole thing won't amount to much. Standing up for each other when it counts is where the rubber really meets the road."

One memorable example of SUFO happened soon thereafter. In early 2008, the Muslim World League, a Mecca-based NGO funded by the Kingdom of Saudi Arabia, announced plans for a World Interfaith

Dialogue Conference. For the first time at a Saudi-sponsored event, mainstream Jewish leaders from the United States and Europe, including Rabbi Schneier, were invited to attend. Excitement in the Jewish community soon turned to dismay, however, when it was learned that the Saudis planned to make Rabbi Dovid Weiss, a virulently anti-Zionist Hasidic rabbi, the preeminent Jewish voice at the event. Weiss had gained infamy in the Jewish community several years earlier when he participated in an international conference on the Holocaust in Tehran, at which Iranian president Mahmoud Ahmadinejad and various participants cast doubt as to whether six million Jews were actually murdered by the Nazis.

Dr. Sayyid Syeed, the Washington-based national director of the Islamic Society of North America (ISNA), who had developed a good working relationship with the Jewish community, called Adel Al-Jubeir, the Saudi ambassador to the United States, and declared that not only would mainstream Jewish leaders decline to attend the Madrid conference if Weiss was made the main Jewish speaker, but he and his team from ISNA would also have to withdraw. As Dr. Syeed recently told me, "The ambassador understood the reason for my gesture and subsequently convinced his side that the whole value of the conference would be lost if they did not replace their choice of Jewish spokesman." Weiss was demoted, and mainstream Jewish leaders ultimately decided to attend. Thanks to Dr. Syeed's stand, the Madrid conference turned out to be a groundbreaking event that promoted enhanced contact between world Jewry and Saudi Arabia and the Gulf states.

Standing Up for Imam Feisal and Daisy Khan during the Ground Zero Mosque Controversy

In 2010, right-wing ideologues, many connected to the Republican Party, seized upon Islamophobia as a weapon to gin up political support in advance of the midterm Congressional elections that November. In May and June, the "Ground Zero mosque" controversy erupted in the liberal and interfaith-friendly New York City. Anti-Muslim talking heads, with assists from political figures like former House Speaker Newt Gingrich and former vice-presidential candidate Sarah Palin, claimed that an application to create a Muslim community center in Lower Manhattan was in fact an attempt to build a mosque five blocks away from the site of the former World Trade Center and defile sacred ground in order to exact revenge on America for its invasion of Iraq and Afghanistan, support of Israel, and other sins.

The perpetrators of this campaign alleged that the gentle Sufi mystic, Imam Feisal Abdul Rauf, was a radical extremist tied to the Muslim Brotherhood—a claim so wildly false as to seem parodic. Yet, if one had no idea that Imam Feisal and his wife, Daisy Khan, were among the most moderate and unequivocally pro-American leaders in the Muslim community (Imam Feisal had written a book entitled *What's Right with Islam Is What's Right with America*), I could see how some might fall prey to the big lie and believe both the smear and the Ground Zero mosque conspiracy theory.

I had the honor to speak on behalf of FFEU at a public hearing of Manhattan Community Board 1 that would issue a recommendation as to whether the community center should go forward. When I arrived at the meeting, the atmosphere was mob-like. Several hundred opponents of the project filled the meeting room to over-capacity, while many more gathered in the crowded hallway, chanting hateful slogans against Islam. Imam Rauf made his presentation, stressing that the purpose of the project was to build not a mosque but a Muslim community center with a small prayer space within. As he spoke, hecklers shouted that he was a fraud, a hater of America, and a hidden supporter of Al-Qaeda. They continued to heckle subsequent speakers who expressed support for the building of the community center.

As I listened to the bigoted chants and took in the bullying and intimidation, it occurred to me that this must have been what it felt like in Germany before and after Hitler assumed power. This was the kind of hate that was directed against my mother as a frightened teenage girl.

Finally, my name was called to speak, and I walked to the podium with my heart in my mouth. I explained that I worked in Muslim-Jewish relations for FFEU, which drew a groan from the crowd; and that I had collaborated with Imam Feisal and Khan on a number of projects and events over the preceding two years and knew them to be people of peace, moderation, and decency, deeply committed to strengthening Muslim-Jewish relations. One heckler roared "Bullshit!" at my comments and was threatened with expulsion by the moderator.

At the end of that evening, the planning board voted lopsidedly in favor of the community center project to a cascade of boos, curses, and vows to resist from many in the audience. Despite the board's approval and strong backing from then-Mayor Michael Bloomberg, the New York City Muslim Community Center was never built. Among other obstacles, the $100 million cost proved prohibitive. But the smear campaign resonated far beyond New York City. Outrage over the supposed plot to defile Ground Zero fired up the Republican base and helped the GOP sweep the Congressional elections of 2010. Islamophobia, which had seemed to be receding in the early years of our Muslim-Jewish coalition building, was back with a vengeance.

On the other hand, Jews in many parts of the country were making common cause with their Muslim neighbors by testifying at zoning board hearings in support of applications by Muslim communities to build mosques. At many hearings, opponents tried to disguise their fear and bigotry with bogus claims that the planned mosques would increase traffic and noise levels, concerns that rarely seemed to get expressed about applications to build churches or synagogues. I testified twice at such hearings, once in support of the McLean Islamic Center in Virginia and the other at the Islamic Society of Baskin Ridge in New Jersey. Both applications were eventually approved after lengthy hearings that dragged on for years.

Gathering Storm Clouds

The years 2015 and 2016 saw stepped-up efforts by Muslims and Jews to stand up for each other in the face of growing incitement, beginning with the first phase of the 2016 presidential campaign and ascendancy of candidate Donald Trump. Trump made statements like "Islam hates us" and, in the wake of a terrorist rampage by a radicalized young Muslim couple in San Bernardino, California, proposed "a complete and total ban on Muslims entering the United States." In November 2015, I joined forces with Catherine Orsborn, executive director of the Shoulder to

Shoulder Campaign, to organize a show of solidarity with the Islamic Center of Irving, Texas (ICI), a large mosque located in a suburb of Dallas where gun-toting Islamophobes had repeatedly rallied outside the mosque to spew hatred of Islam, holding aloft a huge banner reading STOP THE ISLAMIZATION OF AMERICA. For protesters to carry loaded guns while screaming defamatory invective at a house of worship is perfectly legal in Texas. Even the mayor contributed to the venom, falsely accusing the Muslims of Irving of seeking to impose Sharia law on the town.

In response to the appeal by Catherine and myself, Jewish, Muslim, and Christian leaders from across Texas—including some evangelicals—rallied together at the mosque in early December 2015 to denounce the bullying and bigotry and to offer a counter-message: *One Irving for Us All: Through Different Faiths, Let's Relate.* ICI's Imam Zia ul-Haque Sheikh, who invited leaders of the Jewish and Christian congregations to join in the creation of a new Irving Interfaith Council, said at the event, "Don't fear Muslims, but instead make an effort to get to know your Muslim neighbors. It is the people who have never met a Muslim who are protesting outside our mosque with guns."

Rabbi Michael Kushnick of Congregation Anshai Torah, who made the trip to Irving from Plano (on the other side of Greater Dallas) with several congregants, drew applause when he said, "We Jews know what it is like to be persecuted, so I challenge the Jewish community of North Texas to stand up and speak out for the rights of all faiths to practice their religions freely and without fear."

An older Muslim man in Pakistani garb approached me and said emotionally, "You cannot imagine how important it is that you are here. We've felt so terribly alone. Now we know we have friends."

As 2015 segued into 2016, it was clear that FFEU no longer had the luxury to focus our efforts on warm and fuzzy events bringing Muslims and Jews together to encounter each other. Rather, the priority had to be on ensuring that Jews and interfaith allies were ready to stand with Muslims and to push back against escalating Islamophobia being fomented by presidential candidate Donald Trump.

There was also an escalation of anti-Semitism, with numerous personal attacks on prominent Jews by online trolls, particularly against

Jewish reporters and commentators who dared to call Trump out for his bigotry. By the late summer of 2016, with Trump running neck and neck with Hillary Clinton, I decided to organize a series of twinning events leading up to November 8, Election Day. Members of our two communities would vow to unconditionally stand up for each other going forward, no matter the result of the election. I kicked it off in Washington with a wonderful "Spread Hummus Not Hate" event that culminated in a rally at American University, during which the Muslim and Jewish university chaplains spoke together and denounced bigotry against the Other, and two young women leaders of the Hillel and Muslim Student Association spoke in a similar vein. In the following week, FFEU sponsored similar rallies at Rutgers University in New Jersey and in Frisco, Texas.

Three days before the election, I attended an interfaith ceremony at the University of Southern California, which I had organized in cooperation with the USC Center for Religious Life. Holding candles, students from multiple faith traditions, including Hindu, Buddhist, Jain, and Baha'i together with Jews, Christians, and Muslims, spoke of their apprehension about the fearmongering and polarization and offered prayers for peace, compassion, and mutual understanding. Standing in that church courtyard and drinking in the aura of kindness and love from these young spirits, it seemed unimaginable that Americans could elect a bigot as president. Any country that could produce such wonderful young people, so animated by love and hope, had to be better than that. Yet three days later, America, or at least a sufficient minority in the requisite number of states for an Electoral College victory, proved me wrong. On that election day, Americans showed they were not better than that.

Sabeeha:

From Standing Up for Each Other, to Making a Muslim Friend

The presidential elections of 2016 changed the landscape, and with that our purpose in life. Rather than wait for the new administration to define the place for Muslims in America, Khalid and I took charge of our destiny. We had a goal: Educate people about Muslims: the spirit of

Islam, the meaning of its texts, its compatibility with the US constitution, and the American Muslim identity. Our objective: in 2017, to visit ten cities across the United States and give fifty talks.

We emailed our network, which was huge. "Invite Us and We Will Come," anytime, anywhere. That summer, Khalid and I had given five daily lectures on "Being Muslim in America" at Chautauqua Institution—hundreds had signed up. The interest was so intense that each day people would line up an hour ahead of time and stand in the sweltering heat with walkers or walking sticks. Many were turned away, and on every subsequent day, the lines would get longer. We had no name recognition—it was the thirst for learning that drew the crowds. We reached out to the Chautauquans and the Sisterhood of Salaam Shalom.

Within days, we began receiving invitations asking, "When can you come?" Within a week we had invitations from ten cities: from people we knew, from people we could not remember, from coastal cities to the Great Lakes, the mountains in the north, and the desert in the south. We went to towns we had to look up on Google Maps, staying in the homes of people we had never met. On one of these trips, our son asked, "Where will you be staying?"

"At the home of our host."

"Who are they?"

"Some nice people we haven't met."

Often after disembarking from the train, we would just stand there, waiting to be recognized. Then someone would wave, and we knew that it had to be our host. Everywhere, the halls filled up. We were not celebrities, we had no claim to fame—my book had been out for barely six months—it was people's craving for knowledge, the desire to get to know a Muslim, to have a conversation with a couple whose faith has been vilified, and to make up their own minds. Think of all the planning host families put into organizing an event. It takes dedication and drive to organize, mobilize, publicize, host and feed, transport . . . and all for the commitment to repairing the world. We would part by saying, "Please come to New York, and stay with us," and some of them did indeed.

As 2017 came to a close, we had covered twenty-seven cities, clocked thousands of miles, and delivered over a hundred talks in person. Not bad, right? It's testimony to the open hearts and open minds of our fellow Americans, who opened their homes to strangers. This is the America we love.

Bring the Other into Your Fold

A New Year for Jews and Muslims: that year—2017—Muharram and Rosh Hashanah fell on the same day, something that happens literally once in a lifetime. There was a time when it would have gone unnoticed, but in today's climate, the interfaith-ers seized the moment. I received an email from Rabbi Leah Berkowitz, inviting me to join Rosh Hashanah services. I had babysitting duties so I politely declined, but Rabbi refused to take no for an answer and called me.

"I am babysitting for my granddaughter," I said.

"How old is she?"

"Five."

"Bring her."

"She can't sit for long."

"Bring her coloring books. Just come for half an hour, when we blow the shofar."

So we came. My granddaughter ended up dancing with Rabbi Leah on the stage, and actually sat through the rest of the service.

Another call from Leah, this time for Yom Kippur. She asked me to give a talk on what it is like to be a Muslim in New York in current times.

"I am sorry I can't come. I am taking out-of-town visitors on a cruise."

"When does it end?"

"Twelve noon."

Where does it dock?"

"Chelsea Pier."

"Take a cab and we will cover the cost."

"But I have guests with me."

"Bring them."

So I brought my Bible-study dairy farmer friends from rural America to Yom Kippur services. You can believe that day was a first for them: accompanying a Muslim woman giving a talk at a synagogue!

These warm and generous gestures by Rabbi Leah are a glimpse into the heart and soul of America. She had brought her Muslim American friend into the fold and made her part of the holiest of high holidays. This is America at its best. This is *tikkun olam*.

The bigger test came eight months later, when the conflict escalated in Gaza.

Our Conflict, Our Shared Grief

It was the day before Ramadan 2018 when I got an email from Rabbi Avram Mlotek. "Ramadan Mubarak! Are you around today? I would love to come and sit with you for a few minutes simply to be together and mourn the painful loss of life in Israel/Palestine."

Khalid and I had woken up that morning in a state of mourning over the violence in Gaza, disappointed at the silence of politicians, and feeling hopeless for the Palestinians as we watched the celebration of the opening of the embassy in Jerusalem.

"I am tied up this morning. Can you come this evening?"

"I am busy this evening. How about tomorrow morning?"

Back and forth, emails and text messages, calendars were just not coinciding. But the rabbi did not give up, and at 5:00 p.m. the doorbell rang.

This was a first for Khalid and me. *Palestinians are dying, they have lost hope for their place in Jerusalem, and a rabbi comes to us to share our pain.* I flicked through my iPhone and showed him a photo of our six-year-old granddaughter, posing in front of her Ramadan calendar. Each day is a little colorful pocket with a good-deed note inside. Each day she will get her good-deed assignment. He loved it. We settled on the sofa, a painting of Qur'anic calligraphy in green and gold adorning the wall behind, and talked. We talked about the violence, the politics; we listened to one another; we saw things the same way and saw things differently; we looked into crystal balls, visualizing what the future might look like; then Khalid asked Rabbi Mlotek to say a prayer. He sang in Hebrew, a prayer for peace in our walls and in our castles. I prayed for him, and for his family. Khalid later said that he had felt "we were his flock, and he was ministering to us."

Sabeeha and Walter:

Together Because We Need Each Other

Today, America is a scary but exhilarating place in which people of conscience of all backgrounds, dedicated to living in an open and diverse America, are being put to the test. But good things are happening too as a result of the crisis. One great leap forward in comparison to a decade ago is that Muslims and Jews on a communal and personal level are now committed to *standing up for each other.* An infrastructure for fulfilling that mitzvah, that moral imperative, has been created, and there are thousands of people on both sides involved in the effort. Remember the call during the early months of the Trump administration for a "Muslim registry"? No sooner was the threat made than leaders—non-Muslims—issued the statement: "If this happens, we will register as Muslims." The threat went away. Just like that!

As we know only too well, there are moments—especially during upticks in the Middle East conflict—when Jews and Muslims become upset with each other's positions and advocacy and pull apart temporarily. Yet, as has been the case repeatedly in recent years, we always come back together, usually after a hiatus of a few weeks or months. This is not only because so many of us have come to like and respect one another personally—that is certainly a wonderful step forward—but for an even more compelling reason: Muslims and Jews need each other in order to be safe. An America that would persecute one minority faith community will eventually turn against others. The only protection for either community is to stand in solidarity with the other—or with any other minority community that is under attack. Standing Up for Each Other has become standard operating procedure for both communities, and that's a huge step forward for us all.

Part 2

TAPPING OUR ROOTS

*What We Learned from
Our Respective Life Journeys*

CHAPTER 7

BEARING WITNESS FOR OUR MOTHERS

As the two of us dialogued, we were struck by the similarities in the lives of our mothers, Farrukh and Helga: both refugees who fled as teenagers from their respective homes in India and Germany and built secure, productive, and fulfilling lives in their new homelands of Pakistan and America. So before sharing our own life stories, we want to tell you about the traumas our mothers endured and surmounted.

Sabeeha:

In August 1947, British India was partitioned into Hindu-majority India and Muslim-majority Pakistan. Millions of Muslims made the exodus from India over to the land that was to become West Pakistan. On the way across the bitter divide, trains carrying Muslims were attacked by armed vigilantes. Tens of thousands were massacred. My mother and her family boarded a train in Hoshiarpur in the Punjab province of India and headed to Pakistan. My father—Mummy's fiancé—waited for her at the other end in Pakistan.

There are some stories you will never forget. This is one of them, which Mummy told me:

"We heard that trains going to Pakistan were being attacked. During the journey, as we passed by Amritsar, I peeked through the wooden shutters and saw hundreds of Sikh men standing in rows, swords in hand, gleaming in the sun. They looked like they were ready to strike. Aba Jee [Mummy's father] said, 'Away from the shutters!' Crouched in the dark cabin, I thought that at any moment they would attack and we all would be killed. But the train moved on, and the attack never came. I believe the men were waiting for orders to attack."

My maternal uncle, Jedi Mamoon, now eighty-one, told me more about that train ride. When the family boarded at Hoshiarpur, the superintendent of police, who was a friend of my grandfather, offered a police escort. "They will accompany you up to Jallandhar. There my jurisdiction ends. From there on, you are on your own. Remember, do not open the doors; do not open the windows." The idea was for the train to look like a cargo car. It was claustrophobic, for sure. My uncle remembers that the stop in Amritsar, Punjab—where the Sikhs were walking the platform holding swords—seemed to take forever.

Finally, the train they were on pulled out of Amritsar, and when it arrived at the next stop, Aba Jee peeked through the shutters and saw the signpost reading LAHORE, which was on the Pakistani side of the border. Cheers of relief and joy went up throughout the train. Their final destination was Gujranwala. When they disembarked, men were hosing down the blood from a train that had pulled in earlier. Every passenger on that train to Pakistan had been slaughtered.

My family's baggage was to arrive on the next train. Mummy's dress for her upcoming wedding to my father was in that cargo. Daddy went to the railway station to receive the baggage. He returned empty-handed, silent, and stunned.

"What is it, Kazim?" Aba Jee asked my father.

"The train rolled in with blood dripping from the doors. Dead bodies everywhere. The cargo was looted." He was barely audible.

Only the engineer was spared by the mob, so he could drive the train, laden with dead bodies, to Pakistan. The men Mummy saw in Amritsar had attacked the next train. It could have just as easily been Mummy's train, and if so, I wouldn't be writing this story.

Mummy emigrated to Pakistan because she was committed to the idea of a homeland for the Muslims. Months earlier, she had marched in the streets, demanding the creation of Pakistan. She loved Pakistan with a passion. Once a stranger in this land, she made her home there, married, raised her three children there, and thrived. As far as she was concerned, Pakistan was the only place to be. Of course, she had her disappointments, but then anyone, anywhere will face the challenge of their country not living up to their expectations. But she was always hopeful and positive, and fiercely defensive of Pakistan. There were many opportunities for her to make a home with us in the United States, but she would say, "I'll come to the US to visit you, but Pakistan is my home." There she died, and there she lies buried beside Daddy in the army graveyard in Rawalpindi. She never went back to India.

Ultimately, I believe her success in fighting for a homeland—for Pakistan, which was no small feat—shaped her outlook. She learned that if you strive, you can do more than move mountains. You can be part of a movement that creates a nation.

Walter:

My mother was a Jewish refugee from Berlin. In early September 1938, at the age of fourteen, she fled Hitler's Germany with her mother by running across the Belgian border.

When I was growing up, she told me the story of how she and her mother came to the train station in Berlin, the city of her birth, each with a small valise, so that they would appear to be going away for a few days and not create suspicion they were fleeing the country. My mother was an only child, and her father, a successful businessman, had passed away several months earlier. They took a train to Munich, and from there by prearrangement they got into a Gestapo car, driven by Gestapo men who were making nice money for themselves by smuggling Jews out of the country. My grandmother and mother were driven all the way from Munich to the Belgian border—approximately four hundred miles—on special autobahns used only by the military. They had to lie down on the back seat to avoid being seen. By now it was nighttime, and at some point, the driver said to them, "Get out now and run in that direction. Keep running across the field until you see a man waving a white handkerchief. Then you will know that you have crossed into Belgium."

I interviewed my mother about her flight from Germany in December 2004, just over four months before she died.

"We did what we were told and ran across the field, and soon we saw the guy with the white handkerchief. But we didn't know if this was a setup or not. We feared the Gestapo might shoot us in the back at any moment," she told me.

"What were you feeling as you ran across that field?" I asked.

"I was feeling nothing at all. I was trying to survive, and the way to do that was to turn off all emotions and just operate on autopilot."

The guy with the white handkerchief turned out to be a member of a gang of Belgian smugglers, who led them across the border and then proceeded to extort money from them. He nearly raped my grandmother. There was a Jewish man with them, another refugee, who protected her.

They spent the night with those awful smugglers and then were told, "You will have to walk another fifty kilometers [thirty-one miles] from here to Liège [the first large town in Belgium]. You will need to walk at night, because if you are apprehended by the Belgian police in the area near the German border, they will send you back to Germany." My grandmother and mother walked for three nights on trails through the forest in rugged terrain, sleeping in farmhouses during the days—all of which had been arranged by the smugglers—until they reached Liège. Then they moved on to Antwerp for a few months, where there was a large Jewish community, and eventually met up with my grandmother's sister Hilda, who had already left Germany with her husband and was living in Holland.

Just before New Year 1939, the four of them moved down to Nice in the south of France, where they stayed for about eighteen months as they tried to figure out how to get from France to Palestine. But the British were blockading Palestine to prevent Jewish refugees from getting there. Also, at the very moment when they most desperately needed a place to go, America was virtually closed to Jews. Despite pious expressions of concern for the trapped Jews of Europe, the US was unwilling to set aside its harsh immigration quotas and take more than a handful of desperate European Jews. So the four were effectively stuck in Nice.

Then came the lightning Nazi conquest of France in May–June 1940. My grandmother and mother ran from port to port in the southern part of the country in a vain search for a way out, while the Gestapo began rounding up Jewish refugees for shipment to concentration camps. Finally, after weeks of running and hiding, they managed to purchase life-saving visas to Ecuador, which enabled them to purchase train tickets to Lisbon, Portugal. After waiting there for nine months, they went on to New York, after a perilous passage through an Atlantic Ocean filled with German U-boats.

They did not have US visas. The US embassy in Lisbon had put them on an endless waiting list, a manifestation of the overall US policy of turning away European Jews. They eventually managed to secure permanent refugee status in America after a representative of HIAS took my grandmother ashore to meet a New York City judge with the same last name as hers—Ringel—who signed an affidavit saying he would take responsibility for them. While this was taking place, my sixteen-year-old mother was being held as surety on Ellis Island.

My mother's survival story is representative in microcosm of the extreme vulnerability to imminent extinction that millions of Jews faced in the 1940s from Nazi Germany, as the rest of the world, including the United States, largely looked the other way while the Nazis slaughtered Jews. Thankfully, my mother made it out of Europe by the skin of her teeth, but six million of my people were liquidated. In the wake of that catastrophe, the vast majority of Jews understood that if we were to survive as a people, we could no longer depend on others to protect us but needed to empower ourselves and control our own destiny by creating a Jewish state.

My mom became very American and loved America deeply. For her, there was no looking back, to the point where she refused to speak a word of German for most of the rest of her life. She would tell me when I was growing up, "I hate the sound of the German language. It makes me sick to my stomach." When we made our first trip to Europe on the way to Israel when I was eleven, and then another European trip one year later on the way back to the States, we visited many European countries, but not Germany. My mother went back to Germany later in her life, accompanying my father to several scientific conferences, but she totally identified with America. She had a strong feeling for Israel too, but she was first and foremost a proud American. Having arrived in New York at the age of sixteen, she quickly came to speak English without a trace of an accent. Listening to her speak American English, you would have no hint that she was from somewhere else.

My mother had strongly liberal values. For much of her adult life, she was deeply involved in the League of Women Voters, getting women involved in the political process. She was a great supporter of the civil rights movement, an opponent of the Vietnam War, and was involved in many other liberal causes. She loved America with a passion but recognized its imperfections. As a patriotic American, she was doing whatever she could to make her country a little bit better.

Sabeeha and Walter:

As we shared stories about our mothers, we realized they had a number of things in common. They were both highly competent women with strong leadership qualities who accomplished a great deal in what was then definitely a man's world. Farrukh got things done that women in Pakistan of the 1960s and 1970s rarely did—she had the equivalent of an associate degree; she was a homemaker but had good business sense and could move paperwork through a rigid bureaucracy, oversee construction workers building her house, get the municipality to clean the streets, form a neighborhood association to secure the community, and more. For Helga's part, she managed a small office of an advertising agency that did market research, where she employed many young women who looked up to her. She served in leadership positions in the League of Women Voters. She was warm and caring, was a great mentor, and had many strong friendships, although there were moments when the trauma she brought with her from her youth would resurface in bouts of seemingly irrational anxiety.

Neither of us gave much thought to our mothers' traits or their source while we were growing up, but as we compared notes of their escapes, we began to connect the dots. We saw how our personalities and values were affected by our mothers' experiences. Each of us inherited from our mothers a determination to stand against hatred, bigotry, and injustice and work to improve conditions in society. We believe this commitment was solidified in the psyches of both our mothers by the experience of having their young lives put at risk. Each in her own way affirmed the moral imperative of the post-Holocaust slogan "Never Again": the conviction that no person should ever again have to endure the horrors they passed through.

Indeed, our lives have been marked by a common commitment to the cause of justice and peace. Rather than focusing on building successful careers, or making money, each of us has devoted our energies to bettering our communities and all of humanity. That is the precious legacy we received from our mothers, whose memories we deeply cherish.

We would now like to share with you key moments in our life journeys that shaped us into the people we are today.

CHAPTER 8

HOW THE TWO
OF US GOT HERE

Israel and Pakistan: Love of Our Homelands

The lands each of us hold dear—Pakistan and Israel—were cast in the same mold. Both were created at the same historical moment—1947 and 1948 respectively—for the same purpose: to be a homeland for the Muslims and a homeland for the Jews. Israel was created to be, and remains, the world's only Jewish state; Pakistan is the only country in the world created explicitly as a Muslim state. Both were born out of a bloody conflict. Both were largely secular societies in their early years, but as the decades progressed, both countries have moved sharply in the direction of extremism and fundamentalism. As of this writing, Pakistan has not recognized Israel. There are no diplomatic relations between the two countries. That was the vantage point we came from.

The two of us are American—one American-born, one naturalized—yet we each have deep emotional and personal ties to Israel and Pakistan, respectively. That love of the land, that connection, is rooted in the common idea behind the creation of these two nations. But it is more than that.

Sabeeha:

What Pakistan Means to Me

I was born in a newborn land, the "Land of the Pure," far, far away from my home today. Pakistan was four years old.

I have lived forty-nine of my sixty-nine years in the US, and only fifteen years in Pakistan. (The math won't work, so add in the five years of my early childhood in England.) Yet those early years in Pakistan laid the foundation for who I am at my core. Pakistan is the land of my birth, the land of my ancestors, my family home; it's where I grew up, where I got my schooling; it's the nation whose national anthem I sang every morning when the school bell rang. Even today when I, a longstanding American citizen, hear the band play "Pak Sar Zameen," Pakistan's national anthem, I get goose bumps.

At the root of my passion for the land was the creation of Pakistan, the struggle for "a homeland for the Muslims of the subcontinent." When did I first learn about its birth? Was it the stories my parents told me, or what I learned in school? I'm not sure. But what I heard is etched in my DNA.

The land was once India, ruled by the Mughals in its most glorious era (sixteenth to eighteenth centuries), when the Hindu majority flourished for centuries under Muslim rule. By the time of Emperor Akbar's reign in the sixteenth century, the Muslims had assimilated into the Indian culture. Akbar's period was of particular significance. He married a Hindu princess, Jodha Bai, formed a team of advisers drawn from all religions, and started a new faith called Din-e-Illahi—a mixture of Islam and Hinduism—in his pursuit of achieving political and social harmony. Emperors Jahangir and Shahjahan, who were moderate rulers, succeeded Akbar. But things began to change when Aurangzeb, Shahjahan's son and heir, ascended to the throne in 1658. A controversial figure—considered by some historians to have been a religious bigot and a despotic ruler but by others as a pious, austere monarch who meted out justice to non-Muslims—he reversed policies of previous Mughal emperors and alienated the Hindus. He converted Hindu temples into mosques. He sowed the seeds of hatred and acrimony that have endured to this day.

Then came the British as traders, who sowed discord among the Muslims and Hindus to overthrow the Mughal Empire. By 1858, the

British had colonized India. They patronized the Hindus and encouraged their elevation to power in local government institutions, commerce, and trade. Muslims were outcasts, oppressed and relegated to second-class citizenship. My father tells me that as a young man in the 1940s, when he would visit a Hindu friend, his friend's mother served him food in separate dishes, reserved for the outcasts. After he left, his mother would hose down the house. "Muslims were considered unclean," Daddy said. Whenever my father told me this story, I had to look away. A man who carried himself with such quiet dignity—how did he endure the insult!

As India sought independence from the British in the early twentieth century, Muslims feared that their position as an oppressed minority would never change, and independence would mean merely a change of masters, from the British to the Hindus.

"We were afraid that in a Hindu-dominated country, we would have no rights," Daddy told me. "We would be just a notch above the 'Untouchables.'"

The Untouchables—the lowest Hindu caste—are relegated to live in the outskirts of towns, and cleaning toilets was their only profession. Knowing how his friend's mother had treated Daddy, I understood his point about the fate of Muslims if we hadn't separated from India and taken control of our own destiny. Today, that has become all the more apparent as Hindu nationalism is gaining strength under Prime Minister Narendra Modi's regime. Immigrant Muslims are being stripped of their citizenship, human rights of Kashmiri Muslims are being grossly violated, and atrocities against Muslims—lynchings, burnings—continue to escalate and go unpunished across India.

"It was impossible to coexist with the Hindus," I remember my eighth-grade teacher, Miss Jamila, telling a class of twelve to fifteen young girls. In the all-girls public school in Kharian Cantonment, Miss Jamila, a tall woman in her late twenties, her black hair braided in a thick *chutiya* that reached down to her hips and swayed each time she swirled around to write on the blackboard, waved her hand resolutely as she faced the students, seated two to a desk. "Muslims were monotheist, Hindus polytheists; Hindus worshipped the cow, Muslims ate beef; Hindus would not socialize with Muslims—they were the 'outcast.' There was only one solution."

She then paused. That was her style. She would give us a prompt, pause, let us absorb the impact, and then call on us to complete the story; in this case, the story we all knew.

Hands went up.

"Yes." she pointed to my friend Rabia, sitting next to me. Rabia, the most vocal in class, was always the first to raise her hand. "What was the solution, Rabia?"

"A separate country for Muslims," said Rabia.

"Why a separate country?"

"So that Muslims could live in peace," said another student.

"How was the separate country created?"

"Partitioning India into two countries: India for the Hindus, Pakistan for the Muslims," a third student responded. I was the shy one; my hand seldom went up.

"Very good," Miss Jamila said, nodding. She knew we had the correct answers to her questions at our fingertips—after all, they had been drilled into us since who knew when. These preliminary questions were just the warm-up for Miss Jamila to delve into memorable details of the miracle that was Pakistan. With each grade level, as we progressed through high school, the story of Partition and the creation of the country we were proud of became more complex, the pictures more vivid, and the impact more stirring.

Our teachers held us spellbound as we listened to the stories and gazed in awe at the photograph of Mohammad Ali Jinnah—the founder of Pakistan—facing us on the white wall above the blackboard. We watched the story of Partition replayed in movies, documentaries, TV series, and plays. We felt grateful that we were living in a free country. We felt proud—we belonged to a nation that had managed to come into being despite the weak position of the Muslims and the strength of opposing forces.

Walter:

What Israel Means to Me

I have lived sixty-three of my seventy years in the land of my birth, the United States of America, and four years in Israel; one year as a child and three more as a young adult. (There were also three years in Russia, where I was a foreign correspondent during my early forties.) Yet despite the relative brevity of the time I spent living in the Jewish state, I loved Israel for most of my life in a much deeper and more profound way than I did the United States. Indeed, I related to Israel as my true home.

In the beginning, there was *Exodus*. Not the Second Book of the Bible, but rather Leon Uris's sweeping novel about the recreation in the twentieth century of a Jewish commonwealth in the Land of Israel. I first read *Exodus* at age ten. The scope and intensity of the book and its expression of unapologetic Jewish pride overpowered me and impacted my evolving sense of self more than anything I have read before or since.

As a lone Jewish kid growing among gentiles, amid fields, forests, and baseball fields in the rolling, verdant North Hills suburbs outside Pittsburgh, I was transfixed from the moment I picked up *Exodus* and inspired by the story of two fictional brothers of the Zionist founding fathers' generation—Yossi and Yakov Rabinsky—who, impelled by Zionist fervor, left their barren Ukrainian shtetl in the early 1900s and walked all the way to the Holy Land. I was awestruck by the heroic feats of Barak's son, the fearless, utterly self-confident sabra hero Ari Ben Canaan, who smuggled desperate Jewish refugees to Palestine in defiance of the British and fought in the War of Independence. And I fell in love with Karen Clement, the sweet German Jewish girl who survived the Holocaust in hiding, only to be senselessly murdered in the newborn State of Israel by fiendish Arab *fedayeen* (saboteurs).

Exodus presented the conflict over Palestine as being between idealistic, valiant, warm-hearted, and progressive Jews on one side and cruel, venal, and backward Arabs on the other. In truth, the book was a simplistic "paint by numbers" propaganda job, albeit a superbly written one. Despite, or because of, its fundamental flaws, *Exodus* helped solidify American support for Israel for decades to come, and later inspired many Soviet Jews to embrace their Jewishness and connect emotionally with Israel.

I remember the release of the film version of *Exodus* shortly after I read the book, with the ruggedly gorgeous blue-eyed Paul Newman playing the dashing Ari Ben Canaan. I found myself overcome with tears during the scene in which the blue-and-white Star of David flag was raised over the refugee ship *Exodus* in defiance of the refusal by British authorities to allow the ship's desperate cargo of Holocaust survivors to reach Eretz Israel.

For me, that moment in the film was an emotionally overpowering affirmation of Jewish pride and power. I left the movie feeling that the Israelis were fighting not only for their own state, but for me as well. If I could somehow get there someday, perhaps I would become one of them.

I had been far from a proud Jew until then. Raised without benefit of synagogue or Jewish education in an area where we were the only Jewish family, I had by the age of ten come to feel ashamed of my Jewishness. Part of that complex had to do with my experience of confusion and shame over the Holocaust, which had concluded only fifteen years earlier, and during which six million Jews were said, in the parlance of the times, "to have gone like sheep to the slaughter." Or, as a sick joke that came out around that time had it: "How many Jews can you fit in a Volkswagen? The correct answer is 'six.' Two in the front, two in the back, and two in the ashtray." Many sabras, or native-born Israelis, expressed contempt for the vanished Jews of Europe, whom they sometimes referred to sneeringly as "soap" because they had not found the will to fight back effectively against their persecutors and the body fat of some of the victims of the crematoria was, quite literally, turned into soap. Using such a hateful term was a textbook case of blaming the victims, whom the Israeli sabras considered the weak Jews of the Diaspora.

Sabeeha:

It Was a Miracle

How had an oppressed and outcast minority in British India pulled off this miracle—carving out a land for the Muslims—creating Pakistan? Well, the Muslims of India got organized. They formed a party—the All-India Muslim League—to lead the movement and chose a leader to make and push their case. Mohammad Ali Jinnah, a brilliant lawyer, was a graduate of Lincoln Inn in London and an accomplished parliamentarian. His tall form, chiseled features, monocle, clipped British accent, and well-tailored suits lent him an aristocratic appearance. He delivered. In

1940, the party, under Jinnah's leadership, passed a resolution calling for an independent Muslim state.

It was a hard sell. A very hard sell. The Hindus bitterly opposed it. They viewed the concept of Pakistan as secessionist and wanted control over the entire subcontinent. For the next seven years, Jinnah led the negotiations on behalf of the Muslims and stayed the course with remarkable precision. He convinced the British rulers and negotiated the terms of division of the land: Muslim-majority provinces were to be grouped to constitute Pakistan.

My Mother Got Arrested Giving Birth to Pakistan

By 1946, Muslims were taking to the streets demanding a "Pakistan." My mother, a seventeen-year-old burqa-wearing college student, was among them. Mummy got arrested on charges of civil disobedience. Aba Jee, my maternal grandfather, a conservative Muslim, received a call from the police. "We have your daughter in custody. Please come and get her." He never reprimanded her. She was fighting for her homeland, and in his own way, so was he. Mummy would tell this story and say with pride, her voice rising in pitch: "*We* made Pakistan." I often relate this story to my friends with a preamble: "My mother got arrested giving birth to Pakistan." Once one of them asked me, "What did your grandfather say to your mother when he came to get her out of jail?" I don't know. I never asked Mummy. Now that I am writing about it, there is so much I wish I had asked her.

The labor was painful, but the British at last agreed to partition India. In May 1946, they set the date for transfer of power: June 1948. The British created a Boundary Commission under Sir Cyril Radcliffe for demarcation of the boundaries of the two new dominions: Hindu and Muslim. This is where things went wrong—big time.

What We Lost; What We Still Grieve For

The beautiful valley of Kashmir in Northern India has a Muslim majority. According to the agreement, Kashmir was to be part of Pakistan. However, the Hindu leaders wanted Kashmir for India. To forcibly occupy Kashmir, the Hindu leaders of the new India would have to send in their military force through the district of Gurdaspur, which had the only road leading from Punjab to Kashmir. But Gurdaspur was in a Muslim-majority province and had been awarded to Pakistan. We don't know what transpired behind closed doors, but two days later, the decision was reversed and the district of Gurdaspur was awarded to India. With a clear roadway, India sent in the army through Gurdaspur and forcibly occupied Kashmir. The Muslim League protested, but the British Viceroy, Lord Mountbatten, who was known to be close to Nehru, the Hindu leader of India, rebuffed their protests, allowing India to occupy the Muslim-majority Kashmir. India's army remains there to this day. If you look for Gurdaspur on Google maps, you will find it just ten kilometers from the Pakistan border. If you plot the directions from Gurdaspur to Srinagar, Kashmir, you will see why the strategic district of Gurdaspur was carved out and given away to India. To this day, the hearts of each and every Pakistani beat for and weep for the land of Kashmir— as does the heart of yours truly.

In August 2019, Prime Minister Modi stripped Kashmir of its autonomous status. As the world watched, Pakistan set aside its internal problems and raised passionate voices for the rights of Kashmiris. Pakistani immigrants in the United States mobilized to bring pressure to bear on elected officials to call for the end of the lockdown of Kashmiri citizens and restoration of the rights of Kashmiris.

Pakistani immigrants in the United States weren't the only ones raising their voices. Human rights activists and other concerned citizens, appalled by the oppression of Kashmiris, were speaking up. Among them was Walter. Always ready to speak out against injustice, he made the time to lend his voice to draw attention to the plight of Kashmiris.

The Rush to Seal the Fate of a Nation

The next thing that went wrong with Partition was the timetable. Lord Mountbatten decided to fast-track it and disregard the June 1948 deadline. It was rumored that he was in a hurry to return to England, where the position of the coveted First Sea Lord was to be vacant, and he wanted to be back home to secure it. Some dispute that theory and claim the decision was made because riots had broken out between

Hindus and Muslims and there was fear that the whole country would explode. Whatever his motive, Mountbatten moved up the date of the partition to August 1947. This critically reduced the time available for a planned and controlled division. The government was aware of the charged emotions on both sides, had witnessed the riots, yet issues of security, transportation, food, and medical help were disregarded. What transpired is the most dreadful chapter of the subcontinent's history, and it could have been averted had the viceroy given thought to humanitarian issues. As I write this, I can feel my heartbeat quicken.

A Bloody Birth

Pakistan's birth was traumatic, a bloody C-section. One million people died; ten million were uprooted—more than the population of Israel today. As soon as the agreement to partition India was announced, massive migrations began. Six and a half million Muslims made the exodus and trekked over from India to the western part of the subcontinent, to the land that was to be West Pakistan; 4.7 million Hindus and Sikhs moved across to what would now be India. On the way across the divide, hundreds of thousands lost their lives. Punjab became a hotbed of the most horrific violence on the subcontinent. Punjab was a Muslim-majority province, but it was also the heartland of the Sikhs. As a compromise, amid the rioting and bloodshed, Jinnah agreed to give up eastern Punjab to India, so Punjab was split in two. For both Muslims and Sikhs living on the "wrong" side of the east-west divide, it meant migration. Neither side was happy. Sikhs and Hindus killed all the Muslims they could find. Trains carrying Muslims from east to west were attacked and people massacred. My mother and her family were on one of those trains. Decades later, Daddy would tell me, "Both sides committed atrocities."

After the train massacres, Muslims in Pakistan retaliated. A train carrying Hindus from Pakistan to India was attacked and every passenger brutally murdered.

My uncle, Jedi Mamoon, told me, "I was playing by the railroad tracks when the train passed. I saw dead bodies hanging out of the train. Enraged people set fire to houses owned by Hindus, and the night sky glowed in the burnt air. Dead bodies were dumped in the verandah of the morgue, piled like sacks of flour. I was eight years old, and I remember the stench and human body parts being dragged about by stray dogs."

Then there were stories of valor. Daddy told me that just before Partition, Muslim-Hindu riots broke out and curfew was imposed, making it hard for him to stay late at the school to study. He didn't live near the school. So a Hindu friend let him stay with his family, who lived closer to the school. When a Muslim mob stormed the street and tried to break into his Hindu friend's house, Daddy and his friend rushed to the rooftop and took aim with rifles at the mob in the street below to disperse the crowd. In that moment, Daddy and his classmate were not Muslims or Hindus; they were friends.

My grandfather Aba Jee's boss in Gujranwala, the superintendent of jails, was a Sikh—Rugninder Singh. He refused to migrate to India. His house was outside the jail compound, and sensing that his life was in danger, Aba Jee advised Rugninder Singh to move into his (Aba Jee's) home, giving him half the house. One day, when Jedi Mamoon went out to play, he saw men outside the house holding daggers.

"We are going to kill the Sikh you are housing."

Jedi Mamoon ran inside and told Aba Jee.

"Why did you go outside? What if they had kidnapped you?"

Jedi Mamoon was grounded.

"You are not safe here," Aba Jee said to Rugninder Singh, a kind and stately gentleman. "You should go to India for now and come back when things settle." Rugninder left, and for a while wrote letters to Aba Jee: "I am coming back." He did not return. The Hindus and Sikhs left Pakistan, and while a small Hindu population remained in Sindh in southern Pakistan, there were none in the Punjab.

Those Left Behind

Millions of Muslims decided against making the move to Pakistan. All they ever had and owned was in India—their families, homes, property, businesses, jobs—their roots. A friend who is now in her eighties tells me that at the time of Partition, her father had decided to stay back in India. They lived in the city of Aligarh. Her father and uncle would spend the night standing guard on the rooftop, armed with guns, to protect their homes from being torched and their daughters raped. Standing vigil night after night was not sustainable. Living in fear could not be endured. A minority in their city, they lacked a support system. Eventually, they decided to pack up and leave—taking whatever they could carry in their hands—and make the exodus to Pakistan. In the years that followed, close to another million migrated.

In those first few months in 1947, chaos was the new normal. Caravans of people walking over to Pakistan had no home and no family to greet them. All they carried with them was the promise of a homeland. In refugee camps, volunteers logged in the names of the arrivals and the names of the missing children, missing wives, missing fathers. People were scouring the camps, searching for lost relatives. One man sought employment with Aba Jee as domestic help. His married son had gone missing. He and his daughter-in-law would go to the refugee camps every day, hoping to find him. As the months went by, they gave up hope. The man decided that his widowed daughter-in-law should marry his younger son. So, they married. A few days later, the missing son turned up. Sounds like a scene out of a movie script, right? Aba Jee was furious at the father, calling him an *Ullu ka patha,* an untranslatable Urdu epithet. The father sought the advice of a *maulvi,* a cleric, who advised, "Ask the woman what she wants." That is my kind of *maulvi.* She opted for the later model, the younger brother, much to the amusement of the younger crowd around and raising the eyebrows of Aba Jee. The bride had obviously enjoyed her fresh union with the new husband. Aba Jee would rant and rave: "What kind of a joint am I running!" Actually, the term he used was *kanjar khana* (brothel). I down-rated it in translation from X to PG-13. No one remembers what happened to her former husband.

Men and women who were engaged to be married found themselves on opposite sides of the partition lines—they were never united. Brothers were separated: one in the Pakistan Army, one in the Indian. Each time my father's fellow army officer pulled the trigger across the lines of defense, he wondered if it would strike his brother. Families would not reunite until decades later; others never saw one another again.

Jedi Mamoon tells me that Muslims who migrated to Pakistan were of two categories: those who were mobile, of lesser means, with no economic interests in India, who risked little in exploring the promise of a new life, and those who were passionate and deeply committed to the idea of Pakistan. Mummy's family was among the latter. After the agreement to form Pakistan was announced, government officers were given a choice to serve in India or Pakistan. Aba Jee opted for Pakistan.

A Nation Is Born

On August 14, 1947, at the stroke of midnight, the subcontinent of India was officially split asunder into two sovereign states: Pakistan and India, with Pakistan composed of East Pakistan to the east of India and West Pakistan on the western side, with India in between. The next day—August 15—India gained its independence from Britain. In a parting shot, the British gave the two nations something to fight about: Kashmir. I still feel the bitter taste. So does every Pakistani.

The carnage ended by the end of 1947 and early 1948, and people got on with the business of making a new life. At first there was chaos, as in "Who is in charge? Where is my next paycheck coming from? Who owns this house? I left behind millions in property—how much is the government going to reimburse me?" Eventually, that settled too, and in 1948, my parents were finally married.

Walter:

Not Present at the Creation

At that same time, two thousand miles west of Pakistan, in another territory controlled by the British, another new nation was taking shape on the shores of the Mediterranean. Like the Muslims of British India, the Jews of Palestine were demanding self-determination in a homeland of their own. And not just any homeland, but a country that Jewish kings had ruled three millennia earlier, for which Jews the world over had pined and mourned and prayed during two thousand years of bitter exile, vowing every year during the Passover Seder: "Next year in Jerusalem."

Jews in Palestine and around the world had been working to fulfill the dream of a Jewish state for exactly fifty years, since the first World Zionist Congress was held in Basel, Switzerland, in 1897. The congress had been convened by Theodore Herzl, a politically liberal, nonobservant Jewish journalist and playwright who became an advocate of the Jews of Europe returning to Zion after the Dreyfus Affair in France. When a French-Jewish army officer was falsely accused and convicted of spying for Germany, Herzl knew that, even in the most liberal country in Europe, Jews would never be able to overcome deep-seated anti-Semitism.

Now in 1947, in the immediate aftermath of the Holocaust, during which the Allies fighting Nazi Germany did almost nothing to prevent Hitler from systematically liquidating German Jewry, the guilt-stricken world community was ready to assent to Jewish self-determination. On November 29, the United Nations, then headquartered at Flushing Meadow, Queens, just a few miles from my newlywed parents' apartment near Columbia University in Upper Manhattan, voted 33–13 (with ten abstentions) to partition Palestine into two states: one Jewish and one Arab, with Jerusalem a neutral zone.

While the Jews ecstatically accepted the partition plan, the Palestinian Arabs—both Muslim and Christian—emphatically rejected it. They were unwilling to countenance the creation of a Jewish state in any portion of a land they considered their own and in which they had been the majority for a thousand years or more. This irreconcilable conflict led to war between the two sides by early 1948. The Jews gained the upper hand in that struggle. As neighboring Arab states prepared to send their armies into Palestine, the Jewish state's founding father, David Ben-Gurion, rose before a conclave of the World Zionist Organization in a crowded hall in Tel Aviv on the evening of May 14, 1948, to proclaim the independence of the State of Israel, the first self-governing Jewish political entity in more than 2,000 years. After an intense struggle over the next six months, the newly created Israel Defense Forces repelled the invading Arab armies and seized considerably more territory than had been allotted to the Jews in the UN Partition Resolution before signing armistices with their Arab neighbors by early 1949.

What My Parents Said

I recall asking my parents what they felt when they heard the news of the birth of Israel. My father responded, "Strangely, I don't remember us talking much about it at the time." My mother nodded her agreement that the gigantic events in the Middle East had barely penetrated their consciousness, even though my mother had a cousin in Palestine who fought in the Battle of Acre during Israel's War of Independence.

My parents' inattention to events in Israel hardly seems surprising given that they had gotten married in June 1947, only about eight months before the War for Independence began. Their wedding came after a whirlwind romance of about seven months that commenced shortly after my father—recently returned from US Army service in the Pacific—broke off his engagement to his previous girlfriend soon after the families had thrown a lavish engagement celebration at the Waldorf-Astoria Hotel in New York. Then, my father commenced his graduate studies in physics at Columbia University, while my mother continued her job on Wall Street. So, yes, Stan and Helga Ruby had a lot going on in those days.

Nevertheless, in retrospect, given how important Israel would become in their lives and those of their three children, it seems strange to me that my parents barely remarked upon Israel's successful battle for independence. My guess is that like many other American Jews, having just witnessed the destruction of European Jewry, my parents weren't ready to invest emotionally only a couple of years later in a cause that—as it appeared to many at that time—might well end in another crushing defeat and with hundreds of thousands more dead Jews. It could accurately be said that until the glorious events of 1948, the Jews had been on a two-thousand-year losing streak, culminating in the early 1940s in the most terrible slaughter our people had yet experienced.

Sabeeha:

A Military Girl with a British Accent

Daddy decided to join the newly formed Pakistan army. After graduating from the Pakistan Military Academy in Kakul—less than four miles away from Abbottabad, the town where Osama bin Laden was captured and killed in 2011—he was sent to England for five years of training in engineering. Mummy was expecting me and stayed back, joining Daddy later with an eight-month-old Sabeeha in her arms. I spent the first five years of my life in England and returned to Pakistan in the mid-1950s sporting a British accent, while Daddy returned every inch a British gentleman. Pakistan by then had settled into a tranquil and easygoing lifestyle. The next ten years were the best years of its life.

I never experienced the making of the nation. I grew up learning that people made many sacrifices and left their homes, families were separated, all for the sake of religious freedom, for Muslims to have a homeland of their own. I was the beneficiary of that struggle. I grew up in a new land that felt as peaceful and safe as a mother's womb, a young country brimming with sunshine and promise, a land of beauty where the majesty of snow-capped mountains leaves you breathless; where the people, whose sincerity and hospitality warms you all over, are proud to be Pakistani; and where, during the war with India in 1965, I sang non-stop Noor Jehan's *"Ae watan ke sajeele jawaano, mere naghme tumhare liye hain"* ("Oh our nation's young warriors, my songs are for you").

Pakistan's history and culture defined me, with an imprint that still endures. I absorbed its traditions of festivity, its color and music; its celebrations shaped my life. Its values of respect for elders, etiquette, and hospitality are what it means to be a Pakistani. Much of what I am today is a consequence of my birth in a place where I spent my formative years. Come into my home, and I will serve you home-cooked *pulao* rice with chicken curry, as we take in the music of the *ghazal*.

A Handsome Couple

My first memories of Pakistan are of my father in his khaki army uniform with brass buttons on his lapels, and shiny metal insignia of a galloping horse on his cap, standing erect in his military posture; and of my mother, always beautiful, sitting at her sewing machine, happy and chatty. Daddy was one of the first graduates from the Pakistan Military Academy. He had enlisted in the army to impress his sweetheart's father after asking for her hand in marriage. In the late 1940s, the armed forces were the most prestigious institutions, second only to civil service. That my father was strikingly handsome must have gotten him extra credit when my grandfather, who appreciated beauty in all its forms, interviewed his prospective son-in-law. Daddy, with his tall stature, light skin, curly light brown hair, and hazel eyes, could easily pass for an Englishman. Those were the days when sexes were segregated and marriages were arranged, yet somehow, my parents met and fell in love. Add to that the complexity that my father was a Shia and my mother a Sunni—a stunning, gorgeous Sunni. My devout Sunni grandfather agreed to the match. Love trumped all—love for his daughter. Mummy had waist-long jet-black flowing hair, olive skin, dark oval eyes with long eyelashes, arched eyebrows, and a slender nose. Tall, with a graceful carriage, she dressed exquisitely, always. Until the day she died—and I am not exaggerating—she personally supervised the custom design of her clothing. Her charm, wit, and gaiety won over friends at first sight. Ours was a secular family. I don't recall ever seeing my father say his prayers. Mummy would, occasionally in her youth and regularly in her later years.

No Invitation Required

My childhood was full of play—skip-the-rope, *chattapu* (like hopscotch) hopping over chalk markings on the concrete driveway, and hide-and-seek in the bushes on the front lawn. When it rained, we played indoor guessing games: Twenty Questions, Capitals of the World, or Ludo, similar to Snakes & Ladders. We played all afternoon while our parents took their afternoon nap, played when they took their afternoon tea in the shade of the verandah, the floor fan humming away, and played until fireflies started twinkling, when Mummy would call us in. Daddy loved to sing, and he would have my sister Neena and me sit on the rug beside him, and we would sing along as the radio played Lata Mangeshkar and Mohammad Rafi's "*Abhi Na Jao Chor Kar*" ("Don't Leave Me Now").

Often our singing was interrupted by a *tonga* horse carriage pulling up and overnight guests descending—aunties, uncles, cousins, and the nanny, with their suitcases and beddings in a rolled holder. No invitation required, no advance notice, just take the train to a faraway city, hail a *tonga* at the station, and present yourself at the home of your host. The host would never say, "What a surprise!" never ask, "How long are you planning to stay?" and always, when it was time to say goodbye, plead in a yearning tone, "Oh please, stay another day" or "Next time, come for a longer stay." Whether one meant it or not was irrelevant. Squealing with delight, we children would run out, jumping as we hugged our cousins and smiling shyly as we got a pat on the head from the uncles and aunties, totally oblivious to Mummy's predicament. She would be telling the cook to go run to the grocery store and get some mutton for lunch and a chicken for the evening meal. Hospitality required one to serve the most scrumptious dish—chicken. In the 1950s, the only chickens in town were the free-range chicks—as in organic, feeding-on-worms chicks. Beef was deemed unhealthy. It was cheap, and it was considered cheap, because cattle were raised to plow the fields and were used for consumption only after they had expended their useful life as domestic animals.

How my mother managed the constant stream of sleepover guests is beyond me. Somehow, there was always enough room. Even when my father was just a major in the army—a middle rank—every house the army provided us had at least three bedrooms with attached baths, a wrap-around veranda where we would sleep in the summer under mosquito nets, and a wide front lawn. We children loved having company stay "overnight," which generally meant many nights. Who wouldn't? Cousins to play with, and chicken for dinner! Never mind the vertical lines creasing Mummy's forehead as she saw her budget turn bright red. Remember, Pakistani menus are no small feat: three full meals plus high tea. Porridge, fried eggs, and milk for breakfast; mutton and vegetable curry, *daal* lentils, and *chappati* for lunch, and dinner. For drinks, it was water. Coca-Cola was reserved for special occasions. No dessert, no in-between snacks—that was the culture. However, with guests at the table, you had the dessert, coke, and all the other trimmings.

Love for All Things Foreign

I don't remember having a garbage can in the house. Life was minimalist and literally down to earth. Everything was consumed—the term "disposable" was not in our vocabulary. There were no leftovers in the fridge, because as Mummy would say, "Finish your food. There are children starving on the streets." I hated vegetables, but Mummy made me eat them. "You have to get used to eating everything or you will become a picky eater like Daddy." And Daddy would nod, as if to say, "Don't be like me."

The mushy turnips with their awful aroma, the *karelas* (bitter melon), the slimy cabbage, the cauliflower that tasted rotten—I ate it all. Give me *Aaloo gosht* with its steaming potatoes in mutton curry, with hot-off-the-tawa *chappati*, and I am in heaven. Taking a piece of the *chappati*, my mouth watering, I would spoon the curry in it, inhale the aroma of cinnamon and cumin, and *Aaah!* Scraps were fed to the pets. Water was stored in glass bottles and pitchers. Paper was scarce, so we recycled every piece. I never heard the term "junk mail." Groceries were bought daily, and produce was fresh off the land. No cans, no prepackaged foods, no frozen foods.

Foreign goods were the craze. Anything labeled "Made in England" was gold. In the fifties and sixties, a few lucky family members got to travel to the West, and when they returned, they would be sporting an English sweater or would bring us a pack of Cadbury chocolates, which we savored, one square a day.

"This material is beautiful," Mummy would say, caressing the fabric of a friend's shalwar kameez.

"It's foreign," the friend would say, conferring on herself a status of privilege.

Mummy and Daddy would make friends with the American army officers on assignment in Pakistan. We called them *foreigners*. On one of our visits to their home, the *foreigners* asked my parents, "Would you like some wine?"

"No thank you. We don't drink," Mummy said. "But I will take your empty wine bottles." She had been admiring the design of the bottles. So, the next time Chris and Bob came to visit, they walked in with a crate of empty bottles. Mummy used them for storing drinking water, but not until after she had purified the bottles by having my grandmother recite verses from the Qur'an and blow her Qur'anic breath into the sterilized bottles. When the *foreigners* were packing to return back home, Mummy would spend her carefully saved pin money to buy their stemware and Brillo pads.

Just recently, sitting in my New York City apartment, I was talking on the phone with my sister Neena in Pakistan. She asked me, "Do you have plans for this weekend?"

"I have friends coming from upstate New York to spend a few days with us."

"Are they Pakistani or foreigners?" she asked.

We chuckled.

A Room for Grandma

My paternal grandmother, Daadi Amma, lived with us. My grandfather had died when Daddy was a child. Daddy was one of five siblings, and they fought over whom Daadi Amma would live with. Everyone wanted her. The elders were considered a blessing, and taking care of elderly parents was an honor, a sure path to heaven in the afterlife. To this day, nursing homes are nonexistent in Pakistan. It is a son's responsibility to take care of parents, he being the breadwinner. My maternal grandparents would visit but for only a short while (by Pakistani standards), despite Daddy insisting that they stay longer. An overnight stay at *beytee ka ghar*—a daughter's home—carried with it a feeling that one was imposing on the breadwinning son-in-law.

All Rise

"This is a paradise for women," a British woman told my mother. Her husband was a British army officer stationed in Pakistan. She had noticed the "ladies first" culture. When a lady entered a drawing room, men would stand and stay standing until she took a seat. The chatter would shift to a "ladies' company-appropriate" conversation, and when a lady spoke, the men would stop talking and listen to her with flattering nods. "Dinner is served" meant "ladies first." When sitting at the dinner table, a gentleman would pull her chair out and seat the lady. If they walked up to a door, he would rush to hold the door open. If a lady approached a queue at a bank, men would part to move her to the front of the line. Being a lady in mixed company was a treat. Mummy, in her nationalistic pride, often quoted this Englishwoman: "See, even the British say that we women live in a paradise." Till she took her last breath, Mummy believed that if there was one place on God's earth made for her and meant for her, it was Pakistan.

Walter:

First Glimpse of Mount Carmel and Arrival in the Jewish Homeland

For me, it was Israel. Only a few months after seeing the movie *Exodus*, as though a good fairy had decided to grant my deepest wish, my parents gave my siblings and me some astoundingly wonderful news. We would be spending my father's upcoming sabbatical year in Israel, where my father, a physicist, would be doing research at the Weizmann Institute of Science in the town of Rehovot on the coastal plain south of Tel Aviv. I remember being stunned speechless and then feeling almost delirious joy, as if my life were beginning at last. It was 1961, and I was eleven years old.

I approached Israel for the first time aboard an ocean liner, the SS *Theodore Herzl*, bound from Naples to Haifa after spending a glorious month of travel with my family through Europe. Our three days at sea had been no pleasure cruise, however; the sea was rough, and the food, mostly overcooked kosher chicken, was execrable in comparison to the succulent European cuisines we had so recently sampled. Still, I was giddy with excitement as I anticipated the first sight of the Holy Land.

In the early morning light, I awoke to see the gray, looming silhouette of Mount Carmel rising dramatically on the eastern horizon. Looking back on that moment after fifty-nine years, I feel privileged to have had my first vision of the Land of Israel from the sea—not, as happens today, jetting onto the bland, generic tarmac of Ben Gurion Airport. To glimpse Mount Carmel, that headland where the Hebrew Prophets had once done spiritual battle with the priests of Baal, rising dramatically out of the gloom to announce itself, was a primal affirmation: "You have arrived. You are home."

Starting Life Anew in Rehovot

When we landed at Haifa Port and walked down the gangplank to terra firma, I waited until my parents' backs were turned before kneeling furtively to touch my finger to the pavement and then bring it to my lips. I don't think either my parents or their friends, the Benesches—a Pittsburgh physicist family also on sabbatical at the Weizmann Institute who had come to Haifa from Rehovot to greet us—noticed what I did. I loved Israel instantly and passionately but felt embarrassed to openly manifest such "uncool" emotion.

My kneeling down to kiss the earth was a religious gesture, yet it was made by someone who, then and now, is deeply secular and doesn't pray or attend synagogue. My primal first kiss of Israel was indicative of the profound connection that Jews, both religious and non-religious, feel to the Land of Israel.

We drove from Haifa to Rehovot. In those days, the Tel Aviv–Haifa superhighway had not yet been built, and we headed slowly southward on a narrow two-lane road through miles of orange groves and even some banana plantations, passing kibbutzim and a few Arab villages. I was in a state of high excitement, having read in *Exodus* about some of the places we were seeing.

Just before the entrance to Rehovot, I got out of the car with Amy, the Benesches' eleven-year-old daughter and my closest childhood friend, and the two of us walked into town on foot, over the railroad tracks, with the smell of surrounding orange groves suffusing our nostrils. My feeling of connection to the place was instantaneous.

We moved into a new brand-new apartment building in a residential district adjacent to the Weizmann Institute, inhabited mainly by scientists and their families. Our street was called Keren Kayemet LeYisrael (Street of the Jewish National Fund) and was unpaved. More than once, our Volkswagen got stuck in the deep sand of Keren Kayemet, and we had to clamber out of the car and dig ourselves out.

My year in Rehovot remains with me today as a reel of wonderful cinematic memories. My mother enrolled my siblings and me in a Hebrew-language day camp, and for the first month or so, I understood nothing that was going on. The language barrier initially made me even more shy and awkward than I had been back in Pittsburgh, but almost immediately I began to experience a warm feeling of reassurance from the Israeli kids, a sense that "We're all Jews here, so everything is OK. Don't worry, you'll be speaking Hebrew before you know it."

On the last day of the camp, there was a pageant in which my age group dressed up in Mexican costumes with outsized hats and sang a song in Hebrew called "Oh Sombrero." The song seemed fitting to me, because physically the area rather resembled the Mexico of my imagination. The landscape was semi-arid and the most ubiquitous vegetation was the sabra cactus, which has a prickly red fruit that the Israeli personality is supposed to resemble (tough and prickly on the outside, but soft and sweet on the inside).

At night, lying in my cozy bed, I could hear the not-very-distant howling of hyenas in the rolling sand dunes that stretched beyond the *pardesim* citrus groves to the Mediterranean shore, seven or eight miles away. That there were hyenas lurking nearby felt wonderfully romantic, like I was living on the edge of the African veldt.

Soon I became an avid member of the Israel Scouts movement and enjoyed wonderful hiking expeditions through orange groves and sand dunes, often ending with a bonfire under the stars. The Israel Scouts were coed, unlike in stuffy, uptight America. Israelis saw no reason to separate the sexes in their scouting movement just because they happened to be reaching puberty. Equally amazingly in retrospect, I don't remember any adult scoutmasters being along with us on these adventures. The sense that kids of eleven or twelve were already partners in the Zionist enterprise and could be trusted with a great deal of independence in the knowledge that they would do the right thing while learning essential leadership and survival skills was then, and remains, a central and very compelling aspect of Israeli life.

In any case, those hikes with the Scouts greatly increased my love for and connection to the land and were the precursors of many solo walks I would take across Israel's wild areas when I returned to the Jewish state as a young adult. Certainly, my scouting expeditions gave me an instinctive understanding that the pocket-sized Land of Israel was best appreciated on foot. It is a land where every square kilometer holds magical revelations, and to which my new Israeli friends seemed linked organically. It sure as hell knocked suburban Pittsburgh into a cocked hat.

Palmachim Beach, where our family went to swim that summer, was a magical experience in its own right. Right in the center of the beachfront, projecting out into the Mediterranean Sea, was a small grass-covered hill, a *tel* (artificial hill over ancient ruins)—originally a

Canaanite city and later a small Roman port. Who needed to bother building sandcastles? At Palmachim, a kid could dig up real Roman coins in the dirt and debris on top of the *tel*. Once I tried to climb up the sheer sea wall of the *tel* and got stuck after clambering halfway up the steep cliffside. I was paralyzed with fright, unable to climb any higher or get back down. Staring down petrified at the waves crashing onto the jagged rocks, I could see a skate swimming in lazy circles in the sea far below. Eventually, my frantic mother discovered my whereabouts and a rescue party assembled at the bottom of the cliff, before a gallant Australian physicist climbed up to me and managed to coax me down.

Sabeeha:

I Still Carry the Catholic in Me

My youth was not nearly as adventurous as Walter's. For one thing, I hated school. I attended Catholic schools in Pakistan (considered premier schools) where most students were Muslim. The nuns were strict and would hit the knuckles of my hand with the edge of the ruler to punish me for offenses I no longer recall. Sometimes I was made to stand in the corner, facing the wall. I was very well behaved, but a below-average student. Each time I was punished, my classmates bullied me. I never told my parents out of fear that they would be angry at me for annoying my teacher. We were taught to respect and revere our teachers, particularly if they were nuns. In middle school, corporal punishment was replaced with verbal humiliation. We accepted that as the norm. But I have to admit that the discipline, ethics, and moral principles that I came to embrace were inculcated in my formative years in Presentation Convent, which has maintained its prestige as the finest girls' school in Rawalpindi.

When Walter read this piece, he asked why a Muslim family in Pakistan, a country formed on the basis of creating a homeland for Muslims, would send their daughter to a Catholic school. He is not the only person to ask me. The curriculum was secular, of high standard, and the medium of instruction was English. Progressive families held the belief that for their children to compete academically, they had to be well versed in English. The nuns were careful in crafting the curriculum to avoid any semblance of diluting the religious identity of Muslim students. When the Catholic girls went for catechism, the Muslim girls went to a class called Moral Science, which was all about universal values and etiquette. Competition to get into a Catholic school was so intense that often families registered their children upon birth.

Making My Way with Tiny Footsteps

One day, I got locked out. Daddy would drop me off at school on his way to the office, and Daddy's army-appointed orderly would pick me up and take me home on his bicycle. I would ride on the carrier at the back. That morning, Daddy dropped me off, but when I got to the school gate, it was locked. Two girls, my age, in school uniform, were standing by the gate.

"Why is the gate locked?" I asked.

"School is closed. Yesterday they had announced that school will be closed today, but we were both absent from school," one of them said.

"Me too," I said.

We huddled together, not knowing what to do. There was no guard, just a sky-high, locked gate. We hung out and chatted, and after a while, the two girls started walking away.

"Where are you going?" I asked.

"We are going to walk home."

I suppose I can walk home too.

I was seven.

This was the 1950s. No cell phones. No phones at home, period.

So I started walking—a pretty little girl in ringlets, wearing a handsome tailored frock, carrying a satchel, walking on the street, alone. There were no sidewalks, just a dirt path alongside the road—a main artery. I knew the route on the bicycle, so I knew where I was going. Men on bicycles rode by, tinkling the bike bells; *tonga* horse carriages going clickety-clock with the horses dropping clumps of smelly poo, and a few pedestrians. After I passed the bazaar of Lalkurti on my right, a man riding a bike got off and walked up to me. He asked where I was going and why I was walking alone. I told him. "I will walk with you," he said. He started walking with me, bicycle in hand. I don't remember his face, just that he was wearing a shalwar kameez. In my childhood, I was called "chatter-box," so I must have chatted my heart out with my traveling companion, telling him everything about me and my family. As we reached a crossing, he parted, saying in Urdu, "Okay Bia, I have to go the other way now," and rode off. I kept walking, past the open fields, the residential area, the military barracks on my left, the polo grounds on my right, and turned right into Lalazar Colony. How long did I walk before I got home? I just Google-mapped it—1.6 miles—a thirty-three-minute walk. With my little feet, I am sure it took longer. I walked up the gravel driveway to the verandah, where Mummy was sitting at her sewing machine, chatting with Daadi Amma. "Hello," I called out, as in "Surprise!"

She cried out. I don't recall exactly what she said, but it was some-thing like "What are you doing home?" Or maybe "What happened?"

"It's a school holiday," I gleefully announced. Now I could play.

"How did you get home?" That I recall her saying.

"I walked," I replied, feeling proud of myself.

"Alone?"

"There was this man on a bicycle . . ." I proceeded to give the whole story.

Mummy got up and ran inside. Oblivious, I stayed in the veranda, chatting with Daadi Amma. When I went in, I found Mummy crying.

"Why is Mummy crying?" I asked Daadi Amma.

"Because you walked home alone. She is afraid of what could have happened to you."

I remember feeling badly that she was crying, but my little seven-year-old head couldn't appreciate what was going through Mummy's mind. I can now.

What if that *nice man* had lured me?

What if I had tripped and gotten hurt?

What if I had lost my way? Did I even know my home address?

I wonder if it gave my seven-year-old mind a pause: *bad things can happen to little girls*. Perhaps.

I have no idea what transpired when Daddy got home. Did Mummy have a talk with him? Did he toss and turn in bed all night wonder-ing about the what-ifs? Did he talk to Mother Superior, the school principal? From then on, did he wait until I was safely behind the gate before releasing the clutch of his stick-shift Ford Consul? I will never know. No one ever talked about it. And now it's too late to ask.

Walter:
Falling Under the Sensual Spell of Hebrew

While Sabeeha struggled with the discipline in Catholic schools in Pakistan, I entered *kitah vav* (sixth grade) at the Sprinzak School in Rehovot, a few blocks' walk from our home, with some thirty native Israeli kids and five or six American Jewish kids, whose fathers, like my own, were doing sabbaticals at the Weizmann Institute. Within a few months, I was speaking Hebrew relatively fluently and found myself falling under the spell of the language. I loved the sound of Hebrew; its pungently guttural quality filled with throat-clearing words starting with the letter *chet* or the hissing sound of the letter *tsadi*, for which there are no equivalents in English.

The more I learned, the more I relished speaking Hebrew: a modern-day, revitalized version of a 3,500-year-old language through which I felt connected to the biblical Patriarchs and Matriarchs, Kings and Prophets, who had spoken the same words and expressions, while living on the same land. Hebrew is simultaneously brash, breezy, and up-to-the-minute—and a passageway back to time-out-of-mind.

To me the language also sounded sexy, which may seem strange, but I was just entering adolescence and forming crushes on girls in my class, and speaking Hebrew was the means of connecting with them. Or maybe the feeling was deeper than that; there was a strongly tactile and sensual flavor to my ardent love of the land itself.

Whatever formed that perception remains unchanged. The language still sounds alluring to me when I speak it today, after all the decades that have gone past.

Sabeeha:
My Downton Abbey in Pakistan

If you watched the delicious TV series *Downton Abbey*, well, scale it down a hundred notches, remove the glitter and glamor, and you have my home, my mini Downton Abbey. My parents were not rich, but we did have a butler and a cook. In Pakistan, domestic help was the norm—it still is. And I am talking middle-class. Aurangzeb was the butler, valet, chauffeur, orderly, attendant, handyman, and staff manager, all in one. Assigned to Daddy by the Pakistan army, he prepared Daddy's uniform every evening, polishing the brass buttons. In the evenings, he would brief Daddy on the state of affairs. Daddy dressed and carried himself like a thorough English gentleman. Mummy was the epitome of style and elegance.

Mummy never cooked. We had Razia. In the kitchen, she reigned. When the milkman made his morning delivery of fresh-off-the-cow-organic milk, she watched him like an eagle, lest he cheat. When she grew old and frail, Mummy hired a kitchen aide to assist her. Whenever the kitchen aide complained to Mummy about Razia, Mummy would give her an earful on the chain of command. When Mummy was in her eighties, facing health issues, with Razia no longer able to climb the stairs to her sunroom, Mummy hired a lady's maid. And now the sparks really flew, as the lady's maid tried to impress on Razia that she had a direct line to Mummy, and so "shoo off."

Mummy loved her profession of homemaker. She kept a sparkling home, but you never saw her mop the floor. Every morning the cleaning lady swept the house, squatting with a *jharoo* in hand. Every morning, Mummy would instruct Razia on the menu, then give Aurangzeb a shopping list and cash. Next morning, he would give Mummy an accounting, which she noted in her notebook. A lady does not do laundry. Once a week, the *dhobi* came to the house. Mummy would supervise him taking inventory, making a laundry list in her notebook. He would then wrap the laundry in a sheet, place it on his bicycle rack, and go on his way, returning a week later. There was no lady's maid to wait on me—I did say we were not rich. I took the trouble to do my own hair. And though I don't remember, as babies we had an *ayah*—a nanny.

If we were not rich, how come we had all that help? Of course, low labor cost was a big factor, but it was also the culture—still is. And the help guarded their territory with zeal. Should I stoop to pick up something, I would get intercepted with a reprimand: "This work is not for you."

Our living quarters were upstairs; the kitchen was—you guessed it—downstairs. The domestic workers lived in adjoining quarters, off the kitchen. We ate in the dining room; they ate in the kitchen. We lived together as a family; they lived away from their families, who resided in the far-off villages. Sad, and not fair. One year, Aurangzeb went home to get married and returned alone, visiting his wife on holidays. Razia was a widow—her children lived with their grandparents. My parents helped her children with their schooling, getting jobs, and, when they married, with the dowries. Their family problems became our family problems.

Mummy had the foresight to know that one day this culture would die out. I was packed off to the College of Home Economics to train me in homemaker skills, because as she said, "You are not going to have a cook when you get married." Boy, was she right!

I landed in New York, freshly married, half expecting an Aurangzeb to carry my bags. Our first stop was the supermarket. What a downer for a newlywed bride. I had never done grocery shopping. My husband picked out the produce as I watched, aghast. My Prince Charming handling vegetables! Back at the apartment, I was confronted with making dinner. I knew how to cook but had never been responsible for it. Seeing the look on my face, my husband took charge and made dinner, sending me into another shock, as I watched the man of the studio-apartment peel an onion. Eventually I got my act together, but boy, did I miss Razia.

Was there ever a lady's maid/valet love affair in the kitchen? I recall—this was long before Aurangzeb and Razia came into our home—Mummy whispering to my aunt about the rumored attraction between the cook and the maid. I don't remember if anything came of it.

Was there ever a Lady and Driver scenario in the households—an attraction between employer and the help? Not that I know of. But Pollywood—my coined phrase for Pakistani movie industry—couldn't resist. There was the movie *Kaneez* (Maid). And there were plenty of Rich Boy/Poor Girl movies, *Chakori* being a favorite.

Once someone tried to hire Aurangzeb away. He turned it down, saying, "Even if you offered me twice as much, I will stay with them. And if the Colonel [Daddy] pays me half as much, I will stay with them." How did we know this? The person who tried to lure him away told Daddy, saying, "I wanted you to know how much Aurangzeb values you."

Aurangzeb stayed with my parents for almost fifty years, Razia for forty years, leaving only when Daddy and Mummy passed away. As Mummy lay in rest, Aurangzeb and Razia cried harder than any of us. Daddy had settled a pension for them, and they live comfortably. They still come to visit when I go back.

Walter:
Finding Acceptance While Dancing the Hora

Pakistan and Israel were both brand-new countries when Sabeeha and I were growing up, but Israel was far more egalitarian. The mainstream Zionist movement was strongly socialist in those days, and while the ethos of social equality reached its apotheosis on the kibbutz, the ideal of "all Jews are responsible to each other" was also quite strong in towns like Rehovot. In those days, nearly all Jewish Israelis felt closely connected to each other, as they worked together to build a progressive utopia where class distinctions were not supposed to matter. To be sure, the families of Ashkenazi scientists in Rehovot were better off economically and enjoyed higher social status than recently arrived new Oriental Jewish immigrants, from places like Yemen or Iraq, who mainly did manual labor. Come to think of it, a young Yemenite Jewish woman named Penina came once a week to clean our apartment, and she and my mother formed a warm personal connection, albeit with my sister, brother, and me often doing most of the Hebrew/English translation between them. Still, there were no great extremes of wealth and poverty in the new social democratic Jewish state, and the dominant narrative was about equality and mutual support.

This idealistic and inclusive ethic was very strong among children and teenagers, including my classmates in *kitah vav* at Sprinzak School—although there too, the ideal of equality was often honored only in the breach. Take my own infatuation with Michal, a vivacious classmate with long black braids, who lived around the corner from our apartment. The most "in" girl in our class, Michal was charming and self-assured and had a wide circle of friends. Unfortunately, she seemed not to be aware that I was alive. She flirted with various boys named Moshe, who were popular and good in sports. While social dynamics among Israeli school kids differed dramatically from what I had known in America, there was, alas, at least one constant: in Rehovot, like in Pittsburgh, the girls tended to go for the jocks.

Almost every Saturday night there was a class party, held al fresco on street corners in our neighborhood, to which every member of the class was invited for an evening of hora dancing. The hora, which the pioneer generation that founded Israel had brought with them from Eastern Europe, was profoundly communal in nature, with everyone standing in a circle, singing and clapping, as one couple after another skipped together around the center. I used to attend every party but did not participate in the hora dancing at the center of the action, because I was excruciatingly shy and felt possessed of two left feet. Instead, I would stand on the outside of the circle, singing and clapping in time to the music, praying that no one would notice me and invite me to dance.

Then one evening, about halfway through the school year, as I stood on the outside, gazing with admiration at Michal as she skipped around the circle with one Moshe or another, she abruptly dismissed her partner and gestured to me to come and dance with her. Taken aback, I thought for a moment she must have meant someone standing alongside, but then she pointed unmistakably to me and smiled. The circle parted and I hesitatingly joined Michal, to find my feeling of awkwardness rapidly giving way to a flood of rapture. Soon I was skipping around the circle to "David, King of Israel" with my arm around the back of the girl I adored and with the whole class clapping for us. *This is happiness*, I thought. *This is what it means to be alive.*

I was silly enough to believe for a few days thereafter that Michal's asking me to dance signified that she liked me as much as I liked her. Yet it soon became clear that she had merely taken pity on a shy outsider, and by reaching out had sought to bring me into the circle of acceptance. Her gesture worked wonders; far from feeling rejected, from that moment on I felt like a full member of the class. I didn't get the girl, but I got the country.

The Kitah Vav Kids Slap Back

Michal's reaching out to me was an expression of the ideology of inclusiveness that was endemic to Israeli life during the early decades of the state. Every one of the thirty-five or so kids in our sixth-grade class was considered a full member of the unit. Admittedly, some kids were more "in" than others. Hunky, athletic Moshe M., who also happened to be Michal's main squeeze, was clearly more central than someone like myself. Yet it was also the case that no one was "out." Not one member of our class was put down as a nerd or weirdo in the way that so many kids are devalued by their peers in American schools, with their chronic cliquishness.

On one unforgettable occasion, our main teacher—a wizened, bitter man named Yona (in those days, Israeli students invariably referred to their teachers by their first names)—slapped Aryeh, a slow learner who may have been autistic, when he failed to answer a question. Shortly thereafter, the bell rang for a fifteen-minute recess, during which our class members caucused on the volleyball court and decided as a unit that we would not return to our studies until Yona apologized to Aryeh and the whole class. The protest worked. Although the school administration sought to hush up the incident, the parents backed up their kids, and Yona received a severe reprimand.

As shocked as I was by Yona's act—which would never have happened in the more genteel world I had come from—it seemed even more astounding to me that a bunch of sixth-grade kids could confidently go on strike in the face of adult authority. My classmates' courage and supreme self-confidence filled me with admiration. *Chutzpah?* It seemed to me that those sixth graders invented chutzpah.

Looking back, I understand that Israeli parents' indulgence of their assertive children, to a degree that sometimes seems beyond all bounds to outsiders, was then, as it still is today, more than a way to maximize youthful independence, initiative, and self-confidence, though it was certainly all of that. It is also an expression of guilt-induced compensation from adults to their kids for what parents know is coming and are helpless to prevent: watching their fresh-out-of-high-school sons and daughters going en masse into the army, with the real possibility of getting killed.

In Israel, there is a strong feeling that parents are only temporary stewards of their children, who ultimately belong to the collective, to the Jewish state. Yet, as someone who got to experience growing up in Israel, albeit for only a year, I am convinced there is nowhere in the world a more fun and fulfilling place to come of age.

As the year progressed, I fell in love with not only Michal but all thirty-five or so curly-haired sixth graders who came to school every day in blue short shorts, sandals, and the trademark sun hat known as the *kova tembel*. I loved them all because I was so grateful they had collectively accepted me as a full member of the class and, in the process, made me feel at one with Israel and with being Jewish. For the first time in my life, I felt that I truly belonged.

Sabeeha:

Boys Off-Limits

There wasn't a Walter-Michal equivalent for me in Pakistan. High school was an all-girls school. We were now pubescent teenagers, and boys were off-limits. Our only "crushes" were movie stars, with Waheed Murad topping the list. Google him and you will see why. It was in high school when I finally fell in love with school. I also had to stop wearing frocks and switch to shalwar kameez—long shirt and loose, flowing pants. Big girls had to cover their legs. I started acing the exams, competed to gain first position in class, joined the debating team, and became the darling of the teachers. When I went off to the College of Home Economics in Lahore for my undergrad, we were walled inside the hostel (dorm) on the sprawling campus. Male visitors had to be pre-approved by our parents, with their photo kept on file. The warden issued gate passes only when we had an approved guardian to escort us. The most delicious gossip was a whispered "She has a boyfriend." Letters passed through the principal's office, and if she found an envelope to be suggestive of a love letter, as in a heavy envelope, she would open and read it, and if her hunch was right, the poor girl was summoned into her office, reprimanded, and her parents notified. And we would be scandalized. Those were the societal rules, and we were expected to live within those boundaries.

College days were glorious. I joined the Girl Scouts, debating team, singing competitions, acting group, was the Deputy-Head Girl, and crammed
every hour into my studies. In many ways, it was a finishing school, grooming us to perfection, and we girls soaked it all in—without the boys.

A Lady in Waiting

After graduating from college with a bachelor of science degree, I became
a lady-in-waiting-to-get-married. With a bachelor's degree in hand, girls
now had to get married before the pool of suitable young men dried
up. And marriage was to be arranged. Since we couldn't date and, in any
case, knew no boys, we had to wait for a suitable proposal from a suitable family. Each time a proposal came, the entire extended family would
gather to evaluate its merits. When Khalid's proposal came—or rather,
his parents proposed—my grandparents weighed in. They had known
Khalid since he was a child and believed beyond a reasonable doubt that
he was the perfect match. There was only one problem: my parents had
never met him (forget about the fact that *I* had never met him). Nor
was there any chance of meeting him—he lived in New York. There was
push-and-pull, yeas and nays, the votes always ending in a draw. In the
end, I cast the tie-breaking vote. My Prince Charming came riding on
a white plane, and I merrily flew off with him into the west. The year
was 1971, and I had just turned twenty. If you want to know the sweet
and funny details of my arranged marriage and why I said yes, my book
Threading My Prayer Rug is just a click away.

Walter:

Life on the Kibbutz

I was married the same year—1971—and I had just turned twenty-one.
I wed a sweet Baptist girl named Gloria whom I had met shortly before
graduating and had taken to the high school prom. In 1976, the two of
us moved to Israel; but for now, let me return to my first adventurous
year in Israel in 1961–62, which had such an outsize impact on my subsequent development.

During that time, our family made some wonderful trips around
Israel, usually on organized tours with the other families of American

scientists from the Institute. I remember that during our first visit to Jerusalem, I hung over a ledge overlooking the Old City, then under Jordanian control, and deliberately dropped a coin several feet to the pavement below. I then jumped down for a second into what was called no-man's land to retrieve the coin, to the alarm of my mother and our guide, who said that Jordanian snipers had been known to shoot at people who engaged in such damn fool stunts. It was an eleven-year-old's delicious brush with danger.

The most dramatic of all our trips was to Eilat, today a sprawling, tacky Las Vegas/Miami Beach amalgam on the Red Sea, but then a scruffy and isolated outpost of a few hundred hardy Israeli pioneers. We drove through the desert in a car convoy with machine-gun-toting guards to ward off potential attack from the Fedayeen terrorists, who during the 1950s and '60s occasionally crossed the border from Egypt to attack Israeli civilians.

Even more impactful for me were visits with our Israeli relatives, the Sharon family, personified by my Uncle Ze'ev and his wife Penina, who lived on Kibbutz Afek, a communal agricultural settlement located on the verdant coastal plain between Haifa and Akko. On the kibbutzim, which began to spring up across Palestine in the decades preceding Israel's Declaration of Independence, all land was owned collectively; there was no private property or money, but all kibbutz members were provided with adequate food and tiny living spaces free of charge. Decisions were made by a vote of the collective. Kibbutzim still exist in significant numbers, but today are a less important feature of Israeli life and less rigorously socialist.

Ze'ev and Penina seemed to me like heroic figures out of *Exodus*, magically come to life. Ze'ev had emigrated to Palestine from Berlin in 1936 at age sixteen. My mother had accompanied him to the train station to see him off, along with fellow youthful members of his Zionist movement *garin* (collective, literally "nucleus"), all of whom were leaving behind anti-Semitic oppression to build a socialist utopia. For her part, Penina fled from her childhood home in eastern Poland to the Soviet Union to escape the Nazis. After being held in a gulag in Siberia for several years, she was among several thousand Polish Jews allowed by the Soviets to proceed to Palestine in the later years of World War II. Both Ze'ev and Penina lost their parents, siblings, and entire extended families in the Holocaust.

Ze'ev and Penina were among the founders of Kibbutz Mishmar Ha Yam (Guardian of the Sea), which was set up on sand dunes near Akko in 1938 but moved a few miles inland to more fertile land in 1947. At some point in the late 1940s, they became a couple and moved in together, but they never had an official wedding because, as socialist atheists, they objected to having a rabbi marry them in the eyes of a God in whom they did not believe. Ze'ev fought in the Battle of Akko in 1948; their only son, Avinoam, would fall on the last day of the 1973 Yom Kippur War. Their daughter Raya gave birth to her first child, a boy, a year after Avinoam's death and named him Achikam, which means "my brother rises."

I spent the Passover holiday week of 1962 living in the sixth-grade dormitory in the Children's House at Afek, with Raya and other kibbutz sixth graders. Each class in the Afek school had its own living quarters. The kids would come home to the Children's House every evening after a full day of school, work assignments, and an hour-long visit with their parents.

When Raya was a young mother in the 1970s, she was among a group of Afek parents who refused to send their toddlers to live in the Children's House, part of a movement on kibbutzim across the country that within a few years led to the end of the practice of kibbutz children living separately from their parents. That effort was the beginning of a counterrevolution, which, over the past forty years, has largely stripped the kibbutzim—and wider Israeli society as well—of much of their socialist ideology and character.

I remember picking grapefruit with Raya and her classmates in Afek's citrus groves, which had a panoramic view over carp ponds and wheat fields to the rolling hills of Lower Galilee, occupied by Arab villages left intact during the War of Independence. We set up small ladders under the trees and cut the fruit from the trees using pruning shears, filling the bins below. On the way home from the fields, I stopped at the barn filled with milk cows nursing their newborn calves. There is a lovely and lyrical

Hebrew folk song called "Erev Ba" ("Evening Descends") describing a pastoral scene with which I will always associate this memory.[3]

In those days and after I returned to live in Haifa at the age of twenty-six, Ze'ev and Penina were my Israeli lodestars, exemplars of a soon-to-vanish socialist-Zionist lifestyle in which the individual devoted him- or herself unreservedly to the greater good of society, living without money, which was not used on the kibbutz, and only a handful of personal possessions. In many ways, the kibbutz felt like the apotheosis of the communal ideology and lifestyle that I, a self-described 1960s radical, claimed to uphold. In truth, I would never have accepted the myriad restrictions on personal freedom that kibbutz residents readily endured.

We Each Had an Enemy

Sabeeha:
Pakistan at War with India, 1965

As Walter returned home from Israel, Pakistan went to war with India. I was not quite fourteen. For the past seventy years, Pakistan has yearned for its birthright—Kashmir. India and Pakistan went to war over Kashmir in 1965, and India attacked Lahore and Sialkot. Daddy was sent off to war, and I stood on the platform of the railway station in Quetta, trying not to cry, not waving, and trying not to lose Daddy's figure leaning out of the doorway in his khaki army uniform, smiling and waving as the train pulled out. I shut myself in the bathroom and cried. At school, my friends and I were gung-ho about the war. We were going to beat the daylights out of India, and they would regret the day they attacked us. Our spirits soared when the news reports started coming in. We had beaten back those Indians from Lahore and Sialkot. The stories of valor, chivalry, and military skill transformed the armed forces into the most beloved institution. Poets wrote ballads, singers sang love songs, photos of the heroes in uniform adorned the halls and walls, and every young girl dreamed of marrying an officer in a shiny uniform, including me.

---

3 http://www.shira.net/music/lyrics/erev-ba.htm.

We listened over and over again to the patriotic songs of Noor Jehan, the voice that pierced the skies and lifted our hearts with pride and love of country. I prayed in earnest and pleaded with God, "Please bring Daddy home safely." When the guns fell silent, we were jubilant at having won the war, and President Ayub Khan, the dashing field marshal, was our hero. Revisionists will claim it ended in a draw, but from where I was, *we* won the war. We beat back the Indian attacks and prevented them from capturing Lahore and Sialkot—even if we didn't capture Kashmir. But I lost my uncle and cousin on the battlefield, and I knew the feeling of having an enemy, an enemy committed to our destruction.

The ultimate blow came in 1971. I was a newlywed, getting on a plane to fly out to the United States with my husband, when India attacked East Pakistan, and the two countries went to war again. I learned of it when we landed in Amsterdam. Over the next few days, from our new apartment in New York City, as I watched Pakistan lay down its arms and surrender to the Indian army, I experienced my most humiliating moment. And when East Pakistan seceded and pronounced the establishment of Bangladesh, I felt the pain of losing a limb. Half the country lost! Tens of thousands taken prisoners of war! I promised never to befriend an Indian and never to set foot in India. The years since have mellowed me, humbled me, and taught me differently.

Tragedy, loss, and conflict infused me with a yearning for Pakistan to heal the cracks and reclaim its standing. I prayed with intensity for a leader who would restore morale and propel the nation forward. That was forty-nine years ago, and I am still waiting, still praying.

Walter:
An Eleven-Year-Old and the Arab Question

There was another, far less palatable side to the sublime togetherness I found in Israel. If there was such a strong sense of "us," there had also to be a "them." Israel then and now was about a banding together of Jews against the world—and especially against the Arabs. There were almost no Arabs living around Rehovot in 1961–62, which was not happenstance. In fact, there had been numerous Palestinian villages in the region, some of which, like the Jewish towns and kibbutzim in the area, had prospered during the British Mandate period, growing oranges and grapefruits. However, nearly all the residents of those villages had disappeared during the 1948 War of Independence, and their homes were subsequently given to Jewish immigrants or bulldozed out of existence.

We were taught in school that the Arab villagers had run away of their own accord, part of the foundational myth that figured prominently in official Israeli historiography and pro-Israeli literature like *Exodus*. The Palestinians had a diametrically opposed version of 1948: one of forced displacement by the Hagana and Irgun paramilitary organizations and later by the Israeli army. They called it the *Naqba* (catastrophe), which resulted in the removal of more than 700,000 refugees across the new borders with Jordan and Egypt and the destruction of up to six hundred Palestinian villages. In the wake of Israel's successful War of Independence, most of the Western world had accepted the Israeli version. As is often the case in wars, it is the victors' historical narrative that tends to stick.

Once, early in our year in Israel, when our family was driving on the road that ran from Rehovot to Palmachim Beach, we came upon an extended Bedouin family camped out in the sand dunes with their tents and several camels. My father stopped the car, and the patriarch of the clan gestured to us in a friendly manner and haltingly explained via sign language that my brother, sister, and I could have camel rides for a few *grushim* (pocket change). We kids jumped out of the car in great excitement, but the Bedouin women became agitated and began ululating in alarm when my mother emerged after us in a modest one-piece bathing suit. My mother, naturally enough, was frightened and offended by this clearly hostile response and immediately ordered the rest of us back into the car.

Meanwhile, my father had made a bad situation worse by snapping some photos of the Bedouin women, provoking angry cries in Arabic and broken Hebrew about the "evil eye." Amid the tumult, my father also ordered us all into the car and we hightailed it out of there, to the great disappointment of us kids, who understood next to nothing of what had transpired. We complained bitterly to our relieved parents about having been cheated out of our camel rides.

That incident was one of only a few times I can remember interacting with Arabs during our yearlong stay in Israel. The others included a visit to the Bedouin market in Beersheva, a tourist trap. There we kids finally got our camel rides. Also several visits to the *shuk* (market) in Jaffa, an ancient city alongside Tel Aviv in which a small Arab community had been allowed to remain, where my mother loved to buy copper plates. In fact, there were still plenty of Arabs inside Israel's pre-1967 border, especially in the villages of Galilee. But we never visited any of those places on the various tours around the country organized by the Weizmann Institute. Such places clearly didn't fit the Zionist narrative with which we were regaled during these expeditions.

Singing a Shocking Song on Tu B'Shvat

Still, in 1961–62, the trauma of the life-and-death struggle of 1948 was relatively recent and raw, and things were said out loud back then that would become less acceptable a decade or two later. At least that's how I explain the following memory. The occasion was Tu B'Shvat (the fifteenth of the month of Shvat), a holiday known since biblical times as the New Year's for Trees and, in the recreated Jewish state, an occasion for people to plant tree saplings in order to replenish the land and make it fertile.

Our class was out on the streets that Saturday evening of January 20, 1962, singing songs and making merry, dancing horas and flirting like mad. It was cool and misty, after a hard rain. On Ruppin Street in Rehovot, we sang a Tu B'Shvat song lustily, and I remember this snippet:

B' Tu, Tu, Tu, Tu
Ha Aravim Yamutu
B' Azeh Chag?
B' Tu B' Shvat!

On Tu, Tu, Tu, Tu
The Arabs will die
On which holiday?
On Tu B' Shvat!

That is how I recall it: my classmates and I singing with pleasure about killing Arabs as we marched through the streets of Rehovot, and no grownups came out of their homes to tell us it was a hateful, racist sentiment we ought not be expressing. "The Arabs will die" wasn't uttered in a whisper. It was sung right out loud. Such sentiments were *b'aveer* (in the air), part of the psychic landscape. For years afterward, I remembered how much I relished singing that song while bonding with my classmates. Only much later did I ponder the import of the words.

Sabeeha:

I Feel as if I Never Left

As of this writing, I have lived away from Pakistan for forty-nine years. In the beginning, I was determined to return in two years, after Khalid completed his medical residency. We were both so committed to returning that it drove all our decisions. "Let's get a dual-voltage toaster so that it can run on the 220 volts in Pakistan . . . Let's get only flat sheets as fitted sheets won't fit the Pakistani mattresses . . . No need to teach our son Urdu, he will learn it when we return." We did return in two years, but just for a visit. Then again in two years for a visit. Then again, and again. Just a visit. Ironically, as the world shrank, I began to lose touch with the land of my birth. Standing under the Statue of Liberty, I pledged allegiance to the American flag and turned in my Pakistani passport. I switched channels from Pakistan TV and the face of President Zia to watching Reagan telling Carter, "There you go again." I stopped calling Mummy on Eid-ul-Adha, asking her to do the *qurbani* sacrifice of the lamb on our behalf for charity, and instead donated to the soup kitchen at Project Hospitality in Staten Island.

Yet each time I go back, I feel as if I never left.

I love the sounds I no longer miss, of the *Adhan*, the call to prayer, and the music—the strumming of the sitar, the beat of the tabla, the melodious voice of Mehdi Hassan's Urdu *ghazals*. I love the fragrance of raindrops on dust, of the morning bloom of white and soft jasmine. I love the squeeze of a tight embrace every time I get a hug from an aging aunt. I relish the spicy taste of *chana chaat* and the sugary, syrupy taste of the saffron *jalebi*. And I love the warmth of the overbearing hospitality that gives me indigestion.

You can tell a Pakistani woman a mile away. She has style, poise, and grace and is oh-so-sophisticated and polished. Show me a Pakistani woman who isn't always perfectly groomed—as in, any time of the day. A homemaker in particular will always be outfitted in an impeccable colorful shalwar kameez, just in case visitors drop by. Although the practice of visit-by-appointment is catching on, most guests are walk-ins. A truly welcome guest is one who doesn't need to call and is welcome anytime. Around these women, I feel rather out of style. Before I get on a plane to visit Pakistan, I go through a grooming routine lest I appear shabby, crumpled, and worn out. Very often, Mummy—when she was alive—would insist that I go straight to the beauty parlor to get a makeover, shaking her head: "Why don't you take care of yourself!"

Aaah, the surround sound of Urdu in the streets! I pack away my English and relish hearing my voice as I bargain the price of mangoes in Urdu and practice my Punjabi with the help in the kitchen. I have learned to field the nosy questions of my dearly beloved extended family—they mean well. I love being smothered in love.

Pakistanis are notoriously tardy. Not everyone is, particularly the military families, but you get the point. Invited guests will ask, "Should we come to the party on Pakistani time, or *fawji* army time?" My husband and I are ridiculously punctual. You could time your clocks with our arrival. So we show up on time and then sit around while everyone else, believing all the guests will be late so why sit around waiting, takes their time. I can't stand tardiness, but I must admit that it has nostalgic value, a sense of permanence, a welcome-back feeling.

Each time I visit Pakistan, someone's passed on, and someone new has come into the family. There are condolence visits, cemetery visits, and "welcome to the family" visits. With some I shed tears; with others I coo over a newborn baby or offer a compliment: "What a beautiful daughter-in-law!" Each time there are fewer and fewer people I grew up with. Yet, in this changing family of more and more new faces, I still feel welcome. My calendar starts filling up the day I land. Once the dinner and lunch slots are taken, calls for breakfast start coming in. I ignore the rumblings in my stomach after feasting over a brunch, lunch, high tea, and dinner, all in one day. It doesn't matter how many shalwar kameez outfits I take with me, it's not enough.

When I visit Pakistan next, auntie Salma and auntie Mano will no longer be there. They were ailing when I saw them on my last trip. Bed-bound, they lived with their sons and daughters-in-law, who nursed them and kept them company. Never alone, they died at home with family by their bedside. The culture of honor—to serve one's parents—runs deep and endures. At such times, I wonder what's going to happen to me when I am dying of cancer.

P.S. I am not dying of cancer—just wondering about it.

Walter:

Leaving Israel But Holding It Closely in My Heart

I dimly remember my parents' debating whether we should stay in Israel after my father's sabbatical year was done. It was a real option, for my father had been offered a permanent position if he chose to stay. Greatly enjoying the scientific *dolce vita* within the white walls of the Weizmann Institute and at a nearby nuclear reactor not far from the beach at Palmachim, he was keen to stay on. Yet my mother, haunted by her traumatic childhood in Nazi Germany, was frightened by the prospect of again living on the Jewish front lines. My father sought to convince her that we should give it a try, but she'd respond, "I didn't escape being killed by Hitler to risk my sons' lives in Israel's wars."

In fact, my mother relished our year in Israel, too. But because of her life experience, she had a clearer-eyed understanding than my father did of the Faustian bargain involved in preserving the Jewish state. As much as she loved the place, she wouldn't countenance putting her children's lives at risk. She won the argument, and my father reluctantly agreed to return to Pittsburgh. I was disappointed by their decision but was partially consoled by a white lie my parents concocted, that we would likely return two years hence.

If we had stayed and become Israelis, of course, I would presumably have grown into an utterly different person—probably better adjusted and less personally tormented but also more conformist and less cosmopolitan. I was only seventeen during the Six-Day War in 1967, so would have been too young to fight then, but would almost certainly have served in the 1969–70 War of Attrition along the Suez Canal and in the bloody 1973 Yom Kippur War, which claimed the life of Avinoam Sharon, my cousin from Kibbutz Afek.

Would I have survived all that bloodletting? Given that I am possessed of monumental technical klutziness, I suspect I would more likely have blown myself up in a basic training accident than do the heroic thing of getting shot dead by enemy fire—though, on the other hand, the life-and-death nature of serving in an army that fights real wars might have forced me to conquer my technical incompetence, taught me useful leadership skills, and helped calm my raging sense of inadequacy. Maybe so, but my mother ensured not only that I would escape war but also that I would have to face my inner demons and chart my own uncertain path through adolescence and early adulthood without Israel's help. Today, I thank her for it.

Our year-end class trip to Jerusalem came two weeks before my family was to leave Israel. We sixth graders rode up the winding mountain road to the capital on rickety wooden benches in the back of an army truck, laughing, flirting as usual, and singing folk songs. Later, as our class toured a home for blind children in the capital, I made a curious vow to myself: *I will always remember the black smudge on the wall in the stairwell we just climbed.* The challenge had come to me in a flash—to focus my attention on something utterly inconsequential and try to remember it my entire life. I had noticed a greasy stain on the stairwell wall five minutes before and in that instant decided it would nicely fit the bill. It became a benchmark to connect me forever with that magical year in Israel.

Glimpsing Bethlehem from Afar

The other memorable moment of our class trip came during our visit to Kibbutz Ramat Rachel, several kilometers south of Jerusalem, hard on the Jordanian border. The kibbutz had been largely destroyed in fierce fighting during the 1948 War of Independence, and being too close to the border to safely operate, it had been left in ruins as a memorial.

Beyond the tangled barbed wire and signs warning of land mines, I could see the little town of Bethlehem glistening in a verdant valley directly below. Bethlehem was so close I had a clear view of the old town's twisted alleyways and centuries-old stone houses and churches and could hear the braying of donkeys and crowing of roosters. It looked wonderfully exotic compared to the concrete apartment slabs of modern Israel. Yet I couldn't dream of going there, because Bethlehem was in Jordan and sealed off from us.

Certainly, it would have been far better for Israel if that border had remained sealed. It would have been better if, during the 1967 war, the largely secular Jewish state I experienced in 1961–62 had not so eagerly "liberated" and grasped to its bosom the holy of holies represented by the Old City of Jerusalem, Hebron, Bethlehem, and the rest of ancient Judea and Samaria. That ardent embrace of the biblical heartland stimulated the entire settlement enterprise as well as a right-wing religious revival that, over the decades, pushed the largely secular and socialist Israel I knew as a child far to the right, toward the atavistic, messianic outlook that has short-circuited any chance that Israel would leave the West Bank in exchange for peace with the Palestinians.

Though my twelve-year-old self was prevented from visiting the actual Bethlehem, after returning to America I had to confront the metaphorical Bethlehem of Christian religiosity and saccharine Christmas carols. In the place where I was born and raised, for many years, I felt like a resident alien. As we left Israel en route to another lovely European trip to help ease the pain, all I could think about was how I was going to get back to the place I now considered home, the only place I believed I could be happy and fulfilled. It wasn't a question of whether I would come back to live in Israel; it was only a matter of when.

Sabeeha:

Why I Keep Going Back

I have visited Pakistan more than twenty times in the last forty-nine years. When Daddy and Mummy passed away, I believed I no longer had a reason to go back. But I still go, almost every year. I feel the tug. A family wedding, a yearning to see Neena or Jedi Mamoon, or just a feeling that it is that time of the year, and I am on a plane, headed into the sunrise. As the plane descends through the clouds over Islamabad, the land I know reveals itself: flat white rooftops, reddish-brown triangular patches of land framed by the highways, small clusters of green, and the dust flying off the runway as the plane makes its landing.

"You have arrived at Benazir International Airport. Please remain seated."

No one remains seated. "Typical Pakistani," I mutter to myself, trying to avoid the bags from the overhead bins that threaten to slam into my head. Stepping off the plane, I walk into a picture that hasn't changed, not in its color, not in its flavor. The cool railing of the wobbly metal stairs leading onto the tarmac, the security guards with mustaches standing below in their blue uniforms, the beige and green van waiting to shuttle us, the antiquated airport, the special lines for women and children at immigration, the ever-so-polite immigration officer—female, I may add—the *coolies* (Urdu for porters) running with carts to relieve me of my heavy carry-on, the careful scrutiny of security guards matching my baggage tags to the bags, the courteous nod of the guard, and then out into the crowd—people crammed against the railing with expectant looks, straining to catch a glimpse of a loved one. I stop and look around to spot Neena. She waves from the crowd, and I rush toward her. My goodness! Even at this hour—isn't it 2:00 a.m.?—she is dressed up. A quick embrace and I can tell—Chanel No. 5—and as we quickly make our way through the crowd, my nostrils inhale a whiff of sweat mixed with musty clothing: the scent of poverty. I am home.

My first visit back in 1973 was to show off my baby boy Saqib, and because I was yearning to see Mummy and Daddy, and just to be with family. New York was lonely. It was Khalid, baby, and me. As is the Pakistani custom, I stayed back for a few months when Khalid returned to New York. Not working gave me that advantage, and I indulged in being waited upon. Already I felt a twinge of discomfort at being served, but it took just a few days of ease and comfort for me to fall back into my Pakistani ways. Someone to cook, someone to clean, plus a nanny. And Razia's mouthwatering cooking—*Aaah!* I had never learned to make *chappati* flat round bread. If I tried, it was too hard, too crusty, or too crooked. I relished the hot-off-the-*tawa chappati* and would consume two or three with each meal. To call for tea, take a nap while someone watched over baby Saqib, and be in the company of cousins, aunties, and friends was a dream. Saqib, being the first grandchild in both families, was a celebrity and got fussed over to no end. Those were the moments I would yearn for when I returned to New York.

Family weddings are a huge pull. It's a given that when a sibling, cousin, or in-law gets married, you *will* fly out and be there. No excuses! Khalid and I would move our life around to make room and money for these sudden wedding calls. When Neena got married, I was back, this time with two boys. The entire extended family had congregated for the wedding, and everyone wanted to hold baby Asim, while saying to Saqib, "Look how big you got!" The festivities went on for days—the *mayoon* when the bride is grounded so that she can get fussed over; the *mehndi* henna ceremony—painting the bride's hands in floral designs—a bachelorette evening of singing and dancing, sporting shimmering out-fits; the *baraat* wedding reception—a send-off by the bride's parents; and finally the *walima,* the welcome-to-the-family reception by the groom's parents. Exhilarating! Exhausting!

When Saqib was five, I asked him, "What do you like about Pakistan?"

"Two things. Lots of relatives and lots of animals."

Lots of family—that was what my children missed in the States. No grandparents to tell them stories (or babysit), no cousins to run around with, no aunties to bring them gifts. It was that connection I didn't want them to lose after I started my career as a health-care executive and could no longer take extended trips overseas. I would send my children to Pakistan to spend the summers with their grandparents. They bonded with their cousins, picked up Urdu, played with goats and chickens, rode on donkeys in the hill town of Murree, listened to uncles and aunties tell family stories, developed a taste for *kulfi* ice cream and *paratha* bread and an ear for the stringing of the sitar and the beat of the tabla. When Saqib graduated from Haverford College and got accepted to medical school, he made an announcement. He had gotten a deferment and was taking a year off; he wanted to spend a year in Pakistan. He wanted to go back to his roots; learn to speak Urdu fluently; bond with his cous-ins, uncles, and aunts. Khalid connected him with the Association of Physicians of Pakistani Descent of North America, which does public health in Pakistan, and off went Saqib. Asim followed three years later, doing human rights work in the prison system.

When Asim was married in 2007, Mummy and Daddy came for the wedding.

"We are too old to continue to travel. From now on, you should come and see us," Mummy said.

And so I did. Every year, year after year. When Daddy fell ill, I went with the intent of staying for two weeks and ended up staying for three months. I couldn't leave him. I couldn't have Neena be the sole caretaker. After I buried Daddy, I stayed with Mummy for another month before returning home. Now I would go back twice a year to be with Mummy. The first time I returned, I dreaded walking into the house. Daddy would no longer be there, standing on the landing of the staircase, waiting for me.

Mummy died a few years later. Her death was unexpected and sudden, and I wasn't there to say goodbye, but I took the first flight out and was there to bathe her body and bury her. Now there would be no one urging me to come, waiting for me, happy to see me, sorry to see me go.

I still go back.

A Foreigner in the Land of My Birth

Whoops! I just gave away the punchline. But here is what happens. I am dressed in a shalwar kameez and seated in the back seat of a car in a crowded bazaar in Pakistan. My sister is in the passenger seat in front. At the red light, a beggar walks up to the window, cups her hand, and knocks at my sister's window. "*Aapke bachey jeetey rahain.*" May your children live long, she cries out in Urdu. Then she knocks at my window. "Excuse me," she says in English.

How did she know I was from an English-speaking country? Don't I look Pakistani enough?

Departing from Islamabad airport, I get in line for the security patdown. The female security guard beckons the women in the line into her enclosure. "*Aiyee jee,*" she calls out to each woman. When it's my turn, she looks at me and calls out, "Please come here." In English!

I walk into the curtained enclosure.

"Hello. How are you?" she says to me, in English.

When I got to the lounge, I called Jedi Mamoon.

"Explain this to me," I said. "I was born Pakistani; I look Pakistani; I dress Pakistani. What is it about me that beggars and security guards switch to English on me? How can they tell I am from America?"

He told me that the next time I should respond by using an Urdu pejorative. "You should have said to them, O *tera satya naas* (untranslatable)."

But honestly, what gives away my American-ness? Is it my bearing? Whatever it is, I am impressed by their perceptivenes. Because, tell you what: in America, people still ask me, "Where are you from?"

Walter:

My Yearning to Return

After returning to the States with my family, I was consumed throughout my teenage years and young adulthood with the conviction that I could only be happy and fulfilled if I returned to live in Israel. Impelled by that understanding, I would move back to Israel at age twenty-six for a three-year stay that I consider the happiest period of my adult life. Eventually, after my second return to the US, I became a New York–based correspondent for Israeli and American Jewish newspapers, which made it possible for me to visit Israel frequently on reporting as well as personal trips and kept me immersed in Israeli/Jewish issues.

I tried to make modest contributions to resolving the Israeli-Palestinian conflict through my work as a journalist and as part of Encounter, an early internet community promoting Jewish-Palestinian communication and cooperation. While my belief in the justice of Zionism with respect to the treatment of the Palestinians dropped away even before my return to Israel, and my overall outlook has evolved over the decades in a universalist direction that runs counter to the "being a Jew first and foremost" credo that dominated my younger years, I retain a deep personal connection to Israel and to what I might call "Israeliness" that will remain with me for the rest of my life. Despite the Israeli/Palestinian conflict and my own internal conflict over it, Israel still gets me high and always will. Israeli society has an informality, immediacy, and intensity I have experienced nowhere else on the planet.

CHAPTER 9

WE BELIEVED
WE WERE ENEMIES

Can you hate someone you don't know? The answer is yes. It's *because* you don't know them that you fear and hate them. Neither of us hated the other's faith community, but truth be told, for a long time we didn't like them very much either.

Sabeeha:
My First Introduction to Israel
"All countries of the world except Israel," Daddy read from his newly issued Pakistani passport. My father explained to me—his eight-year-old daughter—that Pakistan does not recognize Israel. He told me the story of the creation of Israel, and the only words I remember are "People were driven out of their homes." Those words shaped my view of Israel and have endured. But Daddy also said, and maintained till the day he died, that "Pakistan *should* recognize Israel." Daddy was in the minority.

Who Are the Jews?
I had never met a Jew. Pakistan was and remains a Muslim-majority country, Christians being the only visible minority, with a small Hindu population. Growing up in Pakistan, my impression and perception was shaped by the country's position on Israel, the circumstances of the

creation of Israel, and the plight of the dispossessed Palestinians in the diaspora. The narrative we heard was that the colonists—British, in this case—were committed to weakening Muslim nations, the Ottoman Empire in particular, and that taking away Palestinian land and giving it to the Jews was their strategy for achieving that goal.

In high school, we studied Shakespeare's *Merchant of Venice*. Shylock's character left us with the impression that the Jews controlled lending practices, often to the disadvantage of borrowers. I know now—now that I have lived with and worked with Jews—that they are one of the most philanthropic and community-oriented people, with a strong commitment to social justice. The quality of life in our neighborhoods and cities is made better with their involvement.

Did we study the Holocaust? Yes, world history was a standard part of our curriculum at every grade level. I was in seventh grade in 1961 when we devoted a class session to Hitler's genocide of the Jews. But I don't recall anyone using the term *Holocaust*.

In June 1967, I was a freshman at the College of Home Economics in Lahore, living in the dorm, while my parents lived wherever the army posted Daddy. The *Pakistan Times* was delivered to our dining room just in time for breakfast. The seniors got first pass at the paper, and we, the bottom-of-the-totem-polers, often had to wait until the 4:00 p.m. tea-time break. Anyway, I heard rumblings that war had broken out between Israel and the Arab countries. We were rooting for the Arabs. *Maybe now, after all these years, the Palestinians will be able to go back to their homes.* I didn't go rushing to grab the paper or listen to the news on Radio Pakistan. We were having final exams and I was cramming my notes to memory over and over again. I don't remember it being a six-day war; what I do remember is walking into the dorm one afternoon, after perhaps spending the day in the library, and finding my roommates and friends clustered around on the beds, their faces drawn.

"The *Yehudis* have taken over Al-Aqsa mosque," one of them said, referring to the Jews.

I stood in respectful silence, acknowledging their pain, and then turned around and left, hoping to find a quiet place to study. I needed to stay focused or I wouldn't be placed in the First Division after the finals. Every year during exams, a feeling of nervous tension would flow through the halls and classrooms; this year there was sadness. The Palestinians were not going home.

Daddy, a colonel in the army, sat me down with a map of the Middle East. Exams were over and I was home for the summer. He walked me through the military strategy of the Israelis. I don't remember the details of the operations, but I recall how he summed it up.

"This tiny country defeated all the Arab countries."

Looking at the war through the eyes of an army officer, Daddy was in awe of the Israeli military and what he saw was a brilliant military strategy. He pointed to Egypt on the map, saying, "The Israelis blew up their fighter jets before they could even take off, right there on the runway."

Passionate and dispassionate, he was telling me that being on the right side isn't enough; you have to get your act together.

He wasn't the only one lecturing me on military tactics. I went to visit my maternal uncle, a captain in the Infantry division, and he had me poring over more maps, his finger tracing the movement of Israeli forces, the takeover of Jerusalem, the operation in Golan Heights: a case study on how to fight a war.

When I returned to college that fall as a newly minted sophomore, I dared not bring it up with my roommates. They would be offended; I would be seen as a traitor to the Palestinian cause, and I didn't want to make trouble. Besides, I had my own woes to tend to. The exam results were out, and I had been placed in Second Division. I wonder how the conversation would go today if I were to bring Israeli military prowess up with my friends in Pakistan. They are likely to say that it's America's military aid and unconditional support of Israeli aggression. Just my guess, because I have not had this conversation.

Then Bobby Kennedy was shot. Once again, I was in the middle of finals, determined this time to get that elusive First Division. I lamented over the tragedy with my roommate.

"He was anti-Palestinian," she said.

He was? It didn't matter. Well, it did, but it didn't. He was the handsome, boyish-looking brother of a fallen president, ready to reclaim the lost years of JFK.

"A second brother has been assassinated! That is tragic," I said.

She was silent. It was her turn to acknowledge my pain.

In the autumn of 1969, the Pakistani film *Zarqa* was released. I had been hearing about this movie all summer. The beautiful star, Neelo, a movie veteran, had made her comeback to play the role of Zarqa, a freedom fighter for the liberation of Palestine. It landed her the Best Actress Nigar Award. My friends and I got our gate passes from the warden, Miss Sharif, hailed a black and yellow taxi, and headed to the Alfalah cinema at the Mall in Lahore. We watched as Zarqa was captured by the Israelis, chained, whipped, tortured with cigarette butts, and executed. Seeing her body hang sent shudders down my spine, and I walked out of the movie theater with my legs trembling. That was the moment when the suffering of the Palestinians hit me at a gut level.

I talked to Daddy about it. He repeated, "The Palestinians were driven out of their homes." He went on to say, "The Arab countries keep fighting amongst themselves. They are militarily weak. If they don't build their strength and unify, the Palestinians will never go home."

Zarqa was a super-hit, making Diamond Jubilee, running for over one hundred weeks in a single city; Neelo was propelled into superstardom; and the name Zarqa was forever associated with "freedom fighter." And the Palestinians never went home.

As for me, two years later, I was married off and landed at JFK in New York.

Walter:

How My Perspective on Pakistan Evolved

Let me start by saying that I long had a rather dim outlook on Pakistan that closely mirrored my overall negative perception of Islam as a faith. As an undergrad at the University of Wisconsin, Madison, with a visceral allegiance to the counterculture of the 1960s, I was open to spirituality of the Eastern variety but hostile to organized religion in general and the Abrahamic faiths in particular. Hinduism, with its multiplicity of gods— Vishnu, Shiva, elephant-headed Ganesh, and all the rest—appealed to the hippie in me. I felt deeply connected to ultimate truth and meaning as a result of a transcendental LSD trip during my freshman year in college. On the other hand, Islam, Judaism, and Christianity—especially of the Evangelical variety—seemed to me harsh and judgmental. Truth be told, I was sublimely ignorant of the basics of all three religions and felt little impetus to learn.

Not that I was uninterested in visiting Muslim countries. In 1970, I dreamed of dropping out of college for a year and following the hippie trail from the Spanish island of Ibiza across Greece, Turkey, Iran, and Afghanistan and on to India and Nepal. I had little interest in Pakistan, besides making a mental note that I would need to cross it to get from Afghanistan to India and Nepal. Among the Muslim countries, it was Afghanistan I most dreamed of experiencing, perhaps hunkering down for a few months to smoke a lot of hashish. To me, Afghanistan epitomized Oriental exoticism: the chance to experience, while blissfully high, the rhythms of a world barely changed since the times of the Bible.

As fate would have it, I never dropped out of school or made my hippie trip to India. Both my mother, who controlled the purse strings, and my girlfriend, Gloria, still in high school but planning to arrive as a freshman at the University of Wisconsin, were understandably opposed to my taking off and disappearing into the mists of South Asia.

Like many undergrads in Madison circa 1970, I was highly politicized, but my political concerns focused on the Vietnam War and the Israeli-Palestinian conflict. The India–Pakistan conflict was barely on my radar; that is, until 1971, when India invaded East Pakistan to help it achieve independence as Bangladesh. In that war, my sympathies were totally with India. The Pakistani regime seemed to me cruel, excessively militarized, and murderous in its bloody repression of the Bengalis. Also, President Richard Nixon and his national security adviser, Henry Kissinger, both of whom I hated intensely, were backing the Pakistanis for strategic reasons: Pakistan was a longtime US ally, and India had the backing of the Soviet Union. All the more reason for someone like myself to support India, the land of Gandhi, the apostle of nonviolence, and Nehru, who seemed rational, intellectual, and humanistic compared to the spit-and-polish Pakistani military regime. And how could any young American who was politically and musically conscious in those days forget the Concert for Bangladesh that the "quiet Beatle," George

Harrison, and sitar genius Ravi Shankar put together with the participation of Bob Dylan and other 1960s icons?

Only decades later, mainly because of sustained encounters with
Kashmiri Muslims, did I begin to understand the cruelty of the seventy-year
Indian occupation of Kashmir. Somehow the gentle Gandhian mystique
of India succeeded in blinding several generations of Western progres-
sives to the mistreatment of Kashmiri Muslims. Of course, in the past several years, the triumph of the Hindu-nationalist Bharatiya Janata Party has
seemingly laid to rest Gandhi's dream of India as a secular state. We have
seen a government inspired by a Hindu-first agenda that sanctioned horrific anti-Muslim acts before and after coming to power, including many
killings, the destruction of a sixteenth-century mosque, and the building
of a Hindu temple in its place. And now it has stripped autonomy from
Kashmir and is brutally persecuting its predominantly Muslim population.

Meanwhile, the Buddhist nation of Burma perpetrated what appears
to be genocide on the Rohingya Muslims in 2017, slaughtering thousands and driving nearly the entire population of more than half a million
into exile. I have learned ruefully that Hindu and Buddhist fundamentalism, chauvinism, and xenophobia are every bit as repulsive—and murderous—as the Muslim, Jewish, and Christian versions.

Sabeeha:

The First Time I Met a Jew

Growing up in Pakistan, I had never met a Jew. Well, now I was in New
York City, and guess what? One week into my arrival, Khalid took me to
his hospital's Christmas party. Of his colleagues—medical residents—half
were Pakistani/Indian, and the other half were Jews. Except I did not
know they were Jewish. I don't know who I thought they were, other
than Khalid's colleagues, or why I would even consider what their faith
was. It was later, when Khalid and I were talking about the party, that it
came up somehow. Maybe I mentioned the nice woman whose husband
wore a skullcap, and Khalid may have explained the yarmulke to me.

"He is a Jew!" I said. My brow must have furrowed.

"Bia, they are very nice people," Khalid said. "Most of the American
doctors you met at the party are Jewish."

Now, of course, I understand that, but then, in that moment, I didn't know how to peel off a lifelong prejudice—not a long life, though— already ingrained in me.

They did seem to be very nice people. They were so welcoming to me. They were like—regular people.

I was confused. They were not supposed to be good people, yet they seemed happy to see me, happy that Khalid was married, complimenting him on his "beautiful bride," asking me how I was adjusting to a new place and was I homesick; asking, "Is your family all right with the war breaking out?"; all the right things that good people would say. Yet, didn't they hate Muslims? Weren't they okay with Palestinians being driven out of their homes? I couldn't reconcile good people supporting the actions of the "bad guys" or holding political beliefs that felt so wrong.

I was in my living room one day when I heard the sound of a broom swishing in the foyer. *It must be my upstairs neighbor.* Lonely in winter and eager to make an acquaintance, I stepped out.

"Hello," I said to the elderly lady in a smock, her blonde hair in a perfect hairdo.

"Hi," she said, broom in hand. "So *you* are my new neighbor."

She invited me up for coffee, which I gratefully accepted, and over the next hour, I told her all about myself.

"I will introduce you to women your age. I am too old for you," she said. Her name was Ruth.

Ruth became my go-to for shopping tips, recipes, lonely moments, pregnancy management, babysitting . . . and pretty soon I learned that she was Jewish. Another nice Jewish woman!

When I became pregnant, Khalid asked his colleague—Jewish—to recommend a doctor. By now I was desensitized, and when I learned that my good doctor was Jewish, I didn't bat an eye. My obstetrician recommended a pediatrician, and I guessed even before I knew that he had to be Jewish. And yes, by now many of my best friends were Jewish. Some were wives of Khalid's colleagues, and some were neighbors. The Jewish mothers became my coaches for parenting tips. *Why do people in Pakistan say that Western parents don't care for their children? Their world revolves entirely around raising children.* When I expressed a desire to learn

American cooking, they wrote out recipes on index cards for me. I still have them in my gray metal recipe box, spinach pie being my favorite. We bonded as we sat on the stoop of our garden apartments, watching our babies sleep in their navy-blue carriages, rocking them if they stirred. I don't recall much of what we talked about, but it was just stuff that mommy-talk is made of. Somewhere along the line, I stopped seeing them as Jewish. They were my friends.

Within a year of coming to New York, I had reconciled perception with reality. But I didn't share my "findings" with my family and friends in Pakistan. They couldn't possibly comprehend what I was discovering. Whoever coined the phrase "seeing is believing" wasn't kidding. Yet, when I went to Pakistan for a visit two years later, I found myself using the term "Jewish" in my discourse, as a matter of habit.

"You shouldn't take Saqib to a Jewish doctor," said one family member.

That remark bothered me.

They don't know. They only know the politics, not the people.

"If it wasn't for this doctor, I would have been a nervous wreck." I explained that he would personally answer the phone between 8:00 and 9:00 a.m. every morning, gently instructing me; that he taught me all I knew about baby handling that Dr. Spock could not; that Saqib was thriving because of him; and how much I depended on his counsel to calm me down.

Someone asked me what hospital Khalid worked at.

"Long Island Jewish."

"Jewish!"

There was no avoiding the issue, so I put on my "ambassador for Jews" hat and told it as I saw it.

"They are very nice people." I went through the list. Khalid's boss who gave him the job, gave him a reference for his fellowship in hematology, his mentors, my mentors, our neighbors, my doctor, Saqib's doctor, and my friends who helped me adjust to a new land and a new life.

What I heard back forcefully from my family members was a reiteration of their conviction that Jews hated Muslims. I understood that their only point of reference was the Israeli-Palestinian conflict. Palestinians had been driven out of their homes, were exiled from their homeland, living out their lives in refugee camps, yearning to return home; those who stayed were treated as second-class citizens. They saw images of Palestinian homes being bulldozed in East Jerusalem and settlements being built in the occupied West Bank in defiance of the UN resolution. Israelis were Jews, and Palestinians were mostly Muslim, and in the eyes of a Pakistani, the Jews were the enemy of Muslims, and here I had put my baby's life in the hands of a Jewish doctor and wouldn't stop talking about how nice they are.

But you can't convince people by rhetoric alone. You have to see for yourself—which my parents did when they came to visit us.

Seeing Is Believing

By sheer coincidence, we bought our first house in a predominantly Orthodox Jewish community in Staten Island, whose residents attended a Young Israel synagogue in the heart of the neighborhood. Did I know that being surrounded by Jews would be an advantage in raising Muslim children? This was 1976, and we were parents of two young boys. I no longer had to explain to my children why we celebrate Eid and not Christmas, why Friday and not Sunday is the holy day, why we fast in Ramadan and not in Lent, why we don't eat pork, why kosher meat is halal for us, and, of course, the missing Christmas tree. My parents, who were visiting, were quite taken by our neighbors, their discipline appealing to Daddy's military style.

In a matter of days, my sociable mother had befriended the neighborhood ladies, offering them gardening tips, giving them an earful on Pakistani culture, and even exchanging recipes, kosher notwithstanding. As soon as she would spot Leah or Betty out on the sidewalk, she would rush out and come back brimming with neighborhood chatter.

"Let's go visit Leah," Mummy would say if she hadn't seen her in two days. She would just knock on the door and walk right in. Unannounced. My neighbors got used to Sabeeha's friendly mom dropping in. And when she left, they would ask, "When is your mom coming back?"

Now it was "converted Mummy" returning to Pakistan and dropping the J word. Didn't I say, "Seeing is believing"? She had been most impressed with the children, particularly little Jason, who at Saqib's fifth birthday party just stood by as other children had cake and didn't touch a crumb in our nonkosher kitchen. That a five-year-old could exercise such self-control amazed her. Jason must now be in his mid-forties. He has no idea of the impact he had on my mother, and how often his story was told in the drawing rooms of Rawalpindi, Pakistan. Too bad I don't recall his last name or I'd try to find him on social media.

Walter:

Getting to Know Pakistanis

Once I got involved in Muslim-Jewish coalition building after 2008, two of my closest collaborators turned out to be Pakistani Americans, Dr. Ali Chaudry and Zamir Hassan, both of New Jersey. Overall, I have been deeply impressed by the open-mindedness and progressive approach of my Pakistani American friends, especially in their willingness to directly encounter and befriend Jews, though almost none exist in Pakistan and they have been exposed to so much official anti-Israel invective. Meeting Pakistanis in their twenties and thirties at annual meetings of Muslim-Jewish Conference in Europe has also been inspiring. Many of the participants first connected with their Jewish counterparts online from Pakistan, even at some personal risk. I have found them to be committed to democracy and human values, in stark contrast to the image I had of Pakistan.

Over the decades, my once largely negative image of Pakistan has become far more nuanced. Dialoguing with my coauthor Sabeeha has had a major impact in that transition. Seeing Pakistan through her eyes, in her memoir *Threading My Prayer Rug*, awoke me to her deep sense of pride in belonging to a culture and a country that defines itself first and foremost as a Muslim state, very much in the way Israel defines itself as a Jewish one. The electric sense of connection to Pakistan and Islam that Sabeeha felt growing up there and still evinces today is something I recognize as a mirror image of my experiences in Israel. To be sure, I see the limiting aspects of a society that defines itself as fully and exclusively Muslim in the same way I have come to recognize the limitations inherent in Israel's self-definition. Yet I totally get the abiding sense of connection to the people, faith, language, cuisine, sounds, and smells of Pakistan that Sabeeha expresses.

Who Are the Muslims? Who Are the Arabs?

With my friend Ali Chaudry, I had a fascinating conversation eight or nine years ago about the eruption of Islam out of Arabia after the death of the Prophet Muhammad in 632 AD and its spread within a century to a broad span of the world's surface, from Spain to India. Ali presented that process as having been largely achieved through peaceful means, with most people in the newly conquered lands having freely embraced Islam because they were won over to its truth and beauty and because it offered a far greater degree of social justice than they had experienced before. His perspective clashed profoundly with the version I had learned and believed: that Islam had been spread by Arab armies that conquered the entire Middle East and North Africa, overthrowing the Sassanid Empire of Persia and supplanting the Zoroastrian faith with Islam, driving to the gates of Constantinople and Poitiers before being checked by the Byzantine and Frankish empires respectively.

True, I had also learned that the Muslim caliphs had been much more accepting of the Jewish and Christian communities in the lands they conquered than were Christian kings and popes of the Jews and Muslims they vanquished. In myriad cases, most notably during the Crusades, Muslims were massacred in large numbers. Yet I also believed there were strict limits to Muslim mercy. I had been taught that while Christians and Jews living in Muslim lands were largely allowed to live and worship according to their own lights, they were forced to subordinate themselves to the Muslim rulers, while pagans were given a choice of "convert or die."

Where had my version of the story come from? I had absorbed it from history texts going back to elementary school and extending through university. A central premise of European and American historiography vis-à-vis Islam was that it was primarily spread by the sword. Hearing Ali's perspective was a revelation to me. Now I realized Muslims saw it very differently, and as we spoke, I came to feel that the truth of what had actually happened during the seventh century AD was probably somewhere between Ali's position and my own.

Certainly, there had been Arab armies winning famous battles that led to the capture of cities like Baghdad, Damascus, Jerusalem, Samarkand,

and Cordoba. Yet the version Ali offered helped explain the astonishing success of Arab armies in sweeping out of the desert, rapidly vanquishing the armies of several longstanding empires, and conquering a huge chunk of the known world. The Arabs' secret weapon was a millenarian faith that promised an ethical approach to humankind, focusing on social justice and a higher level of equality than existed in the societies it overcame. Evidently, a lot of the dispossessed embraced Islam because it affirmed that they mattered as human beings and were part of a global community dedicated to truth and justice. Proselytizing must have mattered every bit as much as coercion.

Given this, along with the better treatment of Jews under Muslim rule than in Christian Europe for most of the past 1,300 years and the well-established fact that Muslim Damascus and Baghdad were centers of advanced civilization—in mathematics, literature, and much more—during the medieval period when Europe was in the Dark Ages, why had I long viewed the Muslim world as more primitive than the Christian one? I suspect the reason had to do not only with history books but also my experiences in Israel, both as a child and when I returned in 1976 as a new immigrant. When I visited Bedouin tents in the Negev and on the beaches of Sinai, the men were treated to elaborate hospitality while the women, seated in the back and covered head-to-toe in black robes, appeared totally invisible and dehumanized. As wonderful as it was to be lavished in warm hospitality and sip delicious Arabic coffee suffused with cardamom, it was unsettling to glimpse women in that condition.

Return to Israel

In 1976, I left the University of Wisconsin with a teaching degree and a Christian wife and abruptly moved to Israel, the place I had always felt I needed to return to be happy. An impulsive decision to shake up our lives and try, in the process, to salvage an increasingly shaky marriage seemed to have paid off in spades, at least for me. Within six months, I was covering the north of Israel for the *Jerusalem Post* and other English-language newspapers and living with my wife in Haifa in a gorgeous hilltop apartment.

I felt deeply at home in Israel, organically Jewish, on the cutting edge of history. My life felt suffused with adventure and limitless possibilities. I was hiking through the backcountry of the Galilee one week, communing with kibbutzniks, Bedouin, and Arab villagers along my way, profiling Israeli rock stars the next week, and following Anwar Sadat on his historic swing through Jerusalem the next. I had a wonderful assortment of friends, both sabras (native-born Israelis) and new immigrants from around the globe, who manifested an enthusiastic hands-on approach to life that combined warmth, informality, and openness.

And then there was the view to which I woke up every morning. From my desk in front of our living room window, I looked out over the entire Galilee. My eyes followed the curve of Haifa Bay to the ancient port of Akko (Acre), with its mosques and battlements gleaming in the sun, and then north to where the white cliffs of Rosh Hanikra, which formed the border with Lebanon, jutted out into the blue Mediterranean. Turning east, I could see the sweep of the mountains of Upper Galilee as far as the old kabbalistic city of Safed and beyond. On clear winter days, snow-clad 9,000-foot-high Mt. Hermon loomed on the horizon, perhaps eighty miles away.

One day it hit me that I could see to the end of the world; that is, the end of the world as residents of Israel experienced it. All of Israel's borders were still sealed tight and impassable. From my apartment window, I was able to see as far as Israel's borders with Lebanon and Syria but not beyond them—in short, to the end of the known world.

Directly to the north, the white cliffs and the ridge along the Lebanese border blocked my view of any portion of that land. At the time, Lebanon was caught up in the convulsions of a many-sided civil war that we read about every day in the newspapers. But only twenty-five miles away, for the people of Haifa, that war might have been happening on another continent. Syria, off to the east and bitterly hostile to Israel, remained terra incognita behind the hulking presence of Mt. Hermon.

For all practical purposes, for me and the four million–odd inhabitants of the Jewish state, the pocket-sized Land of Israel was the whole world. My world, the place I worked and played, was the Galilee, a beautiful region that I could—and once actually did—walk across in three days. Size turns out to be elastic. How quickly I and other Americans living in Israel adjusted our perspectives from living in a continent-sized country to one no bigger than New Jersey, but which felt many times larger because there was so much to touch, see, and experience within its confines. I never left Israel from the moment of my arrival there in January 1976 until flying back to America twenty-two months later, but during that time I never felt hemmed in or claustrophobic. Israel was a mythic, larger-than-life place that assumed a size and a presence in accord with the psychic needs of those who cherished it.

Encounters with Israeli Arabs and Palestinians

I was no longer a believer in the *Exodus* version of Israeli-Palestinian historiography. One day in the summer of 1969, the scales had fallen from my eyes while discussing Israel with my father. I blurted out, "Oh, my God, so we really did steal the land from the Arabs? Is that what you're saying?" My father didn't deny it, but affirmed gently that after generations of anti-Semitic pogroms culminating in the Holocaust, self-determination had become an existential necessity for the Jews. To be sure, the impact on the Palestinian Arabs had been terribly unfair, but once the wheel had been set in motion with the large-scale return of the Jews, it was all but inevitable that the Palestinians would resist the intrusion and the two peoples would end up fighting each other. The best that could be hoped for, he said, was that the Israelis and the Arabs would summon the wisdom to make the future happier than the past.

From that moment, I was imbued with the gut understanding that the return of my people to their lost homeland was the direct cause of the dispersion of the Palestinian Arabs, who had formed the vast majority of the people living there in the early decades of the twentieth century. This realization did not alter my abiding passion for the Land and people of Israel. In the fundamental conflict between my head and heart, I had to give primacy to my heart. I loved Israel and needed Israel to survive in order for my own life to have meaning and purpose. Only by returning to Israel could I be happy and fulfilled. Only if I did that, I told myself, could I play a meaningful role in helping promote a new consciousness of equality between Jews and Arabs.

My deeply felt sense of the unfairness of Israeli life toward its Arab minority was buttressed by my work as a Haifa-based feature writer for the *Jerusalem Post*. Soon the Arab villages of Galilee became a regular part of my beat. I wrote articles that exposed the systematic discrimination endured by Israeli Arabs, the descendants of the minority of the Palestinian population who were allowed to stay in Israel after 1948, who by 1975 had grown to around 15 percent of the population of Israel within the green line—the pre-1967 borders of Israel, not including East Jerusalem, the West Bank, or Gaza. (By 2013, due to the higher Arab birth rate, and despite ongoing Jewish immigration, that number had grown to 20.7 percent of the population.) I soon found out that Arab municipalities received a fraction of the government aid for schools, community centers, libraries, hospitals, and other public institutions received by Jewish municipalities of similar size. The vast majority of towns and villages in Israel were then and remain today either Jewish-only or Arab-only, and even the handful of cities like Haifa, Acre, Jaffa, and Jerusalem, in which the two communities have coexisted, tend to be rigidly segregated by neighborhood. Arabs are forbidden to serve in the army on the grounds that they could be security risks. While Israel has made it possible for Arabs to attend universities, it has largely prevented them from finding jobs in the professions and in fields like computers, high tech, and security, since prior army service is a precondition for attaining such positions.

Meeting with Arab students at Haifa University in 1977, I heard their deep frustration that the only job possibilities awaiting them were in the so-called Arab sector (i.e., as teachers and administrators in Arab schools and municipalities or in blue-collar positions in construction or factories). The practical alternative for educated young Arabs in search of career fulfillment was emigration to Europe or America. One couldn't help but suspect that Israeli authorities were purposely creating conditions that made emigration the desired course for the best and brightest among Israeli Arabs.

On assignment for *Israel Horizons,* an English-language magazine published by the quasi-governmental Jewish Agency for Israel, I visited the Arab village of Ibillin in western Galilee to interview a dynamic Greek

Catholic priest and community activist named Father Elias Chacour. He turned out to be one of the most compelling figures I had ever met. Fed up with crying discrimination at the government's foot-dragging over funding the construction of a long-delayed and desperately needed community center in Ibillin, the charismatic Chacour inspired and organized members of the community of all ages to roll up their sleeves and build the community center themselves. This process was helped by the fact that Arabs traditionally built their own homes and are essential workers in the Israeli construction industry.

Father Chacour, who was born in the village of mainly Christian Arab Bir'im in 1939, has written vividly of the experience of being driven out of the village together with his family by the Israeli army in 1948. (The Israel Supreme Court ruled several years later that the villagers should be allowed to return, but the IDF never allowed that to happen.) Father Chacour became an apostle of nonviolence, urging Arabs to win over Israeli Jews by treating them with love and forbearance. His message of hope and reconciliation left a powerful impression on me.

Yet when I returned to Haifa and told Israeli-Jewish friends and acquaintances about my meetings with Father Chacour, and about a return visit to Ibillin during which I was warmly welcomed into the home of one of Chacour's congregants for an impromptu dinner attended by many of the young men of the village, I was greeted with a jarring combination of eye-rolling and condescension. Even some purportedly progressive friends expressed the sentiment that I was a naïve American who misunderstood the underlying realities of the Israeli-Arab conflict and therefore could be easily hoodwinked by the Arabs. A few bluntly repeated variations on an overtly racist saying that one often heard in Israel: that Arabs are prone to offering lavish displays of hospitality, including elaborate banquets, but as soon as the contented and well-fed guest turns his back, they will stick a knife into him.

What I had experienced wasn't a false show of hospitality but rather a genuine expression of human kindness and gratefulness that I, as a Jew, had been willing to come into their homes to dialogue with them. Yet to that, my Israeli-Jewish interlocutors would simply repeat that I understood nothing of the situation; that if the Arabs hadn't harmed me, it was out of a calculation that I was the kind of useful idiot who could be depended upon to write things in the media that would present them in the most sympathetic light. I sometimes asked my challengers when they had visited the nearby Arab villages of the Galilee, and most acknowledged that they rarely, if ever, had done so. Nevertheless, they insisted, as native-born Israelis, they "knew" the Arabs in ways that I, as a well-meaning outsider, was unable to.

My admiration for Father Chacour also caused tension in my relationship with my Uncle Ze'ev and Aunt Penina, whom I frequently visited at their home on Kibbutz Afek. On several occasions, I sat on their living room couch directly in front of a small memorial shrine for their son, Avinoam, which included a tiny eternal-flame keepsake provided to the family by the IDF, and spoke about how Father Chacour had inspired me with hopes for peace and reconciliation between Israeli Arabs and Jews. Conscious of the enormous symbolic power for his parents of that shrine to Avinoam, I believed naïvely that my words might provide my grieving aunt and uncle with hope for a future in which no Israeli family would ever again have to sacrifice a child in war. Yet, instead of greeting my words positively, Ze'ev and Penina would grimace and offer more gently phrased variations of the comments I had heard from other Israelis: that I was a naïve American who didn't understand the Arabs or their implacable agenda.

After one such discussion, I stepped out of the apartment for an afternoon walk through the kibbutz fields and took in the gorgeous vista I never tired of, across the orchards of Kibbutz Afek to the hills of Lower Galilee, where the lovely Arab town of Tamra cascaded down a mountainside. Suddenly, it hit me that Father Chacour's village of Ibillin was just beyond my field of vision, hidden in the hills to the southeast, no more than ten kilometers away. Until that moment, I hadn't considered how close Afek and Ibillin were to each other.

When I returned to Ze'ev and Penina's home and, over a fresh cup of Nescafé, asked, "By the way, Ze'ev, have you ever been to Ibillin?" he replied brusquely, "Yes, of course I have." To which I asked, "When was the last time you were there?" He furrowed his brow and replied, after some thought, "As far as I recall, I was there once in 1943." Ze'ev saw my eyebrows go up but responded forcefully, "Yes, it has been a while since I've been there. So what? Don't think for a moment that just because you were there a few weeks ago and got sweet-talked by that priest of yours that you understand the Arabs better than I do. Listen, I don't need to go to Ibillin to meet Chacour and the others in order to understand what they want, which is to destroy the State of Israel as soon as they can. And one way they are trying to accomplish that is by pulling the wool over the eyes of Jewish dreamers like you."

Was Ze'ev right? Was I a naïve fool or traitor to my own people, oblivious to the true agenda of the Arabs? To Chacour and the other Israeli Arabs with whom I had dialogued, the return of the Jews and the eviction of most of their Palestinian brethren in the event they called the *Naqba* was a national tragedy. Yet I also believed that most of the Arabs I had met were realists who understood that Israel wasn't going away. They simply wanted to achieve the maximum amount of justice and opportunity possible under the circumstances for themselves and their children. It seemed to me that it was very much in the interest of Israeli Jews—not to mention consistent with basic precepts of justice—to meet them halfway.

My positive encounters with Israeli Arabs and the negative reaction to them of many, though not all, of my Israeli-Jewish interlocutors taught me one of the life lessons that has defined my subsequent career in Muslim-Jewish relations: the importance of reaching across psychological barricades and encountering the Other face-to-face. Once one made the effort to build person-to-person ties, Israeli Arabs ceased to be a threatening collective "them" but instead became flesh-and-blood human beings with whom I was able to find common ground and build friendships.

I don't want to give my 1970s self too much credit. Despite my progressive politics, I retained major blind spots. I gave little thought to the suffering of the 1948 Palestinian refugees and their descendants living in woeful conditions in the refugee camps just across the sealed borders I could not cross. I took as an unassailable truth that the Arab refugees had largely fled of their own accord in 1948. The revelations by Israeli historians that, in fact, the Haganah, Irgun, and the newly formed

IDF had intentionally driven a large percentage of the Arabs of Palestine across the border during the War of Independence were still a decade or so away.

Even if I had known, I'm not sure how much it would have changed my perspective. It was the practice of Israeli painters and sculptors to create "artist villages" in places like the abandoned Arab village of Ein Hod near Haifa and in formerly Arab neighborhoods of towns like Jaffa or Safed. It was the so-called *yafeh nefesh* (beautiful souls)—gentle, free-spirited, secular, left-wing types who often lived a bohemian lifestyle—who were the most drawn to moving into old Arab houses and fixing them up. Yet few of these artists who moved into places like Ein Hod seemed to care that it had once been a Palestinian village or that the charming stone houses they so lovingly rehabilitated had once belonged to families who still retained the keys to their former homes and dreamed of returning to them. The attitude conveyed by Israelis—including most in the dovish Peace Now movement—seemed to be a kind of willful amnesia about the extirpation of an estimated 750,000 Palestinian refugees from the territory that became Israel only thirty years earlier. Living among Israeli Jews, I absorbed that perspective as well. I was all for promoting equality for the Arabs remaining in Israel, yet did not see the Palestinians driven out in 1948, and their millions of descendants, as having any relation to me.

I was fortunate to spend my three years living in Israel during a relatively peaceful window of time, between the 1973 Yom Kippur War and the 1982 Israeli invasion of Lebanon. I witnessed big events, including Menachem Begin's coming to power, Anwar Sadat's visit to Jerusalem, and Israel's subsequent withdrawal from Sinai, but no actual warfare. Not surprisingly, therefore, I got a happily distorted picture of the place that airbrushed out the harsher realities. I was swept up in the national euphoria of Sadat's Jerusalem visit in November 1977, which felt to many Israelis and Jews, myself included, like the coming of the Messiah—a sudden opening of the previously impenetrable barriers between Israelis and the Arab world that seemed to utterly transform the situation and portend an early peace settlement. My dear friend Naomi, an immigrant from London who worked with troubled teenagers in a deprived Oriental Jewish town in northern Israel and was a far more dedicated leftist than I, expressed opposition to Sadat's impending visit. She argued that the Egyptian president was embarked on making a separate peace with Israel to get the Sinai back for Egypt but would leave the Palestinians in the occupied territories under permanent Israeli control and bar Palestinian refugees from the 1948 war from ever returning. What came out of my mouth in response was "F— the Palestinians! Naomi, how can you care more about them than about your own people, who finally have a chance for peace?"

That was profoundly unfair, of course, and the truth was that Naomi was clear-sighted enough to understand that Israelis would not have peace until they reached an agreement with the Palestinians, and not solely with the Egyptians.

I left Israel and returned to the United States in the summer of 1979. I told myself I wasn't necessarily leaving for good, just taking another detour in my life journey. Looking back, though, it's obvious that rationalization involved a healthy measure of self-delusion. I had only six months left before my temporary residency would run out, and if I had chosen to stay, I would have been confronted with the necessity of becoming an Israeli citizen and going into the army. Clearly, I wasn't going to do that. Also, with some honest *heshbon hanefesh* (soul searching), I would have had to acknowledge that my encounters with the harsh realities of the Israeli-Palestinian conflict made it impossible for me to transform into an Israeli. If I had come to understand anything during that time, it was that Father Chacour was as much my friend and my brother as my closest Jewish friends and relatives, and that he and other Arabs I had befriended belonged to the land every bit as deeply as did Jewish Israelis. That was something most Jews refused to accept because it put the whole rationale of a Jewish state in question.

I would stay deeply engaged with Israel, visiting at least once a year for the next two decades or so on reporting trips and to reconnect with friends and family members. I stayed within a primarily Jewish context, building what I like to call my so-called career—writing for Jewish and Israeli newspapers, mainly about Israel and Diaspora Jewry in interaction with America, Russia, and the world. Yet I lived mainly in New York rather than in Haifa. The abiding conviction of my youth, that I needed to live in Israel to be happy and fulfilled—the impulse that had impelled me to leave Madison four years earlier and sign up for *aliyah*—immigration to Israel—all of that had somehow slipped away in the interim.

Sabeeha:

Jewish Humor

The year after Walter returned to the United States, Khalid and I moved to Lighthouse Hill on Staten Island. No Jewish neighbors, but my former neighbors would come by, the children's birthday parties being the draw. When they first came, Mummy and Daddy happened to be visiting. I gave my former neighbors a tour and pointed out all the furniture the previous owners had left behind, including a gorgeous china cabinet.

"They left all this for free?" Sue asked.

"Yes."

"They must not be Jewish. A Jewish person would even sell you the heating vents. I should know, I am Jewish."

Daddy burst out laughing. We all laughed, including Sue, but what struck Daddy was her sense of humor. He immediately warmed up to her, and every time he visited, he would ask me how Sue was doing and then repeat the joke. All my family in Pakistan know of Sue, with an affectionate smile.

Must-See Tourist Destination

It's not what you think. Well, it was, but not anymore. In the 1980s when family visited from Pakistan—uncles, aunts, and cousins—we would take them to the standard tourist sites: the Empire State Building, the Statue of Liberty, Central Park, etc. Now, we take them to a synagogue—for Sabbath services. Our friend Jenny invited us for services at the B'nai Jeshurun synagogue, and we just loved the music and dancing. Not to mention that the prayers were so similar to ours. I mean, if I didn't know, I'd think I was holding the Qur'an and not the Siddur Sim Shalom. The first time we did this experiment, taking a Pakistani family member— Khalid's niece—to a synagogue, we walked over to a diner with some of the Jewish congregants afterward and chatted over dinner. This young woman was so taken by the experience, first the services, then dinner with a group of Jews who were giving her tourist tips, that she spent hours that night writing the longest email to her mother and sister in Pakistan. We had successfully recruited another ambassador.

Goodwill Is Infectious

We now have another tool that Khalid is using rather effectively—Facebook. Most of his nieces and nephews don't email—if you want to reach them, use Facebook. So now each time there is a Jew speaking up for a Muslim, or a solidarity event, or just day-to-day examples of coexistence, Khalid posts it on Facebook and tags the young ones in Pakistan. They are the future. Think of their reaction when Khalid posted the photo of Rabbi Sharon Kleinbaum with members of Congregation Beit Simchat Torah, an LGBTQ congregation, on the first Friday after the 2016 presidential election, standing in the rain outside the Islamic Center of New York University during Jumma prayers, holding up signs saying JEWS SUPPORT OUR MUSLIM FRIENDS. Google it; you will see the photo. This was not a one-time showing; they came every Friday for three years, stopping only when COVID-19 forced Jumma prayers to cease. The youth in Pakistan—at least the ones we are connected with—are now saying, "We need to do something like this for the Christians in Pakistan."

There Is a Sad Side

If and when Walter visits Pakistan, I hope he returns with good memories, not like the experience I had when I visited Israel in 1997.

Khalid and I were with a tour group at the Al-Aqsa mosque when a suicide bomber attacked a restaurant in Jerusalem and scores were killed. At that instant, everything changed. We had entered Israel as tourists but exited as potential terrorists. We were stopped, interrogated at every checkpoint, detained at the border crossing into Jordan, and humiliated.

When I say "we," I mean our group of physicians—members of the Islamic Medical Association of North America (IMANA), who had convened for a medical conference in Amman, Jordan, and with their families were making a day trip to Israel and the West Bank.

After saying our Dhuhr (noon) prayers at the Al-Aqsa mosque and visiting the Wailing Wall, we had just sat down to lunch when we heard the news. Feeling terrible about the loss of lives, we boarded the bus to Hebron. Our bus was stopped at the checkpoint and a young man in Israeli army uniform—he couldn't have been more than eighteen—boarded the bus, rifle in hand. He started walking down the aisle while looking each of us in the eye.

This was a bus full of dark-skinned, Muslim-looking men, women, and young adults.

"Where are you going? What is your business?" he said.

"Doctors from America, attending a conference in Jordan," Khalid said, pulling out his passport.

A few more questions, and he disembarked, waving us through.

This happened at every checkpoint. A young boy, rifle in hand, finger on trigger, interrogating us.

At Hebron, as we walked up to the entrance to the Tomb of the Patriarchs, a group of young boys in military uniform stopped us. Their faces were angry, their eyes squinting with hatred. Everybody's papers were checked; more questions. As we walked up, leaving the armed boys behind, I heard a shout, and shooting. One of them had thrown himself on the ground and shot rubber bullets at a lone Palestinian boy walking down the alley.

I felt my cheeks flame. Bystander guilt.

On our return, as our bus rolled through the narrow streets of a forlorn-looking Hebron, we watched through our windows as Israeli soldiers pushed a Palestinian boy against the wall and kicked him.

More checkpoints; more interrogation; more young boys with rifles.

What if any one of them loses his composure and shoots at us?

I couldn't wait to get out of Israel. But not before we glimpsed the tragic sights of the settlements: beautiful villas on the hilltops and shacks of the Palestinians in the valley.

The worst lay waiting at the border crossing into Jordan via the Allenby Bridge.

We got off the bus and walked into the building to be processed. My friend Kausar and her family were ahead of us in line. The young lady at the counter took her son's passport and told him to step aside. Her son was in his early twenties. A uniformed guard escorted him to another room.

"Why are you taking him?" Kausar asked.

She glared at Kausar and told her to be quiet and wait.

They did that to every young man in our group. We parents were told to go wait in the bus.

We waited.

And as we waited, we started despairing.

What are they doing to our sons?

How long are they going to hold them?

All thirty of us, stunned in our collective helplessness, couldn't fathom how our children could be treated like that.

Then we started getting angry.

How dare they hold our boys?

Is this where our US tax dollars are going? So the Israelis can treat our sons like suspected terrorists? Do they really think that a busload of doctors from America came to blow up a restaurant?

"Look at what a few hours of humiliation has done to our nerves. Think of what it is like to live the life of a Palestinian!" one person said.

One by one, the boys were released. As they boarded the bus, we had just one thought.

Let's get out of here.

Back in the United States, I was cautious about sharing my experience with my Jewish friends. I didn't want to offend, so I decided to tell them only if they asked. Of course, they asked. Did I think they wouldn't? I gave them the entire rundown, and they felt really bad. Some felt embarrassed, and then *I* felt bad for *them*. Some were incredulous but knew I wasn't making it up. There was one friend whom I didn't have the heart to tell. He is a devout Jew, very committed to Israel, and holds the land and its people close to his heart. He was most anxious to know my impressions and sent me an email, asking how my trip went. I didn't respond, hoping he would forget about it and I wouldn't have to deal with an unpleasant conversation. Chicken! Well, he didn't give up and one day my office phone rang.

"Sabeeha, I want to know how your trip went."

"I am sorry I haven't called you, but I didn't want to offend you."

"I won't be offended."

I gave him the whole story, just as I told you, word for word.

"All I can say, Sabeeha, is that at least you weren't among the scores that were killed."

"What did they think they would get by detaining our sons?" I asked.

"Maybe to see if anyone bolts."

"Bolts and goes where?"

"Sabeeha, it's a war zone; it's not America. You don't know what it's like to live under the threat of suicide bombing."

"I know now just a little bit of what it is like to live under occupation."

"This is some conversation. I am not going to apologize for them."

"You don't have to apologize. It wasn't your doing."

"Yes, but I feel bad you had this experience."

He had so hoped that his Muslim friend would see the bright side of Israel and return with a positive impression.

After the call—which ended on a strained but "we will remain friends" note—I had difficulty focusing on work. I had wanted him to denounce the treatment of our boys and the youth who had been shot with rubber bullets. I tried to put myself in his shoes, but they felt tight. I could see where he was coming from. Palestinians blew up people; of course the Israelis' guards will go up—one cannot be too careful, too exacting, when scores of your own people have just been killed. But what I witnessed was so much more than that.

He and I have remained good friends. After 9/11, he and his wife drove out to visit Khalid and me. No words were needed—their presence said it all. Whenever a Muslim terrorist strikes, and Muslim bashing gets hyped in the media, he is one of the first to call me and offer support. The four of us—our spouses included—meet up in Manhattan for dinner. We share our woes—family issues, Khalid's health, his wife counsels me on my autistic grandson Omar's transition into adulthood, and just the stuff friends talk about. Our friendship has endured the pain caused by our differing politics.

Our difficult experiences in Israel compelled me to study the history of Jerusalem. The work that gripped me was Karen Armstrong's book, *Jerusalem: One City, Three Faiths*. I introduced the book to the curriculum of the Muslim Sunday school young adults' class at my mosque. If you haven't read it, I urge you to get a copy.

Postscript: When Walter read this piece, he asked how I processed the contradiction between my positive impression of American Jews and what I witnessed and endured in Palestine. For the most part, the Jews I shared this experience with were sympathetic and recognized that what we witnessed and experienced was terrible and shouldn't have happened. Of all people, we Muslims should know that you cannot paint everyone with the same brush. We feel smeared by the bloody colors of violence each time a Muslim suicide bomber takes innocent lives. We cry out, "Don't blame us all for the acts of a few. There are 1.8 billion Muslims in our world. The extremists do not speak for us or represent us." We scramble to put our best foot forward to show that most of us are good people. And we all know—we Muslims, Jews, Christians, Hindus, Buddhists—that some people who share our faith, sometimes, somewhere, in some circumstances, do bad things.

Walter:

Processing Sabeeha's Hellish Experience in Israel

What can I say to offer Sabeeha and Khalid consolation about what happened on their one and only trip to Israel and Palestine? If only I had a magic wand to make the sting of that traumatic memory go away. I learned about their experience only recently, while Sabeeha and I were discussing making trips together to Israel and Pakistan, perhaps as a postscript to this book. I was already anticipating elaborate and delicious feasts with their extended family in Pakistan, exploring her college town of ancient Lahore, and finally seeing the Himalayas, but somewhere in the back of my mind—not very far back—was a keen awareness of the fate of Daniel Pearl, the Jewish *Wall Street Journal* correspondent who was kidnapped, tortured, and eventually beheaded by extremists in Karachi purporting to be acting in the true spirit of Islam by executing a Jew.

I avoided mentioning my safety concerns to Sabeeha. What an irony that I had been worrying about my own well-being on a prospective trip to Pakistan and then finding out she and Khalid had already been subjected to humiliation and intimidation in Israel. Knowing what had happened to them, would I really want to invite Sabeeha and Khalid back to Israel and be put in a position where, God forbid, something similar could happen again?

As I learned in 1997, when I traveled to Israel with a Palestinian American friend I will call Ahmed on a self-styled "Mission of Peace and Reconciliation," the Israeli security people have carte blanche to investigate and humiliate whomever they please among those arriving in Israel, even if high-level Israeli diplomats or political types have sanctioned the visit. Anticipating possible problems before setting out on my trip with Ahmed, I obtained a letter signed by a prominent official at the Israeli Mission to the UN, specifying that the Mission was aware of and approved of our trip and pointing out that I was a veteran reporter for the *Jerusalem Post* and American Jewish newspapers. Unfortunately, that letter and my loud protests in Hebrew had absolutely no effect on the stone-faced Israeli security guys at JFK Airport who held us separately for more than an hour of interrogation about the purpose of our trip and who we would be meeting. After completing their questioning, the security people put each of us through exacting searches of our clothing and persons, a process that in my case included being compelled to lower my pants. The message transmitted to me through this humiliating search was unstated but quite clear: "Walter Ruby, this is what you get for consorting with the enemy."

Of course, there are legitimate security concerns in a country beset by terrorist attacks like the one that took place on the day of the visit of the IMANA delegation. But unlike Sabeeha's Jewish friend, who told her he would not apologize for her terrifying ordeal, I do humbly apologize to Khalid and her and ask their forgiveness for the collective punishment meted out to them that day. It must have been quite clear to Israeli authorities from the outset that the IMANA delegation had nothing to do with the terrorist attack, yet they intentionally set out to make them pay a price for what happened. Her group was punished for the crime of being Muslims come to pray at Al-Aqsa and the Tomb of the Patriarchs.

I wonder whether any of those security people tormenting the IMANA delegation paused to consider that these visitors were influential people in the American Muslim community who might have been persuaded that perhaps Israel wasn't so bad if they had been treated with dignity and respect rather than terrifying them by taking their sons away for interrogation. Almost certainly, they did not. I believe their core perspective that day was that Muslims of any background are intrinsically enemies of the Jewish state, and the only way to deal with them is via the mailed fist, since—they believe—Muslims respect only strength.

Yes, security and military people act like that, and much worse, in many countries around the world. Right here in the USA, ICE agents were empowered by the Trump administration to make the lives of desperate immigrants a living hell, even separating children from their parents and putting them in cages. But to my mind, Israel was supposed to be about something far better and more humane than the sadistic behavior unleashed on the IMANA group. Sabeeha's Jewish friend was willing to forgive the Israelis for hurting her by rationalizing that they have no choice but to sometimes behave that way, given the unending peril in which they live. I am less willing to do so.

What Sabeeha has come to understand through extended personal interactions with Jews, just as I have through such interactions with Muslims, is that her Jewish friends are not personally to blame for the actions of those security officials and do not resemble them in their personal behavior any more than most Pakistanis or most Muslims are responsible for, or act similarly to, the extremists who murdered Daniel Pearl.

Sabeeha and Walter:
It took both of us many years and multiple human encounters with the Other to reach the point where Sabeeha could fully accept the humanity of the Jews and Walter of the Arabs and Muslims. Accepting each other's humanity means understanding that Jews and Muslims are neither angels nor demons but multifaceted human beings. There is a bitter side

to the Muslim-Jewish relationship—caused in part by several generations of conflict in the Middle East and beyond—but there is also a sweet side: the ability to connect with each other on a person-to-person basis, embrace commonalities in our faith traditions, and build ties of friendship and trust. The sweet side is the basis upon which our two peoples can—and, we believe, eventually will—achieve reconciliation. It would be tragic, and against the interests of both our communities, to deny the transformative potential of the sweet, because of our awareness of the existence and corrosive ugliness of the bitter.

For a long time, as this chapter records, we Muslims and Jews believed we were enemies. Now, thank God, we emphatically refuse to be enemies. We simply have too much healing to achieve, too much *tikkun olam* and *islah* to carry out together, for us to waste another minute on fear and loathing. *Maspeek. Khalas.* Enough is enough.

CHAPTER 10

THE SAD TRAJECTORIES
OF PAKISTAN AND ISRAEL

Sabeeha:

The Pakistan I Knew Is No More

On a recent visit to Pakistan, I was staying with my sister Neena in Bahria Town, Rawalpindi. My aunt was living in Lalazar Colony, also in Rawalpindi. What should have been a thirty-minute car ride took over an hour. Not traffic; checkpoints. Random checkpoints that spring up not so randomly—probably a tip, a security threat, or just a drill. Taking a flight? Give yourself extra-extra time for security at the entrance to the airport, at Customs, at security inside the terminal, and then more security. Every car is swiped from underneath, guards will peek inside the car, examine the driver's ID, ask for your airline ticket, and then wave you through as you navigate the roadblocks inside the perimeter. Custom officials open every bag and sift through each item, holding up shirts and shaking them, opening books and fanning the pages, and sniffing bottles of lotion.

How Did We Get Here?

"It's peanuts!"

A former peanut farmer had offered $400 million to President Zia of Pakistan, and that's what the Pakistani president said to President Jimmy Carter.

Peanuts made Pakistan a household word. In the past, often my neighbors would ask, "Now where did you say you were from?"

"Pakistan."

"Oh yes. Pekistain."

"*Paaakistaaan*," I would say, correcting the pronunciation. The *a* in "Pak" as in "palm," the "tan" as in "aahn." Got it!

The "peanut dust-up" between Carter and Zia got Americans talking. My neighbors—they didn't know this—were my focus group for Americans' perception of Pakistan.

"Jimmy Carter offered President Zia four hundred million dollars to fight the Russians in Afghanistan, and he called it peanuts!" one of my neighbors said as we stood on the sidewalk, watching our children race their Big Wheels down the slope.

I didn't know what to say. I had been away from Pakistan for seven years now, was disconnected from the political realities there, and had no insight into the nuances of the offer. What I did know was that I resented President Zia.

In July 1977, an event took place that would squeeze the soul of the nation. A seemingly low-profile chief of army staff, General Zia-ul-Haq, overthrew the government of Prime Minister Zulfikar Ali Bhutto of Pakistan in a military coup, declared martial law, appointed himself ruler, and executed Bhutto. His dictatorship lasted until his death in a plane crash in 1988, taking the US ambassador to Pakistan with him. By then, the damage was done. Zia had imposed a conservative brand of Islam in every sphere of life and paved the way for extremism.

Before I vent my outrage any further, let me explain another watershed event: the Soviet invasion of Afghanistan in 1979. We, the United States, enlisted Zia's support in fighting the Soviets—the peanut offer—and, along with Saudi Arabia, funded, trained, and armed the mercenary freedom fighters, whom President George H. W. Bush referred to with pride as mujahedeen (those engaged in jihad). Have you seen the movie *Charlie Wilson's War*? Do me a favor and take 102 minutes of your time—Tom Hanks and Julia Roberts make the point in ways I cannot. Bottom line: Pakistan fought our proxy war, and when the war was won, we pulled out and left a mess behind. Young warriors, who had tasted the thrill of jihad, crossed the mountains into Pakistan, carrying their zeal and their war with them. What started as a war of atheists vs. mujahedeen took the form of internal sectarian violence and radicalism in Pakistan.

"Why are there tents in the graveyard?" I asked Mummy as we walked through the cemetery to visit the gravesite of Aba Jee and Daadi Amma. I was on a visit to Rawalpindi in 1983, where my parents had settled after my father retired from the army.

"Afghani refugees," Mummy said.

Children in dusty and stained shalwar kameez came running, cupping their hands. Light brown hair, milky skin, pink cheeks, big gray eyes, they gathered around us, expectantly. As soon as I opened my pocketbook, more children emerged, and now I was stuck with my hand in my purse, not knowing how to divvy the rupees.

When we went to visit friends and rang the doorbell, I expected someone to open the door—just like that.

"*Kon Hai?*" Who is it? I heard a voice from the inside.

That's rather un-Pakistani; more like the American way.

"Robberies at gunpoint are taking place in broad daylight," Daddy said. "The militants from Afghanistan have brought guns and drugs into Pakistan."

Only four years earlier, I had gone to the College of Home Economics to get my transcripts. I was applying to the master's program in health care administration at the New School for Social Research in New York City. The clerk, sitting behind two-foot piles of files, handed me my transcripts and told me to have them signed off by Mrs. Shah, the vice principal.

"She has the day off today, but you can go to her home in Gulberg and have it signed," he told me, scribbling her address on a piece of paper.

Mummy was with me. We drove to her house, and as we stepped onto the verandah, Mrs. Shah opened the screen door. Seeing us, she flipped the door stopper to hold the door ajar, smiled, and nodded us in.

Why did she just open the door without asking who we are or what is our business?

I had forgotten that I was not in New York City, that this was Pakistan and hospitality meant having an open-door policy.

She signed the papers. But would she have opened the door to us four years later? By then, crime had made the interpersonal atmosphere in Pakistan more like New York.

That year, in 1983, as always after dinner, the family would gather in the sunroom (without the sun) and watch TV. On this visit, I noticed the change in the look of the female news broadcasters. Every lady had the *dupatta* draped over her hair.

"President Zia's orders," Daddy said.

"That's ridiculous!" I said.

Yearning to listen to Pakistani music, I flipped the channels.

News.

Talk shows.

Religious sermons.

"Zia says music is un-Islamic," Daddy said. "Those who can afford it hold private music events in their homes."

"Any good movies playing?" By now I should have guessed.

"The movie industry is dying. Zia is anti-movies. So, we rent videos," Neena said.

What no one was talking about was the Saudi-funded madrassas. These were a new kind of seminary, focused less on Islamic scholarship and more on training religious fighters who would go into the Afghan field and fight.[4] They were out of sight, and their impact wouldn't be realized until those tiny tots grew into young men, hardened and hard-wired with fire and fury.

Give me your huddled hungry children, and we will feed them, clothe them, and house them and give them religious education was the offer the starving poor with large families couldn't refuse. Desperate parents gave up their children to the madrassas, and those boys had matured into angry and fanatical young men in their twenties and thirties who feared noth-ing. Try deprogramming them! No surgery, no chemo, no radiation will excise the malignancy. Prevention—the only cure—works, but that is a slow change. Give it your best shot, and you are talking at least ten to

---

4 *Frontline*. PBS.org. https://www.pbs.org/wgbh/pages/frontline/shows/saudi/analyses/madrassas.html.

fifteen years to get results. Until then, find workarounds and wait for this generation to die out.

Thirty years later—I am talking 2015—I was having a conversation with a thirty-year-old Pakistani woman, a product of the Zia era.

"We never knew what culture is," she said. "We never knew art. When my parents talked about *mehfil-e-moseeki* music gatherings, I couldn't visualize it."

What she also never knew was what it was like to live in the Pakistan of the 1950s and '60s: to live without the threat of terrorist strikes, go out for a stroll at night and feel utterly safe, walk the bazaars with gold bangles jingling on your wrist, hear a medley of music playing on the radios as you walked from shop to shop, drive through the roads without roadblocks, have electricity 24/7 and not have to live with one-hour-on/one-hour-off load shedding of power, have running water from a tap that would never run dry, and be able to remove your coat in January when you stepped inside a house heated by natural gas that was still flowing. She could not comprehend what she hadn't lived.

Dissed by America

Bill Clinton announced that he was visiting India. He said nothing about neighboring Pakistan. Would he visit Pakistan or just fly over? Newscasters and every authority on diplomacy speculated. It was the year 2000, and I just happened to be visiting Pakistan.

"We don't care if Clinton comes or doesn't. If he comes, most welcome; if not, who cares?" my aunt said with a shrug.

I had forgotten how nationalistic Pakistanis were, and how deep their sense of pride. They were not going to beg him to come, although it was likely that diplomatic pressure was applied behind the scenes. Because he *did* go.

"Clinton is such a *darpoke*," Daddy said, calling Clinton a coward. "His plane landed, and when passengers disembarked, there was no Clinton. Everyone wondered what had happened. Then another plane arrived, and he emerged. What was he afraid of?"

Daddy told me that all the streets had been cleared for his motorcade and Islamabad looked deserted.

The tipping point was his TV address to Pakistanis in which he rebuked them. This is what I was hearing my relatives and friends say:

"He was a guest in our country, and he insulted us."

"He lectured us . . . reprimanded us."

"Patronizing! Telling us how to run our country."

"He visits India, a nuclear power, and gives them a pat on the back, then rebukes us for being a nuclear power."

"America has killed innocents . . . Hiroshima, Vietnam, Iraq . . . and your president lectures *us* on peace!"

Pakistanis felt dissed.

We Are Fighting America's War

I was visiting Pakistan in December 2001, just months after 9/11. The military ruler, General Pervez Musharraf, had yielded to America's demands to join the war on terror in Afghanistan. Pakistan had become the base for US attacks on Afghanistan. This is what I heard from friends:

"Your Bush gave us no choice."

"We have internal problems to deal with; we cannot afford to take on America's war."

"Innocent people are being bombed in Afghanistan."

"Osama bin Laden was America's creation. They used him when they needed him to fight the Russians in Afghanistan. They made him what he is, and now they want *us* to fight him."

That is what I heard; that is what I read in the newspapers; and that is what TV talk show hosts talked about. Pakistanis were angry.

"It's all America's doing."

Your Bush . . . My Bush! Yes, he was my president. I had voted him into office (first term only), yet I recoiled at the finger-jabbing. I was conflicted over the war in Afghanistan, yet as an American, I felt defensive. I heard their anguish. When we wage war, we have no idea how much we impact the lives of ordinary citizens in far-off lands. Or have we become desensitized, being in a state of war for decades?

Sectarian strife had broken out all over Pakistan, from the port of Karachi in the south to the beautiful northern areas in the mountains. Whatever the root cause, be it poverty, exploitation by politicians, or power struggle, Pakistanis pointed the finger at the United States—the CIA in particular.

"India is behind it," many would tell me. *I wouldn't doubt that.* That was when I started hearing the term *RAW*, standing for Research & Analysis Wing, the intelligence agency of India, considered responsible for actively sowing strife and disinformation.

"Israel, India, and America are behind the strife, because we are a nuclear power."

Honestly, I saw this as a cop-out. Sorry, Pakistanis, I love you, but I have to say this: Fix your house. It's easy to shift blame, and though you may have your reasons for believing that foreign powers are behind all your woes, look at what is in your power to fix. For example, don't throw your garbage over the wall; don't stare at women in the bazaars; don't drive through a red light; don't look for a *safarish* to get ahead of the line; don't spend money you don't have on hosting lavish weddings. These issues are not America's doing.

By the way, in case you are wondering, I applauded when Pakistan became a nuclear power. It brought Pakistan up to par with India's military might. Now India would not bully Pakistan, nor will the two go to war again.

Drones!

That did it for Pakistanis. Innocent families were now coping with the loss of a breadwinner, a child maimed for life, a house blown apart. The United States dismissed it as collateral damage.

I was asked when I visited Pakistan: "If American children were maimed, what would the reaction be?"

At a store where I had stopped to shop, the owner, realizing that I was from America, muttered under his breath, "Killing hungry children in Iraq."

When I voted for Obama, I knew I was casting my vote for a man who had committed to launch drone attacks in Pakistan. While I couldn't be a one-issue voter, I experienced that inner conflict when I made the calls for MoveOn.org urging voters to vote for Obama. An American, I was putting America first and was hoping he wouldn't go through with it.

Drone attacks fueled anti-American sentiments and radicalized the vulnerable. Across Pakistan, people resented the attacks and the loss of innocent lives.

"Our lives don't matter!" is what I heard.

The militants retaliated against their own, believing that the Pakistan government was complicit. Suicide bombings shattered lives, livelihoods, and lifestyles. Now when I visit Pakistan, the guard is up.

Airport security in Pakistan is nothing like JFK or LaGuardia. They take it to the tenth degree in vigilance and scrutiny. But TSA could take a lesson or two in customer service from Pakistani security officials. "May I," "Please," "How are you today?" and a smile. During my visit in 2014, the guard who was ushering passengers to bag inspection at Customs stopped me.

"Where are you going?" he asked in Urdu.

"New York."

"Please proceed," he said, directing me to the X-ray machines, bypassing Customs. Why was I cleared when everyone else had to have their suitcases opened and their intimate apparel aired? No idea. Actually, I do. They are experienced and trained to detect, not profile.

Curtained cubicles, manned by female uniformed guards—I should say "womanned by"—pats me down after first asking for permission. One woman watches, another pats you up and down, left and right, back and center. Sometimes I even have my head examined, gently. They are thorough—and professional. This level of security is not a post–9/11 measure. It has been in place for as long as I can remember, and I go back to the 1970s.

And the drones keep striking.

Terrorists are killed.

Women and children are killed.

Another suicide bombing.

Osama bin Laden is captured, killed, and buried at sea.

I was at my computer, doing work for the autism association, when I heard the news. Within minutes, my friends were emailing me: "How are Pakistanis reacting to the news?"

I called my mother.

"How could they not have known that he was hiding there?" Mummy said. By "they," she meant the Pakistani authorities.

In other words, "they" were either protecting him or looking the other way.

If Mummy was wrong—if they didn't know he was hiding there—shame on "them." But if she was right, that was big-time messy and scary.

The official response of Pakistan was one of outrage over breach of sovereign territory. But come on! That aside, couldn't "they" have at least expressed some degree of embarrassment?

On November 6, 2012, I walked into the voting booth of the Armenian Orthodox Church in Murray Hill, New York City, and cast my vote for Barack Obama.

Four years later, in 2016, America elected a new president, and he has put Pakistan on notice, squeezing them financially. Pakistanis are not going to roll over; both their cheeks are bruised. They have a new leader too, Prime Minister Imran Khan, with a charismatic aura that has energized the nation and given them hope. It will serve our US leaders well to get a brief education on the history of Pakistan and its people and know that this is a proud nation; no one can bring it to its knees by withholding aid. Pakistan has given its blood for *our* war on terror and demands that its contribution be acknowledged.

Each time I fly out to Pakistan, I take a look at my will, settle my affairs once again, assure my children that Mummy will be fine, and take off. When I arrive, I am embarrassed. All around me is business as usual. Hustle-bustle on the streets and festivity in the air. Precious resources like water, electricity, and natural gas have become scarcer. There is plenty of blame to go around, both internal corruption and external subversion. Yet its rich culture endures—the hospitality, the warmth of its society, its civility and grace. I am amazed at the resilience of the people and their ability to adapt to security threats. It's the land I love.

Walter:

The 1980s: A Jewish Journalist Unleashed on the World

While Pakistan was going through convulsions from Zia's dictatorship, I left Israel in 1979 and washed up in New York City, where I began

working as a reporter for the *Long Island Jewish World* and other publications. There, I soon met Lyudmila, a twenty-eight-year-old refugee
from Soviet Azerbaijan, who came from an ancient Oriental Jewish tribe
known as the Mountain Jews.

In June 1983, I married Mila, as everyone called her, in a Dostoyevskian
debauch of a wedding at a Russian restaurant in Brighton Beach,
Brooklyn, that included both a Conservative rabbi (Rabbi Paul Kushner,
a friend from the Jewish Federation) and a ribald performance by a belly
dancer. Being the groom at an unabashed Jewish wedding, including
standing under a *huppa* (Jewish wedding canopy) with Mila and stomp-
ing on a glass with my right foot at the end of the ceremony, and later
the two of us being lifted high on chairs by the celebrants, was a wonderful validation of my Jewishness.

Meanwhile, my professional life was also flourishing. As a reporter
for the *Long Island Jewish World*, the *London Jewish Chronicle*, and *Jerusalem
Post* in New York, I was immersed in the life of the organized American
Jewish community and tasked with covering its interactions with Israel
and the larger world. My listening post at the UN, which afforded me
the opportunity to cover visits by Israeli prime ministers Shimon Peres
and Yitzhak Shamir, also gave me the chance to write about ongoing
efforts to achieve Middle East peace. I covered a succession of Reagan-
Gorbachev summits and Reagan's 1985 trip to the Bergen-Belsen death
camp in Germany. I traveled to Asuncion, Paraguay, in a fascinating but
futile search for the notorious Nazi war criminal Josef Mengele.

My journalistic output during the 1980s and 1990s focused mainly on
two overarching issues: the Middle East peace process, which appeared
hopeful for a time but eventually crashed and burned, and the Soviet
Jewry movement, which ultimately made it possible for up to two million Jews to emigrate from the Soviet Union. As a Moscow-based correspondent for the *Forward*, *Jerusalem Post*, and *Maariv* from 1990 to 1992,
I had a ringside seat to cover the post-Soviet aliyah, not to mention the
collapse of the Soviet Union. The emigration of Soviet Jewry proved to
be a great success but also had the unanticipated consequence of adding
a huge, mainly right-wing voting bloc of new immigrants to the Israeli
electorate that since the late 1990s has helped the hard-liners remain in

power. Refusenik human rights activists I had deeply admired—including Natan Sharansky, whose heroic arrival at Ben Gurion Airport I covered in early 1986—became ardent supporters of the Israeli Right's policy of denying Palestinians the same human rights that Soviet Jews had rightly demanded for themselves. That hypocrisy, combined with the ultimate collapse of the peace process, was for me, truly, the saddest of trajectories.

With Arafat in Algiers

Throughout my journalistic career, I believed that one of my core responsibilities as a reporter was to expose my readers—Israelis and American Jews—to objective coverage of those widely considered to be our enemies. I had an unparalleled opportunity to accomplish that when I was accredited to cover the historic Palestine National Council (PNC) in November 1988 where Yasser Arafat implied recognition of Israel and declared the independence of the State of Palestine.

The event was held at a sprawling seaside compound called Club des Pins—an hour or so west of the white hillside city of Algiers. The compound was ringed by the Algerian army for protection, with a gunship floating offshore. Inside, heavily armed and trigger-happy-looking guards eyed the large number of journalists milling about. As the only reporter for an Israeli publication—although officially accredited to the New York alternative weekly *Village Voice*—I felt simultaneously invincible and vulnerable. I was buoyed by the PLO-issued press credentials hanging around my neck and the belief that people in the hierarchy were looking out for me, yet paranoid that if a hard-line faction wanted to show their tough anti-Zionist side, I was the nearest available Zionist to act out upon.

On the first morning, I glimpsed a knot of international reporters surrounding a stocky, chain-smoking, middle-aged man dressed in khakis and rushed over to see if there might be a juicy quote or two to be had. As the mystery commando spoke to the journalists in somewhat disjointed English, I was stunned to realize that he was none other than Abul Abbas, a notorious terrorist leader who three years earlier had led a small group of commandos who seized control of the *Achille Lauro* cruise ship in the Mediterranean, shot dead an elderly American Jewish tourist named Leon Klinghoffer, and pushed him into the sea in his wheelchair.

I jumped into the conversation, asking Abbas directly if he had any regrets about the killing of Klinghoffer. Abbas glanced at me sharply and then rolled his eyes, responding that there was some confusion as to what occurred on the ship. I asked, "So are you suggesting that Klinghoffer rolled his wheelchair into the sea on his own?" Abul Abbas took a long drag on his cigarette and then suddenly grinned broadly and said, "Well, maybe he was trying to swim for it."

As sickened as I was by Abbas's casual celebration of the Klinghoffer killing, I was equally struck by what he said next, evoking the Palestinians' abiding anger at what they saw as a Western double standard. He asked, "Has Israel expressed regret about the millions [sic] Palestinians who were shot at Sabra and Shatila? . . . I wish the names of our victims and martyrs were as well known as the name of Klinghoffer. Can you name ten Palestinians who died from Israeli gas, or ten pregnant Palestinian women who were crushed and killed?" As he spoke, I acknowledged to myself that I could not, in fact, recall any names of Palestinian civilians killed in the conflict with Israel.

On the evening of November 15, 1988, I witnessed PLO Chairman Yasser Arafat reading the Declaration of Independence of Palestine. It was surreal to listen to this strange-looking keffiyeh-clad man, whom I had been taught to consider either a remorseless terrorist or an absurd caricature, intone an often-eloquent call for a Palestinian state imbued with democracy and social justice that would live in peace with all of its neighbors. As I heard Arafat pronounce sentences that seemed lifted directly from Israel's Declaration of Independence about the age-old connection of the Palestinian people with its land and determination to return to it after having been forced into exile, I imagined myself in the crowded Tel Aviv Museum on May 14, 1948, where David Ben-Gurion proclaimed the rebirth of the Jewish state after two millennia of exile. And here was Arafat intoning, "The Palestine National Council, in the name of God and in the name of the Palestinian Arab people, hereby proclaims the establishment of the State of Palestine on our Palestinian territory with its capital Jerusalem (Al-Quds Ash Sharif)."

At that moment, my eyes welled up with tears, followed immediately by a sharp rebuke to myself to cut the crap. Such an empathetic response came uncomfortably close to a betrayal of my people. Then the other side in my internal debate kicked in and reminded me that the PLO's move toward accepting Israel could represent a passageway to a new Middle East in which Israeli and Palestinian children would live in peace and security. *Go ahead and cry tears of joy,* I told myself. *This is a transcendent moment.*

As the conference was winding down, an Arab reporter approached and asked if I would like to come to dinner with Khaled el-Hassan, one of the cofounders with Arafat of the PLO and the organization's chief ideologist. How could I say no? Clearly, Hassan had wanted to meet, but as he rose to greet us at the dinner table where he sat surrounded by several strapping young security men, he didn't exactly seem overjoyed to see me. What followed was a tirade against Israel and Zionism. Seemingly frustrated by the dovish turn of PLO policy, Hassan wanted to signal to the Israeli reporter who had turned up in their midst that nothing was forgiven. Did I realize, he asked, the true extent of the horrors that the Zionist Ashkenazi Jews had inflicted on the Palestinians? What right did Jews from Russia or the United States have to settle in his own hometown of Haifa, when he was denied the right to return there?

I decided against informing Hassan that I was one of those very Ashkenazi Jews who came to live in Haifa. But Hassan was off on another rant, shaking his fist and shouting that the Zionists were "draculas" who sucked Palestinian blood and enjoyed killing for its own sake. The Jews, he said, unlike the Muslims and Christians, did not even have holy places in Palestine. The Western Wall? That was a bogus holy site, he asserted.

Despite some very real feelings of fear, I had no choice but to make clear my identification with Israel. Swallowing hard, I locked eyes with Hassan and said firmly, "In fact, I *am* a Zionist. It is of tremendous personal importance to me that Israel should live. It is for that reason that I came to the PNC, to see if a way can be found for both of our peoples to live side by side in peace."

I braced for an explosion, but Hassan's fury seemed to have subsided. The Jews need not worry, he said. The results of the PNC showed the

Palestinians were ready to accept a two-state solution and live along-side Israel in peace in a mini-state in the West Bank, Gaza, and East Jerusalem. "Not because such a solution is just, which it is not. The truth is that we have accepted the two-state solution because we have come to understand we are not strong enough to drive three and a half million Jews out of Palestine." Given that bitter reality, the PLO owed it to the Palestinian people to at least win them a homeland and end their exile and statelessness.

Why, I asked, if the PLO was ready for peace, had it not gone all the way, renouncing "armed struggle" and explicitly recognizing Israel? Hassan responded, "The problem is that you always ask us to do the rec-ognizing, but you don't ask [Israel]. You ask the existing state to be rec-ognized by the non-existing, which is illogical." One critically needed step toward peace and reconciliation, he emphasized to me, would be for Israel and America to acknowledge the terrible suffering of the Palestinians.

I thought a lot about what I had heard from both Hassan and Abul Abbas about the need for Americans and Israelis to show respect for the Palestinian people. I decided to submit an op-ed article to the *New York Times* urging that Israel and the United States find a way to do just that. Convinced that there had been historic forward movement on the Palestinian side in Algiers, I found it deeply problematic that the story of the PNC in much of the American media had become Abul Abbas's callous comment, "Maybe he was trying to swim for it." If anyone could turn that narrative around, it might be the reporter who had asked Abbas the question.

So I penned a piece entitled "Abul Abbas's Other Remarks," return-ing to the scene and recalling: "When Mr. Abbas posed his last question, I realized that I did not know the names of any Palestinians killed in the conflict with Israel. . . . That Mr. Abbas's comments about the Palestinian victim should have gone largely unreported in the American press con-firms his point—which is that the death of one American is more news-worthy than the deaths of many Palestinians." I concluded: "While there is no question that the PLO must swallow twenty-four years of rejec-tionism and meet the [US] conditions, the Americans and Israelis could ease the process greatly by acknowledging that the Palestinian people are worthy of respect."

I bought the paper first thing on the morning of December 7 and was both exultant and terrified to see my piece on the op-ed page. Several hours later, with heart in mouth, I called Baruch Binah, the spokesman for the Israel Mission to the UN, for whom I had considerable personal affection, to get a sense of what the Israeli reaction would be. Using his nickname, I asked, "Hi, Bube, how ya doing?" He replied icily, "Well, I was doing a lot better until I read your op-ed this morning."

My op-ed confirmed my status as a bête noire to many on the Jewish right, but thankfully, neither the editors of the *Jerusalem Post* nor the consortium of American Jewish newspapers I also wrote for called me on the carpet. People either congratulated me or expressed disapproval—depending on their political perspective—for several days and then largely forgot about it.

Calling Jewish Leaders to Account

By 1992, I had lost my position as *Jerusalem Post* correspondent after that newspaper swung radically to the right under new management and was unable to cover the impact of the electrifying Oslo Accords the following year, including the signing on the White House lawn by Arafat, Prime Minister Yitzhak Rabin, and President Bill Clinton. The euphoria that Israeli-Palestinian peace was about to arrive lasted only about a year. Then came the murderous rampage by Baruch Goldstein at the Tomb of the Patriarchs in Hebron and several devastating terrorist bombings by Palestinians in Jerusalem and Tel Aviv. Finally, in 1995, there was the shocking assassination of Rabin by a right-wing Jewish zealot, followed by the razor-thin election of the hard-line Likud leader Benjamin Netanyahu.

In the immediate aftermath of that crushing blow, I wrote an op-ed that ran in the *Los Angeles Times* and *Newsday* entitled "American Jews Must Say No to Netanyahu's Plans," meaning his fervent opposition to the Oslo Accords and a Palestinian state. In the article, I said the election of 1996 was reminiscent of the 1977 election when Menachem Begin won a shocking upset victory as the first Israeli prime minister officially dedicated to the principle that Israel should retain the West Bank and

Gaza. At that time, the chairman of the Conference of Presidents of Major American Jewish Organizations was Rabbi Alexander Schindler, a liberal Reform rabbi. I had expected Schindler to push back against Begin's announced plans for a massive buildup of Jewish settlements in what he called "Judea and Samaria," yet within a week or two, Schindler announced that he would back the newly elected prime minister of Israel, regardless of his personal beliefs.

My op-ed argued that Schindler's decision in 1977 set the precedent for his successors at the Conference of Presidents and at the America-Israel Public Affairs Council (AIPAC), and that the organized American Jewish community would lobby on behalf of Israel no matter what policies its government pursued. Doing that essentially made our community enablers of Israeli policies that were immoral and self-destructive. I wrote that with the fate of the Oslo peace process on the line, Jewish leaders of the 1990s should learn the lessons of history and not repeat the damaging mistake Schindler made in 1977.

I was proud of the op-ed, but leery of coming face-to-face with Rabbi Schindler, a kindly man whom I liked personally and who had always treated me graciously as a reporter. A couple of days later I glimpsed Alex from across the room at a reception and saw he was looking directly at me. I walked toward him, with an expression and hand gestures conveying that I was sorry for any pain I had caused him. Yet when we came face-to-face, Rabbi Schindler smiled broadly, clasped my hand, and said, "No, no, Walter, you don't have to apologize. You were absolutely correct in what you wrote."

It was a very classy gesture on his part, an acknowledgment that he had been wrong on one of the most consequential decisions of his career. Sadly, I never saw Alex Schindler again. He retired from his position as chairman of the Union of American Hebrew Congregations and passed away several years later.

Encountering the Other

From 1997 to 2002, during the infancy of the Internet, I had the opportunity to moderate an online discussion forum, the Jewish-Palestinian Encounter. This experience taught me the great lesson of the second half of my life: that to achieve peace and reconciliation in Israel-Palestine or any other conflict, grassroots people on both sides need to become involved.

Within days, participants were emerging out of the cyber-ether to take part in deliberations. Within a few months, the forum had attracted scores of regular participants, among them Israelis and Jews, Palestinians and Arabs of all faiths, and people of diverse backgrounds from around the world.

Most of the time the participants managed to accord each other mutual respect and even affection. No one's point of view was fundamentally changed, but much nuance was added to people's understanding of the situation because they were hearing other perspectives that they would otherwise never have encountered and, equally important, getting to know people from "the other side" as human beings. The Other was no longer a sinister abstraction but instead became flesh-and-blood people with spouses, children, jobs, and many of the same challenges faced by those on one's own side of the barricades.

The success of the forum led to the idea of creating Encounter programs on the ground, where we could meet each other face-to-face. Much of the credit for these efforts goes to Maria Espinosa, a brilliant and determined Spanish woman with impressive connections on the ground in Israel-Palestine. It was thanks to Maria that a few of us found ourselves living during the summer of 1999 in a Catholic convent school affiliated with the Latin Patriarchate of Jerusalem in the town of Bir Zeit, several kilometers north of Ramallah inside the territory of the embryonic Palestinian state. Among the participants were Chahine, a Tunisian who taught computer programming to young Palestinians in Bir Zeit, and an Israeli political cartoonist named Avi Katz, who taught computer graphics. Maria and I liaised with peace activists on both sides of the border, planning a conference on the need for Israeli-Palestinian cooperation on land-use issues, which we held at Al-Quds University in East Jerusalem.

A broad spectrum of people in Bir Zeit spoke to me about life under the Palestinian Authority, with the reports largely focusing on widespread corruption among the leaders of the new Palestinian Authority. Palestinian Christians, in particular, wondered out loud if they had a future in an overwhelmingly Muslim Palestine. Many said they felt less free than before. As one middle-aged man confided, "We didn't have any rights living under Israeli occupation, but at least we could travel anywhere in the country. I could take my family to the beach or to Al-Aqsa to pray. Now it has become almost impossible for us to move." The Israeli network of roadblocks, put in place after Oslo, meant that most Palestinians were more hemmed in than ever despite living in territory under the flag of Palestine.

It was easier for me as a privileged guest from abroad. I had the chance to explore my little piece of Palestine, walking through villages and clambering up hillsides, feeling completely safe as a Jew among Palestinians—something that would become impossible just over a year later with the failure of the 2000 Camp David Summit and the eruption of the Second Intifada. On near-perfect summer afternoons a large group of us—Palestinians, Jews, and assorted NGOniks—would gather in an ornately decorated outdoor restaurant called Ala Kefak, situated in a verdant valley filled with fig, olive, and pomegranate trees. After a feast of Palestinian and Lebanese specialties, we would sip Arabic coffee spiced with cardamom, pass around a bubbling hookah, and talk and laugh. At those moments, peace seemed to be on the way. The very idea of renewed bloodshed was unthinkable.

Through the experience of living among them, I had come to care deeply for the Palestinians, and felt they had become part of me. Unlike some Israeli leftists who advocated a two-state solution so they could "separate" from the Palestinians, which they claimed would be "good for the Jews," I could no longer look at the conflict exclusively from the Jewish perspective. Israel/Palestine was an organic whole, and we were all its sons and daughters. Yes, I believed, it would be necessary to divide the Land into two states to allow both sides to exercise self-determination. Still, if we could learn to celebrate together our love of the land, over a period of decades the borders would become increasingly irrelevant. What was needed was for Palestinians and Israelis to sit together in places like Ala Kefak.

Two States, One Common Land

A year later, the Second Intifada broke out, including multiple acts of terrorist violence. While many of my Jewish and Israeli friends moved sharply to the right, I moved left. Despite my anguish at the deaths of so many Israelis in bombings, I felt aggrieved that Israel had more than doubled the population of Jewish settlers in the West Bank during the Oslo years, making a return to the 1967 lines—the minimum the Palestinian Authority felt able to accept—almost impossible to achieve. The effect of the accelerated settlement building at a time when Israel should have been winding down the settlements sent the message to the Palestinians that the strategic choice of nonviolence they made in 1993 had yielded them little. Ultimately, it seemed Israel had chosen settlements over peace. The governing elites on both sides were unwilling to encourage Israelis and Palestinians to take part in people-to-people encounter efforts.

Yet, I remained convinced there was a viable alternative to endless conflict. That belief was informed by a dialogue I had with a participant in Encounter, Aref Dajani, a Palestinian American. Aref's father had been driven out of the family's ancestral village of Beit Dajan, only a few kilometers from Rehovot, in 1948. Talking to Aref helped me to appreciate that it was unreasonable to expect Palestinians like himself to give up their love for, and connection to, their former towns and villages in the citrus-scented coastal plain that become Israel in 1948, just as it was wrong to expect Jews to give up their love for the olive-tree-covered hills, villages, and towns of the West Bank, the land where Abraham, Isaac, and Jacob had once tended their flock. That reality needed to be addressed in any peace construct.

Seeking to fill a void, Aref and I wrote a manifesto entitled *Two States, One Common Land*, which was published in the prestigious *Israel-Palestine Journal* and in shorter form in the *New York Jewish Week*, arguing that, while it remained necessary to create two states, Israelis and Palestinians could over time learn to celebrate, together, their connectedness and belonging to the whole of the common land they both loved.

A Personal Tragedy

For me, the collapse of the prospect for Israeli-Palestinian peace is a personal tragedy. It has felt like everything I believed in and worked for has gone up in smoke. During the Encounter years, I had developed a philosophy of people-to-people engagement as the path to reconciliation in relation to Israel-Palestine, but now I felt I had nowhere to apply it.

As peace slipped further away and violence escalated, I realized I needed to take a sabbatical from the conflict in order to protect my own sanity. I was fortunate, several years later, to find a viable alternative path to people-to-people engagement through my involvement with Rabbi Schneier in strengthening Muslim-Jewish relations in America and around the world. Also, after having divorced Mila at around the same time, I met my third wonderful life partner, Tanya, originally from Ukraine, who has given me personal happiness and inner contentment ever since. Still, I felt a gaping hole at my core where my connection to Israel-Palestine had once been. As the years flew by and I approached the fateful age of seventy, I knew I needed to go home one more time.

A Two-State Solution May Be Over, But the Dream of Reconciliation Lives On

At the end of February 2020, I returned to Israel for the first time in more than ten years as a participant in a mission organized by Project Rozana, an international not-for-profit focused on saving the lives of desperately sick Palestinian children in need of cancer treatment or kidney dialysis by helping to transport them to hospitals in Israel. The organization also helps defray the cost of providing advanced training to Palestinian doctors and medical personnel in Israeli medical institutions.

The minute I touched down at Ben Gurion Airport, I felt a rekindling of my sense of deep connection with the sights, sounds, and aromas of the country. Yet, on a daylong excursion to the Palestinian cities of Hebron and Bethlehem prior to the mission, I was stunned—and frankly horrified—by the exponential growth in the number and size of Jewish settlements, which had swallowed up much of the countryside of the southern West Bank.

On the first morning of the mission, our group of directors and supporters of Project Rozana from the United States, Australia, Canada, and Israel took a bus up a steep, winding road to the hilltop Palestinian town of Beit Jala, where we met with Palestinian and Israeli social service and human rights activists to celebrate the recoveries of two Palestinian children, Narmen, ten, and Muhammad, eight, both of whom had survived treatment and surgery for cancer in Israeli hospitals. Alongside the two children sat six or seven Palestinian and Israel volunteer drivers who together had transported the two and their caregivers multiple times to hospitals for diagnosis, operations, and post-op care. Without their help, the two children and hundreds like them would not have survived. Their financially hard-pressed parents could not have paid the cost of a taxi—about $200 for each round trip between their homes and the hospitals.

The Palestinian drivers, four young men in their twenties, explained why they are motivated to get up before 5:00 a.m. to drive sick children long distances to the checkpoints in heavy traffic before dropping them off and heading to their day jobs before 9:00 a.m.: "I agreed to drive the children one time at the suggestion of my friend, but after that first time, I was hooked. I do this to help save these beautiful children, who could be my little brother or sister. It feels wonderful to make such a difference for them."

One of the Israeli volunteer drivers, a woman of about seventy, told me, "I am not able to end the Occupation, but at least I can help these children survive and hopefully live to see a brighter future. . . . It is important for me to let them know that I, an Israeli, care about them."

I met Israelis who had lost loved ones in bombings by Palestinians and Palestinians whose family members were killed in shootings by Israeli soldiers, but who nevertheless find the psychic strength to extend hands of love and compassion across the checkpoints and work together with people on the other side. If they have witnessed and endured all that they have and still not given up on achieving peace and reconciliation, what possible justification had I to throw up my hands and turn away? *The very least I can do*, I told myself, *is to stop bellyaching about the collapse of my dreams, and instead support their holy work to the best of my ability.*

During the remainder of my trip, I saw much that convinced me that what I witnessed in Beit Jala was representative of something bigger: an unprecedented cultural-political coming together showing that a new Israeli-Palestinian identity was forming. An April 2020 poll by the Israel Democracy Institute showed that 77 percent of Israeli Arabs feel they are part of the state and share with it a common destiny—the highest percentage ever. The situation seemed much transformed among the Palestinians in the West Bank as well. During our visit to Ramallah, I felt a palpable lessening of anti-Israel militancy compared to what I had discerned on previous visits. The possibility of the eruption of a long-predicted Third Intifada seemed far away.

How to explain the birth of a Palestinian-Israeli identity at a moment when relations between the two peoples appeared to be hurtling backward? And why has Palestinian rage apparently abated at a time when the prime minister of Israel appeared poised to annex large sections of the West Bank; a plan that was, at least temporarily, put on ice after the agreement between Israel and the United Arab Emirates to establish diplomatic relations?

I came to the conclusion that the positive change in tone and the evident reconnecting of Israeli Jews with Palestinians in people-to-people contacts is directly related to a visceral understanding on both sides that the two-state solution is all but dead. Israelis and Palestinians argue over whose fault that is—and there is plenty of responsibility on both sides—yet both agree that a shared future is virtually fait accompli.

No one would be happier than I if the two-state solution could magically be resuscitated, but in the real world it appears likely that the choice now is not between one state or two but what kind of joint state will come into being. Will it be one based on democracy and equality of opportunity for all inhabitants, or one based on apartheid? I have come to believe that Israel-Palestine will evolve over the coming decades—with starts, stops, and retrogressions—into a joint state or a confederation based on equal rights for all. That will ultimately happen because Israelis and Palestinians alike are heartily sick of conflict and because Israel is too integrated into an international order based on humanistic values to accept permanent brutalization of a subject people.

Alas, my dream of two states living side by side in peace may be over. Yet I continue to dream: that all the people of Israel-Palestine will one day share—and together rejoice in—their Common Land.

CHAPTER 11

WHO AM I?

Our Shifting Identities and Embracing the Promise of American Pluralism

Sabeeha:

So what am I?

A Pakistani?

If length of stay is an indicator, I have lived less than one-fourth of my life in Pakistan.

If the color of one's passport is an indicator, mine is blue, not green.

Dress? Take a look at me any time of the day, and it's stuff off the racks from Target and Macy's.

Language? Even in the privacy of our apartment, I converse with Khalid in English. I wonder when that transition occurred.

Books? Urdu books take up only one of the fifteen shelves on my book racks and zero on my Kindle or on my holds list at the New York Public Library.

Politics? Ask me: Who was the president of Pakistan in 2020? Let me think. I guess the answer is that I have to look it up. All I can tell you is that it has to be a member of Prime Minister Imran Khan's party, Tehrik-e-Insaaf. Shame on me! My ignorance about world politics makes me so

American. Had I been Pakistani, I would have been on top of the who-
is-who in our world today.

National identity? Somewhere along the line, I started saying "our
foreign policy" instead of "the foreign policy of the United States." US
has become *We*. But even today, when I listen to "Pak Sar Zameen," the
national anthem of Pakistan, tears well up.

Social life? Scrolling through my calendar, I see breakfast with Liz,
coffee with Hazel, dinner with Ann . . . keep looking . . . book club—
no Pakistanis there . . . checking the Ramadan calendar: two Ramadan
iftars with the Muslim-Jewish Solidarity Committee. *Don't give up, there are
bound to be Pakistanis somewhere on that calendar* . . . Interfaith book club?
Yes! One of the members, Kausar, is Pakistani—or was. But wait! I do
meet up with my Pakistani Home Ec classmates living in the US once a
year in Wherever-USA—a mini-reunion of sorts. And don't two of my
Pakistani friends from Staten Island occasionally come into the city and
we meet up for dinner—like twice a year? All those *mehfil-e-ghazal*, weekend Pakistani music parties—when did those become a thing of the past?

Friends? Now that's a good one. Friends from high school? I am still
in touch with Najma in Pakistan. College? We are as close today as we
were back in the sixties. We have a college Facebook page, WhatsApp
group, and are chatting, sharing videos, and giggling away. But my relationship with them is cloudy—I hang out with them in the cloud—they
are scattered all over the globe. Friends whom I reach out and touch, curl
up with on my sofa (pre COVID-19), are Toni, Jenny, Michele, Janay . . .

What about all those Groups oxygenating my calendar? Writers'
Group—no Pakistanis; Writing Circle—no Pakistanis; Sisterhood of
Salaam Shalom—one Pakistani; Daughters of Abraham in Dialogue—
getting warm—four Pakistanis; Qur'an Club—bingo—all Pakistani.

Music? I never transitioned to American pop or rock. Beyond being
aware of what they look like, I know next to nothing about Lady Gaga and
Beyoncé. Give me the soul-stirring ghazal and sitar anywhere, anytime.

Food? Aha, bull's-eye! Steaming biryani, succulent kebabs, and the
spicy aroma of chicken curry. You can sniff your way to my apartment as
soon as you get off the elevator.

My final Pakistani score: 2.5 out of 11.

Yet, checklist aside, if you look into my heart, you will hear the musical beat of a Pakistani; if you peer into the microscope, you will see the colorful Pakistani genes brightening the surface; and if you give me a tight hug (women only, please), you will inhale the scent of a Pakistani.

So what am I?

A Pakistani-Muslim?

It's a long story, but I have carved out my own version of the faith, one that is not quite aligned with the Pakistani variety.

In Pakistan, I would read the Qur'an in Arabic; in America, I read it in Arabic and English.

In Pakistan, women wear makeup; I have chosen not to, for religious reasons.

In Pakistan, women do not go to the mosque for prayers; in America, I practically planned the building of our mosque (co-planned, to be exact) and ran the mosque's Sunday school (co-ran) from behind the scenes.

Pakistanis believe that a Muslim man can marry women of the Book—Christians and Jews—but a Muslim woman cannot marry outside the faith. I believe that Muslim men and Muslim women can marry men and women of the Book. (References provided upon request.)

Pakistani women cover their legs. I have no problem wearing calf-length skirts.

Pakistanis believe that a woman cannot lead a mixed prayer; I will argue that she can. That argument has gotten me into boiling water with some Muslims here at home in America—from women no less. I haven't taken the risk of raising this in Pakistan.

A Pakistani's Muslim identity is defined by one's sect: Shia, Sunni, Ahmadi, et cetera. In fact, the Pakistani Constitution considers Ahmadis as non-Muslims. I, on the other hand, will disregard sects, referring to myself as "just Muslim," and believe that anyone who professes to be a Muslim is a Muslim. I have no right to judge.

So what am I?

A Pakistani-Muslim-American?

Being hyphenated twice is more than I can handle. And since I failed the first two tests, let's move on.

A Muslim-American?

Now we are talking. I am Muslim, and I am American. I am an American, and I am a Muslim. But am I a Muslim first? Will I get into trouble for even asking the question? Probably.

An American Muslim?

I think in an American mode, I think of Islam in an American context, my politics are American, my causes—for the most part—are American, my community service is American . . . and I am a believing, practicing, and committed Muslim. From my vantage point, the two are inseparable. My politics, causes, and service are deeply ingrained in my being Muslim. My faith drives my associations, my commitments, and my priorities. As a Muslim, I hold these truths to be self-evident: that all people are created equal, that they are endowed by their Creator with certain unalienable rights, that among these are life, liberty, and the pursuit of happiness.

An American.

When I toggle back and forth between MSNBC and Fox News and read the opinion pages in the *New York Times* and the *Wall Street Journal*, I strive to be open to all that is American. So help me God.

When I rinse the dishes in the soup kitchen of a church on Christmas Day, I feel wholeheartedly American. I am not that holy, just wholly American.

When I rush to the library to pick up a just-published book by Walter Isaacson, David McCullough, or Gloria Steinem, I feel literally American—pun intended.

When I give to the National Autism Association and Muslim Advocates, retweet a post by Black Lives Matter and Wajahat Ali, laugh at Dean Obeidallah's stand-up comedy, "like" a page from Pantsuit Nation and Daughters of Abraham, join the trending #MeToo conversation: I commit myself to the American dream.

A Muslim woman's American dream.
An American Muslim's dream.

The Transition

When did the transition take place? Was it a slow process of integra-
tion over five decades? Or was it events, people, and circumstances that
reshaped my identity? At a gut level, it was need (i.e., what I needed at
that time) for myself and for my family. When I was young and lonely—
in the early 1970s—I craved the society of Pakistani friends. A homemaker, raising two little boys, I yearned for adult company—female, of
course—someone with whom I could talk in Urdu, talk Pakistani. I
wanted my children to have Pakistani children for friends—Muslim children. Not that I ruled out American friends for them—not by a long
shot—but I didn't want them to miss out on being Pakistani and being
Muslim. So, our efforts—my husband's and mine—were to build a social
circle of Pakistanis. It wasn't easy. There just wasn't a critical mass. In that
void, we started drifting away from religious practices as the environment that nurtured that practice was missing. There were no mosques,
no Islamic community centers, almost no Muslims in my neighborhood.

As the boys started growing up, we began to worry about their religious identity, as did other families who were cruising on the same ship.
Out came the prayer rugs, copies of the Qur'an, Muslim-ish clothing
from the back corners of the closet, and we turned our focus to establishing a children's Sunday school—Islamic, of course. Raised as a secular
Muslim, I grew up strong in faith but knew next to nothing about Islam.
When my children asked questions, such as "Why do we pray five times
a day?" or "How do you know that the Qur'an is God's word and was
not written by Prophet Muhammad?" I realized that I had never asked
these questions when I was growing up. There was no need to. Pakistan
was a Muslim society, everyone was Muslim, no one challenged you or
asked questions, so I was blissfully ignorant. Khalid and I did what any
parent would do when they didn't want their children to see how ignorant their parents were. We scrambled to educate ourselves. We had to
stay just one level ahead of our children, who were learning fast, thanks
to the Sunday school. We also had to practice what the Sunday school

preached, as in praying five times a day and fasting during Ramadan. The need to bring our children into the fold of Islam made me a practicing and "knowledgeable" Muslim.

What made me a practicing American? At first, it was my professional career. As a student at the New School for Social Research, I made friends with my fellow students—women and men. They became a regular fixture in our home, became friends with Khalid, and played with our boys. My social circle expanded to include non-Pakistani homegrown Americans. We remain in touch to this day. As a health-care executive in a hospital, I embraced the corporate culture of America with zeal and pride. I was impressed by the professional conduct of my colleagues, the work ethic, and the commitment to put the patients first and foremost. The hospital's mission became my mission, my cause. I marveled at the ease with which my colleagues had accepted me into the fold—a Muslim woman of Pakistani origin, brown skin, Pakistani-British accent—enhancing my respect for American professionalism. I was swept away. This was where I wanted to belong. I soaked up every ounce of mentorship my preceptors generously offered and adopted the image of an American executive.

Twenty-five years later, our grandson Omar was diagnosed with autism. I left my career to launch the New York Metro chapter of the National Autism Association. We had moved to Manhattan and the autism community—a community I needed—became my community. An all-American community—no Pakistanis. It was the post 9/11 era; I delved into interfaith dialogue. To raise awareness about Muslims, I needed the support of faith communities, and over time, people of all faiths became my family. Only in America! Then I wrote my memoir, and a whole new world of friends opened up—mostly American-born. After the 2016 presidential elections, Khalid and I got onto the Islam-101 speaking circuit, and now I can't keep track of all my new friends. The Pakistani weekend singing parties are a thing of my musical past. *This* is my life. An all-American life. I still relish the opportunity to wear a sparkling shalwar kameez, chat in Urdu, and sway to Shafqat Amanat Ali's love song "Aankhon Ke Saagar," but life has taken me on a different path.

Is There an Identity Crisis in the Next Generation?

Yes, and no.

I cannot speak for all Muslims in America, or any one Muslim community for that matter, but I can share what I have experienced in my limited sphere. My Muslim network is for the most part composed of immigrant families, mostly of Pakistani/Indian descent. My contemporaries—immigrant Americans—had a full-blown identity crisis, and each dealt with it based on their circumstance, their sense of security or insecurity, and their attitude. Now in their sixties and seventies, many are still struggling. Just last year, I overheard a conversation between a mother and daughter:

Daughter: What should we plan for Thanksgiving?

Mother: It's not my holiday.

Daughter: You have lived in this country for forty years; it *is* your holiday.

She did manage to drag her mother across the generational divide for that year. I have no doubt that it will replay year after year.

The second generation is wholly American, but not without their share of confusion.

"Mom, my friend Linda is having a sleepover on Saturday. It will be so much fun." She is a tween.

"You can't go."

"What do you mean I can't go? Why not?"

"Because I said so. In our culture, girls don't go to sleepovers."

"*Your* culture. This is not Pakistan. In *my* culture . . ."

Mom has the last word, and now daughter doesn't know how she is going to explain this to her friends. Will she be cast off as un-American? She huffs and puffs, scoffing, "Stupid culture!" to no avail.

I almost choked when my son announced that he was going to the high school prom. But neither my husband nor I intervened. I often wonder how we would have handled it if our son had been a daughter. Would my double standards have kicked in? Those were the times when I didn't miss having a daughter.

"Muslims can't date," Mom tells her teenage daughter.

How does the daughter feel listening to her girlfriends chatter about their boyfriends and compare notes on their weekend dates? Less American?

"Muslims don't drink alcohol," Dad tells his son.

Does he go to the bar with his friends anyhow? Does he order seltzer as he tries to explain himself? Or does being appointed the designated driver for the group make up for being the odd one out? Or does he choose to go to the library instead, justifying to himself that it is time better spent? In those moments, does he feel less American?

Their politics and entertainment are totally American. While Dad may be listening to ARY Pakistani news, and Mom may be watching *Humsafar*—a Pakistani soap opera on JadooTV—they are scrolling through their Instagram and TikTok and scrambling to get discounted tickets to Rihanna's concert. Some seek the benefit of both worlds when slapping their knees in rhythm to a tabla performance by Zakir Hussein, or swaying at qawwali devotional music by visiting Pakistani qawwals; they savor Mom's biryani and dance the bhangra at a traditional wedding, the young ladies twirling in their sparkling shalwar kameez in a hundred colors.

Many cross the boundaries set by their parents and live a double life. They date, but their parents don't know. Remember the movie *The Big Sick?* They carry the burden of a dual identity. This reminds me of a talk Khalid and I gave in Winchester, Virginia. A woman in the audience—a white American—asked a question—actually, shared a story. Her son had been dating a Muslim girl of Pakistani descent. He would bring her home, and they all got to know her and fell in love with her. But she could not tell her parents that she was seeing a non-Muslim. Eventually, she broke up with him because she knew that she would not be able to stand up to the ire of her parents. The lady got teary-eyed as she told the story, saying how much she had liked this young lady. In such moments, I don't know what to say.

All this aside, their politics and civic engagement are totally, 100 percent American. No confusion there. No overlap or crosscurrents whatsoever. Yes, you will see Linda Sarsour raise her voice for the rights of the Palestinians as she will for the rights of the Jewish Americans; Muslim youth groups will be raising funds for the Rohinga refugees and for Hurricane Sandy; Kashmiri Muslims will speak up when atrocities are committed in Kashmir, as they will when synagogues are defaced with swastikas. They will protest the separation of families at the Mexican border and march in protest of police violence against African Americans. I recently watched with great pride as our granddaughter Laila marched in a demonstration in the aftermath of the killing of George Floyd, holding aloft a banner reading BLACK LIVES MATTER. Our American Muslim younger generation is committed to the principle of upholding the rights of all human beings, Muslims and non-Muslims alike.

In that commitment, our children are totally American.

Walter:

My Evolving Identity

Who am I? Jewish, Israeli, Jewish American, American Jew (is there a difference?), or a cosmopolitan human being whose ultimate loyalty is to all of humanity? The truth is, my sense of identity and connection has shifted a lot over the years and will, I'm sure, remain a work in progress for as long as I exist. Yet, at the age of seventy, it is time for fresh reflection on these issues or, as they put it in that lovely Hebrew phrase, to do serious *cheshbon hanefesh* (accounting of the soul) and reach some tentative conclusions.

Much of my life's work has been about getting comfortable and getting whole with myself. I spent the first part getting whole and happy with being Jewish, and during the past decade have finally come to amicable terms with the American part of my being. I am now in a position to grapple meaningfully with mysteries of my identity, hopefully helping to role-model positive Jewishness and Americanness while building alliances with the Muslim community and affirming the common humanity that binds us all.

Healing My Jewish Self-Hatred

My second sustained period of living in Israel had healed my angst about being Jewish, even though I ultimately decided not to reside permanently in the Jewish state. Somewhere in the early 1980s, during my salad years as a journalist for Jewish and Israeli papers and living in the New York Jewish community—the largest in the world—I had the revelation that being Jewish was the most important thing in my life. I had come to

revel in a newfound sense of fluency in the nuances of Jew-to-Jew communication, whether in English or Hebrew, and felt empowered by my
ability to operate effectively within the Jewish community as a journalist, to be a player on the team while spotlighting the community's foibles
and inconsistencies in my reporting. Indeed, "Jewish journalist" became
an identity that fit me perfectly: at once part of and an observer of the
Jewish community, simultaneously belonging to the tribe and maintaining an independent perspective.

During those years, I often defined myself as a *yachas cham* Jew (an
untranslatable Hebrew term I would roughly render as "warm connection," "warm relations," or "good vibrations"). My use of *yachas cham*
relates to an experience I had in 1977 while working on a feature article
for the *Jerusalem Post* about rock and roll stars in Israel, sitting in a Tel
Aviv recording studio listening to a laid-back Israeli rocker named Dani
Litani record a song by that title. The song seemed evocative of Israeli
society, both in its breezy "no bullshit" credo concerning romantic relationships and the "warm relations" that bound all Israelis in one big
Jewish family. Even today, the warm and gently ironic spirit of the Israeli
rock music of the 1970s, as expressed by Litani and musical geniuses like
Shalom Hanoch, Arik Einstein, and Ariel Zilber, remains the soundtrack
of my Jewish identity.

Though I chose not to become Israeli, my experience living in Israel
gave me the needed kick in the ass to become happily Jewish. I remain
so to this day, full of enthusiasm for life despite my abiding sadness at the
collapse of the peace process and of other dreams of my youth.

There are major gaps in my connection to *yiddishkeit* (Jewishness).
I remain uneducated about Judaism as a faith and allergic to religious
practice, though over the years working as a journalist I did glean a lot
about Jewish ritual. Ironically, given the Israeli soundtrack playing in
my head, I am part of the effort by many American Jews of my generation and younger to create a positive and sustainable American Jewish
identity in which commitment to Israel is less at the core than during
my youth. Instead of genuflecting to the Jewish state, we are focused
on values like *tikkun olam* and commitment to serving people in need
from all backgrounds. Some of us are religiously observant, and some are

not; some are Zionists, and some post-Zionists. Whatever our individual positions on Israel, we have in common that we have chosen to live as committed Jews in the Diaspora. For that to work, our faith identity must be about more than blind support for a Jewish state that is moving in a direction that clashes with our pluralist and humanist values. The challenge is to remain committed to doing what we can to contribute to the fulfillment of the dream of Israeli-Palestinian peace and reconciliation while creating vibrant forms of Jewish connection in the place where we live, America. For many of us, it is about embracing and enhancing our Jewishness while also working to build friendship and trust with our Muslim brothers and sisters.

Healing My American Self-Hatred

During my years in Encounter, when I was in my late forties, Maria Espinosa once said to me, "Walter, you are so American!" I cringed at that statement, which so contradicted how I viewed myself, as being as un-American as I possibly could despite having been born and raised in this country and having lived all but seven years of my life here. At different points, I had tried to identify as Jewish, Israeli, quasi-European, or indeterminate cosmopolitan. Anything but American!

Why was that? I imbibed much of my youthful anti-Americanism from my father, an "egghead" from the 1950s who abhorred America's commercial culture and sneered at Disneyland and Coca-Cola. He pointed out to me what he identified as the vapidity and soul-shattering ugliness of this commercial culture, represented in the shopping centers and gas stations on highways like Roosevelt Road that ran along the southern edge of Glen Ellyn, Illinois, the leafy, lily-white, *goyische* suburb where our family lived during my teenage years. Why he and my mother chose to live and raise their kids in such religiously, culturally, and politically dissonant places as the North Hills of Pittsburgh and Glen Ellyn, which went 80 percent for Goldwater in 1964, rather than in more Jewish areas, remains a mystery. To some degree, it seems to me, my father relished living among the Philistines so he could sneer at them while simultaneously affirming that he was a full human being rather than a ghettoized Jew.

My father's narrative of an ugly, sterile American culture was greatly reinforced for me by the counterculture of the sixties, which began infiltrating into the seemingly inhospitable soil of Glen Ellyn by 1967. Within a year, that consciousness transformed me and a small group of like-minded rebels who coalesced around a self-described "mock-rock" band called Xeno and the Stoics (I was Xeno). We went from being high school nonconformists/nerds given to parodying school spirit and the in-crowd to politicized and increasingly angry dissidents with a visceral loathing for the so-called American way of life, characterized by capitalism, militarism, and racism. That process was accelerated by the Vietnam War, which potentially threatened the lives of teenage boys like me a year or two short of draft age.

During my college years, I was a believer in the coming revolution, which we thought would arrive within a decade or so, when American society would be turned upside-down by the consciousness of the counterculture and we would peacefully transform into a society based on cooperation, not competition; sharing, not personal acquisition; and above all on our love for humanity, our precious Earth, and all of creation.

The truth is that I still believe in the sixties' vision and feel privileged to have been part of it. History moves in waves, and I am convinced that in time, the days of our children and grandchildren, America and the world will finally fulfill the dreams of my generation.

It took me a lot longer to let go of my American self-hatred than my Jewish one. Living in Israel and later in the Soviet Union and traveling widely as a journalist to quite a few dictatorships taught me that America wasn't nearly as bad as I had thought. In fact, as the decades went by, I had to admit that America was a decidedly more decent and humane society than many I had encountered. In 2009, I witnessed firsthand how excited members of a visiting delegation of European imams and rabbis were to see Muslim Boy and Girl Scouts at a mosque in northern Virginia pledging allegiance to the American flag. Such a vision, one visiting French imam declared, would be hard to imagine in his country, where Muslims were considered tolerated outsiders at best, but not truly French.

That experience illuminated for me that America, with all its faults, remains a unique country animated by a pluralistic and democratic universal ideal: namely, that immigrants from around the world, of varied religious, racial, and ethnic backgrounds, can come and be accepted as fully American, with a shot at realizing their individual American dreams of life, liberty, and the pursuit of happiness. One does not have to belong to a particular race, ethnicity, or religion to be considered fully American. That is decidedly not the case in France and other European countries I had long considered better than America.

After 2009, I came to appreciate, and even celebrate, the American dream for the first time. I had spent my life trying to make a small contribution to bringing Jews and Arabs together in Israel-Palestine but had seen those bright hopes go up in smoke because of religious and ethnic particularism. America is very far from perfect in this regard: our history has been forever scarred by the original sins of the enslavement and persecution of African Americans and genocide of Native Americans. Nevertheless, it appeared in 2009, after the election of Barack Obama, that our country was moving to finally acknowledge and overcome those sins. I came to believe that the American model of belonging offered the best hope for troubled humanity. At least that appeared to be the case in Obama-era America, before the native land I had finally embraced turned to the abject bigotry and greedy acquisitiveness represented by President Donald Trump.

Vanquishing Trumpism and sustaining the vision of a religiously, racially, and ethnically diverse society where everyone has a fair shot at fulfilling their dreams is imperative not only for America but all of humanity. Upholding the American vision is about saving the world. So I'm planning to fight for the soul of America alongside my friend Sabeeha and like-minded people of conscience of all faiths, colors, and creeds.

Jewish American or American Jew?

Am I a Jewish American or an American Jew? For me, it is emphatically the latter, because that formulation gives primacy to the Jewish part of my being. Indeed, even though I have chosen to live in America, not Israel, and speak English almost all the time as opposed to my beloved second language of Hebrew, and even though I now embrace the American part of my identity, I am a Jew to my core, both psychologically and genetically. When I did a DNA test recently, the results came back as 99.5 percent Jewish—and, bizarrely, 0.5 percent Chinese. My American roots are of relatively recent vintage: the two sides of my father's family arrived in New York from Russia in 1874 and 1891 respectively, while my mother arrived from Germany in 1941. By contrast, my Jewish gene pool goes back 4,000 years, into the mists of antiquity.

Many American Jews worry about being accused of dual loyalty, of caring about Israel more than America. On more than one occasion, Trump provoked nervous laughter among supportive American Jewish audiences when he spoke about how good he and his administration have been for "your country, Israel." For my part, I've never been hung up about the dual loyalty issue. I am who I am: a Jew first and foremost. America will just have to figure out how to deal with that. Also, for most of my life, I *did* care more about Israel than about America. That is no longer true. And though I'll continue trying to contribute to the healing of Israel-Palestine, my main job is joining with my Muslim brothers and sisters and people of conscience of all backgrounds in the sacred task of healing America. This is where I'm making my stand, and I am doing so as a proud, unabashed American Jew. *Zehu zeh* (that's it)!

A Human Being Above All

So, I am both proudly Jewish and American, but I am a human being above all. That may sound like a no-brainer, but many of my Jewish and American compatriots emphasize their Jewishness or their Americanness over their humanity. To me that's profoundly misguided from a moral perspective. In *The Merchant of Venice*, Shakespeare's great character Shylock demanded recognition of his humanity, even as he was cursed by Renaissance Christians as a perfidious Jew:

> *Hath not a Jew eyes? Hath not a Jew hands, organs,*
> *dimensions, senses, affections, passions? Fed with*
> *the same food, hurt with the same weapons, subject*
> *to the same diseases, healed by the same means,*
> *warmed and cooled by the same winter and summer, as*
> *a Christian is? If you prick us, do we not bleed?*

Yes, absolutely, yes! We have eyes and hands, and if you prick us, we definitely bleed! But the same logic applies to the 99.9 percent of humanity that is not Jewish, too. They also have eyes, hands, and bleed when they are cut. Palestinians are as resplendently and fully human as are Jews, and so, for that matter, are Christians and Muslims, Blacks and Whites, French, Germans, Russians, Pakistanis, Nicaraguans, Ethiopians, and Burmese.

Yes, Jews were persecuted and murdered by fellow human beings for two thousand years, culminating in the Holocaust that took the life of my great-grandmother, Bette Katz. Yet now that we have achieved power and a state of our own, we need to remember that we are not exalted above the nations but rather at one with them. If we are a Chosen People, as affirmed in the Torah, it is because we were chosen by God for a particular mission or destiny, not because we are intrinsically different or better than other nationalities or religions.

I used to stay up nights worrying that Israel would be destroyed by terrorists who would slip a suitcase atomic bomb into the cities of Tel Aviv and Haifa and ignite them. Now my existential fear is not primarily for Israel but for the whole planet because of the threat from climate change and the accelerating disasters it is spawning. I am terrified there will be no sustainable future for my son and stepdaughter and their eventual children and grandchildren, as well as for everyone else on this planet. Fear for the survival of my own tribe has become fear for the survival of humanity.

In my life and work, I'm fighting for human survival alongside my brothers and sisters from all racial, ethnic, and religious backgrounds, and I'm doing so as an American Jewish human being. All of us, all almost eight billion, bring our diverse histories and cultural effervescence to our common struggle for life. May we rejoice in our diversity! Let it be a source of harmony and strength as we stand together to save our planet and our species.

Sabeeha and Walter:

We Both Choose to Be Americans

Each of us love our people. We sang and danced with them in the citrus groves of Rehovot and the campus grounds of Lahore, but we ultimately embraced America, Americans, and the dream of America. This land has given us the freedom to exercise our choice—to practice our faith, to wear it on our heads, be it the hijab or the kippah if we choose to. America has bestowed upon us the right to cast our vote for those who speak for us and vote out those who don't. America holds to be self-evident that every Jew and every Muslim is created equal and each of us has the liberty to express our opinions in the public sphere, on the air-waves, in a range of ideologically diverse newspapers, or with the handle of a tweeting bird. America has given us the opportunity to pursue our calling and nurture our talent—a Home Ec grad turned hospital execu-tive turned author, a journalist turned community organizer and peace advocate. And isn't it wonderful that here we are, two people arriving at the age of seventy faster than we might like but still very much in the process of reinventing ourselves? We hate to invoke the cliché "only in America," but it sure feels that way.

Here in America, we have been challenged and made smarter and more empathetic. We have been made bigger by being among people who are not like us. Here our differences don't make us feel different but rather united in our common humanity through our diversity. This is where we have pursued and found happiness and fulfillment—most of the time. This is the land that gives us hope. This is where we feel most at home.

Part 3

CONFRONTING THE ELEPHANTS IN THE ROOM

CHAPTER 12

THE ISRAELI-PALESTINIAN CONFLICT

A Dialogue

Should Muslims and Jews intent on relationship building discuss the Israel-Palestine conflict with each other? It's a hard conversation to have even when we have areas of agreement because of the correct perception that the Other has not walked in our shoes. Feelings are strong on both sides, and there is truth in both perspectives. So if participants in Muslim-Jewish relation building don't feel ready to have this conversation, fearing it might sabotage their budding but still fragile entente, they should not be pressured to do so. While there is no hard-and-fast rule, we believe individuals on both sides should wait until they feel ready for it, until they feel close enough to each other that they can have that conversation without risking the progress they have made.

In the case of the two of us, we have built solid ties of mutual respect, friendship, and trust—and, equally important, a sense of common purpose in standing together against fear and bigotry here at home. So we decided we were ready to have a candid conversation about Israel-Palestine in all of its scope and intensity without destroying what we had created together. We recognize that we may be less far apart from each other's positions than many of our Muslim and Jewish compatriots.

Nevertheless, the conversations we have held over the past two years were still difficult. They brought up emotions from very deep within us that we had not necessarily expected to share.

We don't hold out these conversations as a model. There is no right or wrong way. In our case, we just turned on the tape recorder and let it rip, but with each of us cautious—perhaps overly so—not to go into a place that would offend the other to the point it might damage our relationship. So the conversations were at once freewheeling and controlled. Contradictory, yes, not to mention messy and frustrating, but that's the nature of the beast when Muslims and Jews talk about the Middle East. It ain't ever going to be perfect, and it ain't ever going to be final. You do the best you can.

Conversations between Sabeeha and Walter

August 18, 2017

Avoiding the Elephant

Sabeeha: When I came to America in 1971, I was intimidated by the large Jewish presence and their vocal commitment to Israel. On the other hand, I was also impressed, particularly with their dedication to social justice and family values. Very impressed. They embraced us as neighbors, as colleagues, and quickly we became friends. All that made it difficult for me to raise a sensitive issue and express my feelings about how the Israelis treated the Palestinians and the circumstances under which Israel came into being. I respected my friends, and I did not want to offend. And somewhere along the line—I can't pinpoint exactly when—I began to accept the idea that Israel had a right to exist. Not that I ever rejected it, but I was too overwhelmed by my pain for the Palestinians having been driven out of their homes. Eventually, I made that shift in my thinking that both have a right to exist with dignity—in the land they both call home.

In my mind, two issues are paramount: The right of return of the Palestinians, and the settlements. Regarding Jerusalem, I presumed that because the UN had passed a resolution that it will be an international city, that this is how it would be settled. My overriding concern was human rights and civil rights of the Palestinians. It still is.

Today, in interfaith dialogues, Muslims and Jews still avoid talking about the Israeli-Palestinian issue. On a few occasions when this issue comes up in interfaith groups, there have been enough voices saying, "Let's not go there." So, we don't.

Walter: In the Jewish-Muslim communication and cooperation efforts I was involved in, we didn't have an absolute prohibition on discussing the Israeli-Palestinian conflict in the same way that you have in the Sisterhood of Salaam Shalom. Our approach was to ensure that when we had a Muslim-Jewish event, we didn't want it taken over by a debate over Israel-Palestine. Yet we also didn't participants to perceive that we were trying to sweep the issue under the rug. While we often encouraged twinning partners to start their programs with a prayer for peace and a joint expression of the sorrow both feel about the conflict, we urged the participants to then focus on how we can connect with each other here in America.

I wasn't sure when I started ten years ago whether this formula was going to fly and feared it would be hard to get people to accept the ground rules. Thankfully, that turned out not to be the case. Most who got involved accepted the rules because they came to see the Muslim-Jewish dialogue as too precious to risk by delving into the Israeli-Palestinian conflict.

On Jerusalem

Sabeeha: I believe it's time that you and I tackle it. May I go first? What do you think about our administration's decision on moving the US embassy to Jerusalem?

Walter: Well, it made me very sad that the US government is now accepting the line that has been ascendant on the Jewish right for many years that "Jerusalem is our city. It belongs to the Jews"—which is wrong because it is the cradle of three faiths and also because 35 to 40 percent of the population of Greater Jerusalem is Palestinian Arab. To claim that it is all ours is false, and the idea of annexing East Jerusalem out from under the Palestinians is morally troubling. Some of this process I have seen up close. There is a beautiful neighborhood called Silwan down below the slopes of the Old City. It is built in a majestic canyon where there are also some very interesting ancient sculptures—both Jewish and non-Jewish. Silwan has been a Palestinian village for many centuries, but in recent years militant Jews, with the support of the Israeli government, have been buying up Palestinian houses and moving Jewish settlers into old Silwan. They have ways of buying houses surreptitiously, offering people a lot of money through shell companies—and then after they get control of a house, they cover it with the Israeli flag and post armed guards around it. A lot of this is very ugly and antithetical to Judaism as I understand it. In my opinion, Jerusalem should be the capital of the people of both states.

Sabeeha: My take on the decision is no different. I was offended. I felt it was morally wrong. Like you, I consider Jerusalem a place holy to all three faiths, a decision the world community made when the UN resolution was passed.

On the Right of Return

Sabeeha: I feel the pain of those who yearn for the Right to Return. I have friends of Palestinian heritage, and I feel their sorrow deeply. It's painful to hear them relate stories of their parents who lost their homes and the land they call home. Then I have Jewish friends who say to me that the Palestinians should move on and not look back; that Arab countries should accommodate them; that the Arab countries are contributing to this problem by not giving them citizenship because they want to keep this problem alive. I feel that if any community or person has a yearning to go back home, they should be allowed to. It is their right. Any people whose ancestors were expelled, centuries spent in the diaspora, knows what displacement feels like. Why do to others what you don't want done to you?

Walter: One area where I am not in agreement with you is the Right of Return. I understand and deeply sympathize with the tragedy of those people who left in 1948, either were evicted or decided to flee the fighting—their tragedy and that of their children, grandchildren, and great-grandchildren. God, all these generations. Yet, to implement a policy of "anyone who wants to come back, please do so" would end any possibility of a Jewish state. The premise of the two-state solution is that we would have two states: one Jewish and one Palestinian. But that won't work if the Palestinians claim the right to come back to the Jewish state as well as the Palestinian one. Maybe we could have a symbolic number of returnees to Israel—some have suggested 50,000 to 100,000 people—but we could not have just anybody who wants to come home, because that would be millions of people and their descendants. The premise of the two-state solution as propounded during the Oslo period was that the vast majority of Palestinians who wanted to return to their homeland would resettle in the new Palestinian state, not inside Israel.

If it's a one-state solution, maybe then it doesn't matter as much whether the returning Palestinians settle in the West Bank or pre-1967 Israel, but even then the Israelis would oppose it because they would fear it would push the Palestinian share of the population of the common state way above 50 percent and create a situation in which the Palestinian majority could vote the Jewish State of Israel out of existence by democratic means. The majority of those who were expelled in 1948 have since passed on, but it would really overwhelm Israel to give a free and open pass to all the descendants of those people to come back to within its borders. I don't think there would be enough land.

Sabeeha: It's not fair.

Walter: Right. It's not fair. Definitely not. But then, there are many things in this world that are not fair.

Sabeeha: I have been reading *My Promised Land* by Ari Shavit, an Israeli. The forced expulsions of Palestinians from Deir Yassin and hundreds of towns and villages by the Israel Defense Forces, four hundred Arab towns and villages depopulated, people marched out of their homes and sent into exile, the denial that the Palestinians even existed, sent tremors down my spine. It was a human rights catastrophe. Palestinian refugees need reparation for the wrongs done to them. I cannot accept the argument that political considerations override human rights. The Palestinians are a homeless nation, and no practical argument makes that existence morally right.

Walter: I understand and deeply respect your feelings on this difficult issue. I personally would support Israel issuing a statement of profound sorrow for the displacement and suffering of an estimated 700,000 Palestinians that happened during Israel's creation, as well as making financial restitution payments to the descendants of the 1948 refugees. But it is clear to me that the consequences of an unrestricted return, possibly by millions of Palestinian refugees—mostly the descendants of those forced out in the 1948 war—to inside Israel's boundaries as they existed from 1948 to 1967—would be disastrous for all.

On the Settlements

Sabeeha: Shall we talk about the settlements? It is an invasion. On moral grounds, on grounds of national integrity—of the Palestinians—the settlers don't belong there. It is not their land. But I also don't see the problem going away. The longer that takes and the more settled the settlers become in their homes, particularly the generation that was born there, then moving them out becomes tantamount to eviction, as it was for the Palestinians who were expelled.

Walter: Yes, to me, the settlements have always seemed like madness: Why would Israelis intentionally create a situation like that? The Palestinians of the West Bank and Gaza have now lived for fifty years not so much as second-class citizens as noncitizens, people who are basically without human and political rights. The Israelis have many excuses for why this has happened. They say, "Why didn't the Palestinians negotiate with us at this or that moment?" or "Why didn't they make this or that concession?" But the fact is that the Occupation has continued for more than fifty years, and it's very hard to fathom what that means in terms of human suffering.

On the Two-State Solution

Sabeeha: By default, I believe that we are headed toward a one-state solution. Jerusalem has already been given away to Israel by the US administration. So, if it becomes one state, normal circumstance requires that all citizens have equal rights, which means it would not be a Jewish state but a state of all the people. I have doubts that the hard-liners would allow that to happen. That would result in Israel being no longer a democracy. It's not a pretty picture. What do you feel?

Walter: That's exactly what I feel. Given that Israel has given me so much joy, to see it going in such a hopeless direction is horrifying. It feels like a big part of my life is ending in failure. So, for me, it's everything you said and on a deeply personal level. It's hard to see how it plays out, but the hard-liners would certainly not allow a state of two peoples with equal rights to come to fruition any time soon. Yet maybe over time— over a generation or two—I believe a binational state essentially will evolve by force of circumstance. You have these two populations within a very small physical space.

One thing I want to say, Sabeeha, is that I have a very deep devotion and love for Israel as a Jewish state, and for me to contemplate the state of Israel as not a Jewish state is personally painful. But I think, "OK, I'm not going to live to see that anyway, and therefore if that's the way it evolves, so be it." I personally see a functional binational state as much preferable to endless conflict, which would be horrible for both peoples. The level of suffering, the physical casualties, the death count, all have been much greater on the Palestinian side because the Israelis are better armed, but there is also tremendous suffering on the Israeli side, both physical and psychological, with no end in sight.

Nine months later, May 15, 2018

Jerusalem and Gaza Conflict

Sabeeha: Today is the day after the move of the US embassy to Jerusalem and the eruption of violence in Gaza. I have been getting emails from the Sisterhood members—Jewish members—expressing their pain over the violence and their feelings that this move was unnecessary and provocative. I have also received an email from Rabbi Avram Mlotek, who wanted to come and sit with Khalid and me and talk about the sorrow about what is happening in Gaza. How do *you* feel about it?

Walter: First, I am so glad to hear that Jews have been reaching out to you, knowing that this event is hurtful to you and Khalid. How do I feel about it? I feel so numb at this moment, to be honest with you. I just saw something now—Ben Wedeman, a veteran Israel-based correspondent from CNN, saying, "This was the day the hope of peace finally died." And that is such a crushing thing to say, but it feels very much on target.

Sabeeha: How do you feel when people say, "That is the reality on the ground." To me, there are many sad realities on the ground. We don't need to etch them in stone and say, "The sad reality is here to stay." It's spin.

Walter: Well, Wedeman is a journalist and he was looking for a hook for his piece, and perhaps he was too definitive in his formulation that all hope for peace is over. Yet the truth is that no one sees any hope right now. The deadlock has been going on for such a long time. Now that the issue of Jerusalem has been taken off the table, as Trump puts it, it seems to have brought the deadlock to a kind of climax that will lead us all to a new paradigm—whatever that is.

Sabeeha: Khalid was saying yesterday that the one-state solution will not prove to be a solution because the Palestinians will be disenfranchised, their rights curtailed, and whoever has the ability to leave will leave the land. They will just die out. That was his worst-case scenario.

Walter: I have to say I agree with Khalid in the sense that that has been the strategy of Netanyahu and the Likud Party all along: if pushed hard enough, the Palestinians would ultimately leave, either by being expelled or deciding to leave on their own. My question to Israeli friends has long been, "Why would a succession of Israeli governments—duly elected and reelected by the people of Israel—deliberately follow a policy of doing everything possible, over many decades, to prevent a two-state solution?" If Israel claims to desire such a solution, why would it keep building settlements across the West Bank to prevent the creation of a Palestinian state that would have territorial contiguity? It makes no sense to have a State of Israel with 50 percent Palestinians or more, so why would you create such a scenario? This long-term strategy only makes sense if what Khalid is saying is correct.

How steadfast can any people be—including the Palestinians—to remain living under occupation for many decades before they decide to leave their homes and emigrate? But one important factor limiting the efficacy of an Israeli strategy of pushing the Palestinians to leave is that with new limitations on immigration to Europe and America, it becomes harder and harder to leave. It's difficult enough nowadays for Palestinians to leave East Jerusalem or the West Bank and find a desirable place that will welcome them, but in Gaza there simply isn't a way out. They can't leave because all the borders are sealed and something close to two million human beings in Gaza are condemned to live in an open-air prison. The creation of that situation was largely caused by conscious policy decisions by Israel carried out over more than a decade, and it is appalling that, as much as I love Israel, I can no longer defend the indefensible.

You know, over the decades I have had so many conversations like this one with non-Jews who were criticizing Israel's treatment of the Palestinians, and invariably I end up defending Israel or at least trying to provide context, offering mitigating circumstances for behavior that I find morally indefensible in my heart of hearts. Yes, Israelis fear for their survival, and yes, they have solid reasons for that fear, but it doesn't justify occupying another people and denying them basic rights for half a century.

So, as you and I were starting this conversation, I was already anticipating that I would say to you something like, "Sabeeha, I understand and respect your concerns about the human impact of Israeli military actions in Gaza, but you need to understand that Hamas refuses to recognize Israel and is dedicated to its destruction based on theological beliefs; and if people are throwing stones and projectiles and launching burning kites at Israeli soldiers or shooting missiles into Israel, what are you going to do? You can't just let them knock down the fence. They might very well kill Israeli civilians."

But I'm not going to say that, because while all of those concerns and fears are very real and valid, I cannot any longer play the game of rationalizing the killing of Palestinian civilians who behave in desperate ways because they are being kept in desperate conditions for years without respite. It is up to Israel—the stronger party—to offer some solutions to this problem besides shooting demonstrators, even those who throw stones or burning projectiles, not to mention civilians being blown up by bombs dropped on apartment buildings in Gaza City.

Obviously, I'm not the only Diaspora Jew who goes through these tortured moral calculations. The hardest part is that an army is killing a large number of civilians and that's *my* army doing that. It's a Jewish army, dedicated to protecting Jewish lives and representing the highest ideals of the Jewish people, presenting its highest moral calling as being "the purity of arms," which implies that it will only shoot lethal weaponry when there is no alternative in order to preserve the lives of its soldiers. But after so many years, I can't pretend that is even remotely true.

Israel claims to represent not only its citizens but all the Jews of the world, so I feel a moral obligation to speak out. But I continue to love Israel, so I can't make common cause with many folks—including many on the political left with whom I agree on other issues—who would like to make Israel disappear. It is traumatic all around, but the trauma I'm enduring is infinitesimal compared to existential fear experienced by Palestinians and Israelis alike.

April 2019

Golan Heights and West Bank

Sabeeha: I am outraged at our president's statement to recognize Golan Heights as part of Israel, and Netanyahu's announcement to annex the settlements in the West Bank into Israel. They have defied the UN resolution and norms of national integrity of the Palestinians. The lengths leaders will go under the guise of national security! They have legitimized occupation. How tragic is that!

Walter: I agree. While I do not advocate Israel now returning the Golan Heights—so close to the Israeli heartland at this point—to a Syrian regime that killed hundreds of thousands of their own people and is closely allied with Russia, Iran, and Hezbollah, it was totally wrongheaded for Trump to recognize Israel's unilateral annexation of the Golan. This is spitting on the international principle of the nonadmissibility of obtaining territory by force of arms. It is wrong when Russia grabs Crimea militarily from Ukraine and then annexes it, and it is wrong when Israel does the same vis-à-vis the Golan Heights.

January 2020
The Trump Peace Plan

Sabeeha: My heart bleeds for the Palestinians. First expelled, then humiliated, and now squeezed out. What an unjust plan: the most fertile land—the Jordan River valley— carved out for Israel in exchange for deserted deserts; Palestinian land carved into pockets surrounded by Israel; noncontiguous patches connected by tunnels and bridges; no control over defense; no share in Jerusalem; and a Palestinian state contingent upon "conditions." It's not a peace plan; it's a plan to vanquish the Palestinians. A people can endure only so much suffering.

Walter: Reading about the Trump-Kushner-Netanyahu dead-on-arrival "Peace of the Century" plan, I keep coming back to that moment a year or so ago when someone asked Jared what he was offering to the Palestinians in his peace plan, and he replied with the following chilling words: "The Palestinians want to pay their mortgage." That's it. One hundred years of a battle for liberation and self-determination comes down in Kushner's mind to an abject surrender to Zionist maximalism and a craven desire to pay the mortgage to landlord Israel for their meager and constantly shrinking slice of their homeland.

Israeli annexation of big chunks of the West Bank turning the supposed Palestinian state into a noncontiguous Bantustan muddle, with every far-flung settlement allowed to remain, is totally unacceptable to Palestinians and every fair-minded friend of Israel. It will not lead to a viable two-state solution but to a one-state apartheid situation. This is a guaranteed lose-lose for both peoples that perpetuates the conflict for many decades to come.

The Challenge at Home in the US

Our struggle at home continues. We recognize that there are forces right here that threaten Muslim-Jewish relationship building, and those forces are directly linked to the Middle East conflict.

Walter: Intense passions continually get whipped up on university campuses across America over the Israel-Palestine issue. There is great stridency coming from both the communities. The Palestine advocacy has been extremely passionate in ways that I think have sometimes been destructive. I am thinking of one example that took place at Rutgers University several years ago. Jewish students were receiving little pieces of paper under their dorm-room doors reading "You are hereby evicted." They were stunned and then they would read in small letters at the bottom of the page: "as were the people of Palestine by the Zionist occupiers." That kind of advocacy serves to inflame rather than illuminate and has made the work of strengthening Muslim-Jewish ties on campus much more challenging. A lot of Jewish people on campuses say they feel almost persecuted and feel stigmatized.

Sabeeha: The Middle East conflict is also creating a schism within our respective communities. In 2018, the Islamic Society of North America (ISNA) canceled Wajahat Ali's talk at its annual convention after the publication of his piece in the *Atlantic* on his visit to the settlements in the West Bank. Likewise, a synagogue in New York City canceled the talk of one of its Jewish congregants because of his association with CAIR-NYC. Muslims and Jews in the US outcasting their own!

Walter: In truth, liberal American Jews have grown increasingly alienated by Israeli policies, although most still feel connected to the Jewish state. The fact that Israel has mostly collaborated with Trump has been a source of shame for many Jews. Even for people more centrist than I, it becomes ever harder to retain reflexive support for Israel and/or lobby on its behalf through their Jewish community councils and organizations like AIPAC. Quite a few polls have measured this. One by the American Jewish Committee released in October 2018 showed 77 percent of Israelis approved of President Trump's handling of US-Israel relations, while only 34 percent of American Jews did. Fifty-seven percent of US Jews disapproved, while only 10 percent of Israelis did.

The poll also showed the two communities differ greatly on matters of religion and state, particularly on the ultra-Orthodox monopoly over religious affairs in Israel. The vast majority of American Jews identify as either Reform or Conservative, the more liberal streams of Judaism that have a very small foothold in Israel.

Sabeeha and Walter:

Where does this leave us? Is the difficult relationship between our faith communities only about the Palestinian-Israeli conflict or does it run even deeper, going back to ancient history and our respective scriptures?

CHAPTER 13

IS THE QUR'AN
ANTI-SEMITIC? IS THE
TORAH GENOCIDAL?

Is Islam anti-Jewish? Is Judaism anti-Islamic? Extreme voices from our respective communities will say yes, and yes. We offer a resounding no.

We acknowledge that not only do some Jews believe that Muslims hate Jews, but some Muslims believe that in the Qur'an God admonishes the Jews and therefore Jews cannot be trusted. Likewise, some believe that the Torah compels Jews to kill all their enemies.

Are these people right? Let's set the record straight.

Sabeeha:

The Qur'an

Muslims believe that the Qur'an is the divine word, God speaking to human beings. In the Qur'an, God says that Jews are "People of the Book" to whom the Torah was revealed, and "We made them excel the nations."[5] He promises to reward the Jews (and Christians) for their

---

5 Qur'an 45:16. "And We gave the Book and the wisdom and the prophecy to the children of Israel, and We gave them of the goodly things, and We made them excel the nations."

good deeds.[6] He allows Muslims to marry Jews[7] (the Jewish partner is not required to convert to Islam), thereby permitting Muslims to engage in the most intimate relationship of trust and interdependency, both as companions and as parents to the children they create together. In my humble opinion, this is the highest honor that can be placed on a human being: to enter into a relationship of marriage. No anti-Semitism here.

God instructs Muslims to unconditionally honor and uphold the Torah[8] and calls upon them to believe in the holy scriptures sent to Prophets Moses, David, and Jesus; that the message in the Qur'an is no different from what is revealed in the Torah and Bible and to hold all prophets in high regard. "Say you: 'We believe in God, and in that which has been sent down on us and sent down on Abraham, Ishmael, Isaac and Jacob and the Tribes, and that which was given to Moses and Jesus and the Prophets, of their Lord; we make no distinction between any of them, and to Him we surrender.'" (Qur'an 2:129–132).

Regarding Prophet Moses:

He is by far the most prominent character in the Qur'an. His name is mentioned 136 times, whereas the Prophet Muhammad's name is mentioned only four times. The Quranic narrative concerning Moses includes most of the details one finds in the Old Testament—from his being abandoned on the Nile as a baby, to his adoption by Pharaoh's wife, to his escape to Midian, to the burning bush, to his defiance of Pharaoh and his miracles, to the Exodus, to the parting of the sea, and the golden calf.[9]

---

6   Qur'an 2:62. "The believers, the Jews, the Christians and the Sabians—all those who believe in God and the last Day and do good—will have their reward with their Lord. No fear for them, nor will they grieve."

7   Qur'an 2:221; 5:5. "As to marriage, you are allowed to marry the chaste from among the believing women and the chaste from among those who have been given the Book before you (are lawful for you)."

8   Qur'an 5:68. "Say, O people of the scripture, you are standing on nothing until you uphold the Torah, the Gospel, and what has been revealed to you from your Lord."

9   Mustafa Akyol, *The Islamic Jesus. How the King of the Jews Became a Prophet of the Muslims* (New York: St. Martin's, 2017), 87.

It's all there.

The Qur'an exonerates Prophet Aaron from the sin of taking any part in the calf-worship.[10]

When prayer was first instituted for Muslims, they faced Jerusalem in prayer, the focus being on the spiritual center of Judaism and Christianity. It was an expression of solidarity and continuity with the People of the Book. Later God instructed the Prophet to change the direction of their prayer in order to face the Kaaba—the house that Abraham built[11]—in order to return to the faith of Abraham.[12] This act unified all monotheistic faiths by reminding Muslims that Prophet Abraham is the prophet of Jews, Christians, and Muslims and we all share a common identity. To this day, Muslims all over the world turn in prayer to face the house that Abraham built.

There are verses in the Qur'an admonishing the Children of Israel for breaking the pledge and worshipping the golden calf, for breaking the Sabbath law, and for the slaying of the prophets. These verses, when quoted out of context, have fomented hatred of the Other.

Just as it distinguishes between the righteous and the unrighteous of Prophet Muhammad's followers—and in order to dispel any such confusion of the superiority of the outer definition of Muslim over non-Muslim— the Qur'an explicitly distinguishes the righteous from the unrighteous of Jews and Christians (and by implication of all religious groups). . . . Indeed, family disputes can be of the worst kind, but let us bear in mind that there is no criticism that the Qur'an has addressed to either Jews or Christians that Jews and Christians have not addressed to themselves or

---

10   Qur'an 20:90–91. "And, indeed, even before [the return of Moses] had Aaron said unto them: "O my people! You are but being tempted to evil by this [idol] – for, behold, your [only] Sustainer is the Most Gracious! Follow me, then, and obey my bidding. But they answered: "By no means shall we cease to worship it until Moses comes back to us!"

11   Qur'an 2:144. "We shall indeed make thee turn in prayer in a direction which will fulfill thy desire. Turn, then, thy face towards the Inviolable House of Worship; and wherever you all may be, turn your faces towards it [in prayer]."

12   Karen Armstrong, *Jerusalem: One City, Three Faiths* (New York: Ballantine Books, 1996), 223.

their tradition. Neither can any Muslim deny that many of these faults are universal . . . and have also existed in the Muslim community.[13]

Scholar Carlos Gourgey has examined this issue in "The Qur'an and the Question of the Jews":

Before addressing the Jews, the Qur'an begins at the beginning, with the story of Adam. It recounts the creation of Adam and his wife, their blessings by God and placement in a beautiful garden, their disobedience and their fall. Then the Qur'an recounts the history of the Jewish people, their disobedience and their fall. After that, the Qur'an calls all believers to faith. . . . There is a strong echo of the Hebrew Prophets in these passages, as they call upon proper care for the poor, the orphan, and the wayfaring stranger. . . . Here the Qur'an is establishing a spiritual history of humanity and calling people to turn to the original Abrahamic faith. . . . Jews are singled out not because they are worse than anyone else, but because their story, preserved in their scriptures, is the human story. . . . By their uncompromising self-criticism and willingness to record their story with all its flaws, the Jews performed a great service to humanity in redirecting us to the proper path. An anti-Semitic interpretation of the Qur'anic passages about the Jews is not consistent with the Qur'an's inclusive statements quoted above. Holy scripture is powerful and must be handled with care. There will always be those who quote it selectively and use it for an incendiary purpose. Individual Muslims may continue to interpret the Qur'an anti-Semitically, just as individual Christians may continue to interpret the New Testament anti-Semitically. But in both cases such interpretations are inconsistent with the overall message. Abrahamic faith moves toward justice and compassion, and it is in the light of that standard that all fundamentalist forms of that faith should be judged.[14]

---

13   Imam Feisal Abdul Rauf, *What's Right with Islam: A New Vision for Muslims and the West* (New York: HarperCollins, 2005), 37.
Qu'ran 49:13. "O' Mankind. Behold, we have created you all out of a male and a female, and have made you into nations and tribes so that you might come to know one another."
14   C. Gourgey, "The Qur'an and the Question of the Jews" (2018), http://www.judeochristianity.org/quran_antisemitism.htm.

Imam Rauf's unifying message sums it up: "Jews and Christians are people with the true religion, the *din-al-fitrah*, strengthened and informed by scripture and prophets. No Muslim may deny this without contradicting the Qur'an."[15]

References to Jews or other groups reflect the conduct of people at a particular point in time and are not meant to vilify an entire faith community for all times to come.

The Prophet Muhammad

Muhammad was a Semite—so, no anti-Semitism there either. He married a Jewish woman, Safiyah and a Christian woman, Mariyah, and set the example of interfaith marriages with People of the Book. No anti-Semitism there. Let us continue: When he performed the Hajj—the pilgrimage to Mecca—he instituted rituals honoring Prophet Abraham. For the next fourteen hundred-plus years up to today, Muslims all over the world have been making the Hajj—more than two million every year—and walk in the footsteps of Abraham. They circumambulate the Kaaba—the house that Abraham built—and commemorate Abraham's sacrifice of the ram. On that day, Muslims worldwide celebrate the holiday of Eid-ul-Adha by sacrificing a lamb or goat to honor Abraham's sacrifice. Why the focus on Abraham? To remind Muslims that we—Muslims, Christians, and Jews—are all children of the same Patriarch. Same roots. Anti-Semitic? Hardly.

When Muhammad migrated to Medina, he entered into a covenant with each of the Jewish tribes living there, offering them protective status and freedom of religion. Referred to as "The Scroll of Medina," the covenant stated that "Muslims and Jews are one nation (ummah), with Muslims having their own religion and Jews having their own religion."

Prophet Muhammad often conferred with rabbis on religious matters. When he observed Jewish tribes fasting on the tenth day of the New Year, Yom Kippur, he asked why and was told Moses fasted on that day to commemorate the day God saved the Children of Israel from the yoke of Pharaoh. The Prophet then fasted on that day in solidarity with the

---

15   Imam Feisal Abdul Rauf, *What's Right with Islam*, 36.

Jews. To this day, Muslims observe this practice of the Prophet and fast on Ashura, the tenth day of our New Year, which also happens to be the anniversary of the assassination of the Prophet's grandson Hussein.

As we were working on this chapter, Walter asked me about an episode in the Prophet Muhammad's life during which a battle with the Jews of Medina resulted in seven hundred Jews being beheaded. In my limited knowledge of Islamic history, while I was aware of tension between Muhammad and some of the Jewish tribes of Medina and the reasons behind it, I was unaware of the violence associated with this episode. I struggled with the dilemma. My love and respect for the Prophet informed me that he would not commit such violence; he was the personification of the Qur'an, which urges us to be compassionate and forgiving. Knowing that this faith-based argument wouldn't hold water with a wider audience, I researched it and came across conflicting accounts. Some biographers of Muhammad confirmed what Walter had related; others disputed it.

Martin Lings and Karen Armstrong relate that when the Banu Qaynuqa—a Jewish tribe that had entered into a solidarity pact with the Prophet Muhammad—broke their covenant and allied with the Quraish, the enemies of Muhammad, in order to oust him, they were exiled.[16] Then the Prophet's army suffered a crushing defeat against the Quraish at the battle of Uhud, and a second Jewish tribe—Bani Nadir—broke the treaty and aligned themselves with the Quraish. They too were exiled.[17] When the Quraish launched yet another attack against the Prophet's army, a third Jewish tribe—Bani Qurayza—broke the treaty and joined the Quraish in a coalition army with the exiled Jewish tribes. The Quraish and the Bani Qurayza tribe were defeated in the Battle of the Trench. The Quraish retreated, and the Prophet's army besieged the Bani Qurayza. Both sides agreed to arbitration. The arbiter, Sa'd ibn Mu'adh, a former ally of the Qurayza and now a Muslim, ruled that the

---

16   Karen Armstrong, *Muhammad. A Biography of the Prophet* (New York: Harper-Collins, 1993), 183–185.
Martin Lings, *Muhammad: His Life Based on Earliest Sources* (Lahore, Pakistan: Ever Green Press, 1983), 161–162.
17   Karen Armstrong, *Muhammad*, 193–194.

tribe had violated the treaty and therefore were charged with treason. As a result, all the seven hundred men were executed (Karen Armstrong)[18], or "according to some accounts more and to others less" (Martin Lings). The women and children were made captive.[19]

That is one version.

I conferred with Imam Rauf.[20] He explained that the Bani Qurayza defected at a critical stage in the war, creating a national security risk, and had the Quraish succeeded, the entire Muslim community would have been wiped out. After the war, the question was, what to do with the tribe? The arbiter, Sa'd ibn Mu'adh, who negotiated the agreement between the Bani Qurayza and the Muslims and who himself died from wounds he sustained in this war, decided that the men should be put to death and the women and children taken as slaves.

Here is what else I learned.

Biographer Omid Safi, director of the Duke Islamic Studies Center at Duke University, reasons: "Virtually every one of the episodes that documents tensions between Muhammad and the Jews is open to some measure of historical suspicion." On the question of whether the first tribe, the Banu Qaynuqa, was actually exiled by the Prophet, Safi questions the veracity of the historical narrative. His source? The Hadith, the main traditions of Muhammad—as preserved in the two most authoritative collections, Bukhari and Muslim—which seem to locate the expulsion of the tribe as taking place after the death of Muhammad.[21]

This revelation stopped me in my tracks. Of course, the question that popped into my mind was exactly what you are thinking. Why attribute the expulsion to Prophet Muhammad? Safi's take: "To give a contentious decision some measure of legitimacy."

Shakes one's confidence in historians.

---

18   Karen Armstrong, *Muhammad*, 207.
19   Martin Lings, *Muhammad: His Life Based on the Earliest Sources*, 221, 231–232.
20   Author of *Moving the Mountain, What's Right with Islam, Islam: A Sacred Law,* and *Defining an Islamic Statehood.*
21   Omid Safi, *Memories of Muhammad: Why the Prophet Matters* (New York: HarperCollins, 2010), 134, 135.

Safi's narrative on the Banu Nadir tribe is consistent with that of Armstrong and Lings. The tribe had attempted to poison the Prophet, and this violation of the treaty resulted in them being banished. But it is the clash with the Jewish tribe of Banu Qurayza that Safi considers "one of the most ambiguous and potentially problematic events":

> *There is a great deal of scholarly debate about the authenticity of what took place, and given the clashes between Arabs and Jews in the twentieth century, this is one instance in which the question of what actually happened is of paramount importance.*[22]

Safi draws attention to a detail I had not yet encountered. After the Banu Qurayza surrendered, they were handed over to the former rabbi of the Jewish tribe of Banu Qaynuqa. Because this tribe had previously been allies of the Aws tribe of Medina, the fate of the Banu Qurayza was entrusted to a leader of the tribe of Aws called Sa'd. Sa'd ruled that they should be dealt with harshly and according to Deuteronomy 20:12; namely, their men would be slaughtered, and their women and children would be made captive.[23] Safi states that if such an episode did take place, it is a reminder of the harsh treatment of the vanquished in an age before the Geneva Conventions and our modern notion of human rights. The contentious episode is used by those who want to point to a fundamental tension between Muslims and Jews; its symbolic power is intended to override the innumerable examples of coexistence. According to Safi, notable scholars have questioned the authenticity of this episode. For one, there are no indications in the Qur'an that Jews and Christians can be dealt with in such a horrific manner (my sentiments were confirmed). Second, if Muhammad had agreed to this harsh treatment, his consent would have set a legal precedent for later Muslims. No such reference exists in the early legal tradition. As a consequence, some of the leading scholars of early Islam, such as Walid N. Arafat, have concluded that the episode was fabricated a few

---

22   Omid Safi, *Memories of Muhammad*, 138.
23   Omid Safi, *Memories of Muhammad*, 138–139.

centuries after the Prophet Muhammad's death, when there was in fact tension between some Muslims and some Jews.

According to Safi:

Perhaps the most measured conclusion has been reached by Gordon Newby, the leading historian of the Jews of Arabia, who says that while there were important tensions between Muhammad and the Jews, Muhammad's under-lying policy was not anti-Jewish, since many Jews remained in Medina and the surrounding regions. The fundamental issue seems instead to be one of political loyalty: Were the Jewish tribes fundamentally loyal to Muhammad's community—and to their own political covenant with that community—or were they allied with the pagans of Mecca?[24]

Mustafa Akyol, an Islamic scholar, author, and senior fellow at Cato Institute, questions the verisimilitude of the Banu Qurayza killing, quoting Indian Muslim scholar Barakat Ahmad, who argues that Muslim historians have failed to take into account the fact that the historical source of the Banu Qurayza affair, the biography of Muhammad by Ibn Ishaq, written during the Abbasid caliphate some 120 to 130 years after the Prophet's death, was strongly influenced by the environment in which it was written, namely Ibn Ishaq's own reaction to Jewish life under the Abbasids. Also referencing scholar Walid N. Arafat, who believes that the story is a later invention, Akyol quotes: "To kill such a large number is diametrically opposed to the Islamic sense of justice and to the basic principles laid down in the Qur'an."[25]

Yet even if the mass execution had really happened, as the mainstream view holds, one should note that it took place not as a commandment of the Qur'an but as a result of the customs of the time. "We cannot judge the treatment of the Qurayza by present-day moral standards,"

24   Omid Safi, *Memories of Muhammad,* 140.
25   Mustafa Akyol, *Islam Without Extremes: A Muslim Case for Liberty* (New York: W.W. Norton, 2013), 57–58.

argues Norman A. Stillman, professor of Judaic history. "Their fate was a bitter one, but not unusual according to the harsh rules of war during that period." Stillman also reminds us that, in the Old Testament (Deut. 20:13–14), the Israelites were enjoined to do the same thing to their enemies: slaughter of adult males and the enslavement of women and children, which was, after all, "Common practice throughout the ancient world." [26]

Akyol puts forth a crucial question:

Are all things that Muhammad did normative for Muslims? Or do some of them reflect not the everlasting rules and principles of Islam but rather those of the Prophet's time and milieu? Some modern Muslim theologians, and even some classical ones, who address the question above have come to the conclusion that the "historical" and the "religious" aspects of Muhammad must be separated. The Prophet brought a message relevant for all ages, in other words, but he lived a life of his own age. [27]

Dr. John Andrew Morrow,[28] scholar of Islamic studies, contends that this entire episode is disputed by both Muslim and non-Muslim historians and cannot be treated as historical fact.

So what *did* happen? *Which* version is correct? Whereas only God knows for sure, the version each of us accepts depends on the direction of our leap of faith.

What Would Jesus Have Done?

This was Walter's question to me after reading what you have just read. Assuming that the incident *did* take place, the punishment was indeed harsh, particularly coming from the Prophet Muhammad who was establishing precedence for all times to come. Would Jesus have countenanced such an act?

---

26 Mustafa Akyol, *Islam Without Extremes*, 58
27 Mustafa Akyol, *Islam Without Extremes*, 58
28 Author of "The Covenants of the Prophet Muhammad with the Jews" (2013); "Islam and the People of the Book: Critical Studies on the Covenants of The Prophet" (2017).

Good question. I pondered, reflected, and went back to the books.

First, a qualifier: I love Jesus and I love the Prophet Muhammad.

Jesus was a preacher. Muhammad was a preacher, a political leader, head of state, commander-in-chief of armies, chief military strategist, chief negotiator for foreign affairs, administrator, promulgator of the law, and a husband, father, and grandfather.

What would Jesus the preacher have done? Jesus taught us to love our enemies, do good to those who hate us, and turn the other cheek.

Karen Armstrong offers this explanation:

> *Jesus was not a head of state, as Muhammad had become after Hudaybiyah [peace treaty with the Quraish]. He [Jesus] did not have to concern himself with the maintenance of public order, a job carried out by the religious establishment that he is said to have reviled and by the officials of Rome. If he had been responsible for social legislation, he would in all probability have been forced to resort to similarly draconian methods because in most pre-modern societies the laws had to be enforced with a severity and brutality which seems horrific to us today.[29]*

In my humble opinion, the execution of the men of the Banu Qurayza tribe, if it actually happened, was not about their being Jewish. It was a consequence of treason in war by a tribe who happened to be of the Jewish faith. Nevertheless, parties who wish to keep Muslims and Jews apart have exploited this event—whether or not it is historically accurate—to stoke hatred. Let's hope that reason prevails, and we can focus instead on eras of coexistence between our two faith communities and on many heartwarming stories of friendship and cooperation.

For example, are our Jewish readers aware that Muslims believe that Prophet Moses mentored Muhammad? Tradition has it that one night Muhammad was taken on a flight to Temple Mount in Jerusalem and then to the heavens for an audience with God. God instructed Muhammad that he and his followers pray fifty times a day. On the way back through the heavens, Muhammad met Prophet Moses, who

---

29   Karen Armstrong, *Muhammad*, 228.

inquired about his visit with God. When Muhammad told him about the fifty prayers, Moses asked him to go back to God and ask for a reduction. So he did. God reduced it to forty. Moses told him to have it reduced further, stressing that his followers would not be able to comply. So back and forth he went until God said that five was his final number. So five it was and five it has been. If it weren't for Moses, guess what! Every Muslim child is told this sweet bedtime story.

Then there are incidents and eras that are exemplary reminders of coexistence. Let's take a look.

Muslims Bring Jews Back to Jerusalem

When the Caliph Umar captured Jerusalem in 638 CE in a bloodless conquest, he asked the Christian patriarch Sophronius to take him to Temple Mount. Umar was horrified to see that the place had become a garbage dump. He had to crawl on his hands and knees to get to the platform. He commenced to use his hands to clean up the debris and litter, and others, seeing him, joined in the cleanup. Once the place was cleaned, he stood there and recited chapters of the Qur'an that mention Prophets David and Solomon and the Temple. He then consulted the group of rabbis who had traveled with him from Tiberias to determine the site of the Temple. Based on their best guess, Umar selected the site for a mosque to be built on a spot away from the temple's location. Umar then invited seventy Jewish families from Tiberias to settle in Jerusalem. Jews had been previously forbidden by Byzantine authorities from living and worshipping freely in the Holy City. Umar assigned the area around the Pool of Siloam to the Jews. They were also allowed to build a synagogue—known as "the Cave"—near Herod's western supporting wall, possibly in the vaults underneath the platform. The Muslim conquest of Jerusalem gave the Jews new hope. The Muslims had not only liberated them from the oppression of Byzantium but had also given Jews the right of permanent residence in their Holy City.[30] Jews, who had been banished by Romans for five hundred years, were able to come back to Jerusalem.

---

30   Karen Armstrong, *Jerusalem: One City, Three Faiths,* 229–233.

When the Christian Crusaders conquered Jerusalem in 1099, they massacred both the Muslim and Jewish communities. After Salahuddin Ayub, the Kurdish general, retook Jerusalem from the Crusaders almost a hundred years later, he invited Jews back to the Holy City.

Jews under Muslim Rule

Historically, Jews fared better under Islamic rule.[31] According to scholars, from the eighth to the tenth century, somewhere between 85 and 90 percent of all Jews lived among Muslims.[32] Until modern times, many Jews considered life under Islamic rule preferable to that of medieval Europe, and often they found safe haven in Muslim lands after being persecuted in Christian ones.

One such place of fruitful cooperation was Muslim-controlled Spain.

From 800 to1200 CE . . . the Cordoba Caliphate ruled much of today's Spain amid a rich flowering of art, culture, philosophy, and science. Many Jewish and Christian artists and intellectuals emigrated to Cordoba during this period to escape the more oppressive regimes that reigned over Europe's Dark and Middle Ages. Great Jewish philosophers such as Maimonides were free to create their historic works within the pluralistic culture of Islam.[33]

Artisans worked in the palaces, synagogues, and mosques. Modern-day visitors may view identical motifs made by the same artists. The very recognizable one is the six-pointed star followed by the eight-pointed star. Hasdai Ibn Shaprut, a Jewish scholar, physician, and diplomat, served as foreign minister in Caliph Abd-ar-Rahman III's reign in Cordoba.

Professor Mehnaz Afridi, director of the Holocaust, Genocide, and Interfaith Center at Manhattan College, a Muslim woman, examines this period critically:

The "golden age" of Jews living under Muslims was not all that golden; Jews and Christians were allowed to participate in their own communities

31 Mark R. Cohen, *Under the Crescent and Cross: The Jews in the Middle Ages* (Princeton, NJ: Princeton University Press, 1994).

32 Omid Safi, *Memories of Muhammad*, 210.

33 Imam Feisal Abdul Rauf, *What's Right with Islam*, 2.

but were also required to pay punitive taxes and live publicly according to the laws of Islam. . . . Between the tenth and twelfth centuries, there was indeed a flourishing of art, architecture, poetry, and language. Major thinkers such as Maimonides, Nachmanides, Moses Ibn Ezra, Solomon Ibn Gabirol, and Judah Halevi could work in an Islamic civilization in Spain. . . . Things changed for Jews in Arab lands, however, with their confinement in the fifteenth century to ghettos or mellahs.[34]

That assessment of the glorious and not-so-glorious history of Muslims and Jews living together in Al-Andalus needs to be understood and acknowledged by both communities.

The Holocaust

During the ethnic cleansing of Muslims in Bosnia in the 1990s, members of the Jewish community in the United States wrote passionate articles protesting the genocide of the Bosnian Muslims by the Serbs, recalling the time when the predominantly Muslim population of neighboring Albania provided shelter to the Jews during the German invasion in 1943. True to the credo of "Never again," the American Jewish Joint Distribution Committee financed the evacuation of both Jews and Muslims from Sarajevo during the siege. "We have strong historical obligations to the Muslim community here, because they accepted us here 500 years ago," said Ivan Ceresnjes, a lawyer and president of the Jewish Center in Sarajevo. "Throughout much of that time, Sarajevo was one of the few places in Europe—perhaps the only one—where Jews lived without a ghetto, freely, and with full rights as citizens."[35]

There are stories to the contrary as well.

After the violence of Judaism's first encounter with Islam, Jews fared better under Islamic rule. Anti-Semitism became prevalent in Arab lands during

---

34   Mehnaz M. Afridi, *Shoah through Muslim Eyes: The Holocaust: History and Literature, Ethics and Philosophy* (Boston: Academic Studies Press, 2016), 187.

35   John F. Burns, "Jews Evacuate 200, Muslims included, in Bosnia," *New York Times,* November 15, 1992, https://www.nytimes.com/1992/11/15/world/jews-evacuate-200-muslims-included-in-bosnia.html.

World War II, with earlier roots in the political actions of the British [in Palestine], and the Balfour Declaration of 1917: "During the 1930s, Britain's commitment to the establishment of a homeland for the Jews in Palestine affirmed in the Balfour Declaration of 1917 came under increasing pressure in the face of Arab opposition to Jewish immigration to Palestine." Violence flared within Palestine in 1929 and most especially in 1936. Why did the Arab world become so seduced by anti-Semitic propaganda? The Nazis understood the importance of their influence on the Arabs/Muslims, and worked to maintain it. The mechanism by which they were able to influence so many Arabs was the growing resentment of the increasing number of Jews migrating to Palestine. Arabs were already resentful of Jews, as they were seen as European enemies and imagined to be more powerful than they were. Shortwave radio broadcasts helped nurture this resentment.[36]

Nazi Germany's Arabic-language propaganda targeted Arabs in colonial lands, exploiting their humiliation and vulnerability. "The assertion the Jews 'have always been' and were in 1941 'enemies of Islam' remained a staple of Nazi radio broadcasts that highlighted the Koran's anti-Jewish passages.[37] . . . The Nazi regime presented itself both as a supporter of Arab anti-imperialism aimed at British and as a friend to the Arabs and Muslims, based on common values and a common hatred of the Jews and Zionism."[38]

Fascist Italy broadcast Arabic programs from 1934 to1943. In August 1941, a US Office of War Information report estimated that there were about 90,000 shortwave radios in the region, including in Aden, Egypt, Iraq, Palestine, Syria, Saudi Arabia, Algeria, and Morocco.[39] The history of Muslim-Jewish coexistence became forgotten history.

In that awful landscape, there are emerging stories of Muslims as rescuers of Jews in Albania, Morocco, Turkey, Iran, and such major cities as Kosovo, Sarajevo, and Tangiers. Many Muslims who risked their lives

---

36 Mehnaz M. Afridi, *Shoah through Muslim Eyes*, 184.
37 Mehnaz M. Afridi, *Shoah through Muslim Eyes*, 186.
38 Mehnaz M. Afridi, *Shoah through Muslim Eyes*, 192.
39 Mehnaz M. Afridi, *Shoah through Muslim Eyes*, 184–185.

to rescue Jews did so based on Islamic principles of social justice at a time when religion was being persecuted, whether Islam or Judaism. Albania rescued all of its Jewish citizens during the Holocaust as well as Jews from other countries who took refuge there. Albania was 70 percent Muslim and 30 percent Christian. In Norman H. Gershman's *Besa: Muslims Who Saved Jews during World War II*, there are many narratives of Albanian Muslims who saved Jews.

Morocco was another example. In 1940, Morocco was ruled by the French Vichy government, which under the influence of their German conquerors, decreed that Moroccan Jews should be gathered and held in prison camps.

Sultan Muhammad V of Morocco issued an order that he would not implement certain anti-Semitic laws on his citizens. He argued that, according to Islam, one cannot base one's laws on race, and the Vichy government declared people Jewish if their parents were Jewish, regardless of whether they professed to be Jewish. The Sultan asked for two amendments: first that the Jews in Morocco become defined by religious choice, not ethnicity; and second, that the Jewish institutions, such as schools and communal Jewish life, not be constrained.[40]

Ulkumen Selahattin, who was the Turkish consul general on the island of Rhodes, helped about fifty Jews by asserting that they were still Turkish nationals. Since Turkey was a neutral country, the Germans left these Jews unharmed.[41]

The book *In the Lion's Shadow: The Iranian Schindler and His Homeland in the Second World War* discusses the life of a junior Iranian diplomat named Abdol Hossein Sardari. "He saved hundreds of Iranian Jewish families by challenging the Third Reich's racial laws, arguing that Iranian Jews were not Semites but from Aryan stock, and asserted that while their religion was based on the teachings of Moses, they were not racially Jewish."[42]

---

40 Mehnaz M. Afridi. *Shoah through Muslim Eyes*, 198.
41 Mehnaz M. Afridi. *Shoah through Muslim Eyes*, 204.
42 Mehnaz M. Afridi. *Shoah through Muslim Eyes*, 205.

The last example I share is that of a Muslim woman, Noor Inayat Khan. "[Khan] was a wartime British secret agent of Indian descent who was the first female radio operator sent into Nazi-occupied France by the Special Operations Executive (SOE). She was arrested and eventually executed by the Gestapo."[43]

The names of seventy Muslims are among the more than 27,000—the vast majority in European countries conquered by the Nazis—listed by Yad Vashem, Israel's official memorial to victims of the Holocaust, as the "Righteous Among the Nations," heroic people who risked their lives and those of their loved ones in order to shelter or protect Jews during Nazi Germany's reign of terror.[44] Ulkumen Selahattin is among those.

Walter:

I want to start my portion of this chapter by affirming how much I appreciate the thrust of what Sabeeha has written above, elucidating the numerous ways in which Islam was accepting and respectful of Jews and Judaism during its formative period and remains so today. She mentions among other things how Islam praised the People of the Book (Jews and Christians), affirmed the divinity of the Torah, God's covenant with the Jews, and Islam's adoption of the Patriarchs, Moses, King David, and Solomon and many of the Old Testament prophets as prophets of Islam as well. She points out how the Prophet Muhammad affirmed Jews and Christians are worthy of going to heaven if they live righteous lives according to their own understanding without becoming Muslims; that Islam allowed marriage between Muslims and People of the Book.

According to authoritative sources, Muhammad forgave a Jewish woman, Zaynab bint Al-Harith, after she attempted to poison him out of anger that he had made war on her people, the Jews of Khaybar. As narrated by Alfred Guillaume, a mid-twentieth-century British Arabist in his *Life of Mohammad; A Translation of ibn Ishaq's Sirat Rasul Allah* (an

---

43   Mehnaz M. Afridi, *Shoah through Muslim Eyes*, 206.
44   Tom Bousfield and Catrin Nye, "The Muslims Who Saved Jews from the Holocaust," BBC Asian Network, https://www.bbc.com/news/uk-england-london-22176928.

eighth-century biography of the Prophet), Zaynab tried to kill the Prophet by serving him a meal of poisoned lamb. Muhammad survived after chewing a morsel of meat, which he immediately spat out instead of swallowing, but Bishar ibn-al-Bara, a companion who shared the feast with Muhammad, died from eating the lamb.

When Muhammad confronted Zaynab, she readily confessed her crime, telling him; "You know what you have done to my people. I said to myself, if he is a king, I shall ease myself of him, and if he is a prophet, he shall be informed (of what I have done). So the apostle let her off."[45] Guillaume goes on to cite Ibn Ishaq in asserting that four years later the Prophet would die prematurely from the delayed effect of having chewed the poison meat, informing the Umm Bishar, the mother of his late friend, shortly before his own death, "I am now feeling a deadly pain from the food that I ate with your son at Khaybar."[46]

As Reuven Firestone, a Jewish scholar of Islam and pioneer in Muslim-Jewish relations, pointed out in his book *An Introduction to Islam for Jews*, "According to the tradition, it was a Jew who was responsible for the death of God's last and most beloved prophet."[47] Indeed, imagine the impact if Muslims had blamed the Jews as a people for the attempted killing of the Prophet Muhammad by Zaynab, and for his eventual death. Actually, we don't have to imagine how that would have impacted Jews living in the Muslim world. We need only look at the horrific situation of Jews in various Christian lands where they were denounced as Christ-killers and suffered systematic persecution, including murderous pogroms, for nearly two thousand years. It is telling that nothing remotely like that occurred in the Islamic world.

Sabeeha also shared how the Muslim Caliphate encouraged Jews to return to Jerusalem and rebuild Jewish life in the Holy City after the Muslims conquered it from the Byzantines in 636 CE and points out that for the most part, Muslims allowed Jews to live in peace, if not

---

45 Alfred Guillaume, *Life of Mohammad; A Translation of ibn Ishaq's Sirat Rasul Allah* (Oxford University Press, 1955), 516.

46 Alfred Guillaume, *Life of Mohammad*, 516.

47 Reuven Firestone, *An Introduction to Islam for Jews* (Philadelphia: The Jewish Publication Society, 2008), 41.

equality, and to practice their faith unhindered in Islamic lands stretching from Spain to Samarkand in Central Asia—again in vivid contrast to the situation of the Jews in Christian Europe. Sabeeha's summation moved my thinking in a direction more favorable toward Islam as a religion of peace and brotherhood and reminded me how much of a reformer Muhammad was in the context of the time and place he lived. The willingness of Muhammad and the Islamic leaders who followed him to allow the People of the Book to go on practicing their faiths was a huge step forward from the way both the Jews and Christians treated adherents of rival religions.

Yet I have not been totally put at ease. Years ago, I read a set of Qur'anic passages that had left me with the feeling of a pervasive hostility for the Jews in the core document of Islam. A recent rereading did not change my previous perception, despite all of the reassuring counterevidence put forward by Sabeeha. For example, in the translation of the Qur'an into English that is widely considered to be the most accurate and least hostile to the Jews of any modern-day translations—by a twentieth-century Jewish convert to Islam named Muhammad Asad—there are nevertheless plenty of verses that feel quite hostile to even the most tolerant of Jewish ears—my own. These include sections in which the Jews are chastised for a wide variety of wrongdoing, including killing their prophets (5:70), worshipping other gods (9:30–31), breaking their covenant (2:83), claiming that heaven is exclusively for the Jews (2:94), slandering God (4:50), spreading corruption (5:64), mocking Islam or mocking the faith of Muslims (5:58), and being ungrateful to God (45:16–17).

For example, in Qur'an 2:83–85, God notes that the Jews made a "solemn pledge" to uphold a series of promises, including exclusively the God of Israel; giving support to the poor and orphans, being constant in prayer and charity, and not shedding each other's blood. Nevertheless, God upbraids the Jews: "Save for a few of you, you turned away, for you are obstinate folk. . . . And lo, We accepted your solemn pledge that you would not shed one another's blood, and would not drive one another from your homelands. . . . And yet it is you who slay one another and drive some of your own people from their homelands."

God then queries the Jews: "Do you then believe in some parts of the divine writ and deny the truths of other parts?" Noting that He is "not unmindful of what you do," God promises them "ignominy in the life of this world and on the day of Resurrection commitment to the most grievous suffering."

In Qur'an 2:89, God seems to scorn the Jews for their rejection of the new faith brought forth by the Prophet Muhammad, stating, "Whenever there came onto them a (new) revelation from God, confirming the truth already in their possession . . . they would deny it." God says it was "vile . . . false pride."

Qur'an 5:64–66 states: "The Jews say, 'God's hands are shackled.' (In fact) it is their own hands that are shackled and rejected (by God)." Blaming both the Jews and the Christians for rejecting the Prophet Muhammad, the Qur'an specifies, "We have cast enmity and hatred among the followers of the Bible (to last) until Resurrection Day; every time they light the fires of war, God extinguishes them. . . . If the followers of the Bible would but attain to (true) faith and God consciousness, we should indeed efface their (previous) bad deeds, and indeed bring them into the gardens of bliss . . . and if they would but truly observe the Torah and Gospel and all (the revelation) that was bestowed from on high upon them by their Sustainer, they would indeed partake of all the blessings of heaven and earth. Some of them do pursue a right course; but as for most of them—vile indeed is what they do."

I have expressed my consternation and sense of hurt about these quotations over the years to an assortment of imams and lay Muslims and invariably have been told that the Qur'an is only repeating condemnations of the Children of Israel that appear in the Torah for betraying God and the Covenant that Moses brought down from Mt. Sinai and the Israelites solemnly agreed to.

For example, they point to the Book of Jeremiah in the Torah, in which that Prophet predicts the coming overthrow of the Kingdom of Judea and the destruction of the First Temple in 586 BCE by King Nebuchadnezzar of Babylon because the Jews had abandoned Hashem and worshipped the Canaanite and Phoenician deity Ba'al, even sacrificing their own children to that God. In the Book of Jeremiah, God, speaking through the Prophet, accuses his Chosen People of all manners of sins and iniquities and seems to revel in the downfall of his people and their loss of independence.

"Is Israel a bondsman? Is he a home-grown slave? Then why is he given over to plunder? Lions have roared over him, have raised their cries. They have laid his land a waste, his cities desolate, without inhabitants. . . . See that is the price you have paid for forsaking the LORD your God. While He led you in the way" (Jeremiah 2:14–17)

So, indeed, why should the Qur'an be labeled anti-Jewish for condemning the Children of Israel for disobeying or abandoning God, when the Torah castigates the Israelites for the same transgressions? Part of the explanation lies in the well-known psychological phenomenon in which individuals, peoples, and religions allow themselves the luxury of self-criticism and self-parody without extending to people from outside their community the same right to criticize them. We saw a related phenomenon in the contretemps over Representative Ilhan Omar of Minnesota, who was accused of anti-Semitism for having complained that pro-Israeli lobbying groups like AIPAC use money and power to pressure members of Congress to support US aid to Israel. Many American Jews have acknowledged this reality, and some have leveled this same criticism for years, but if a Muslim American congresswoman says it is "all about the Benjamins" and expresses resistance to being pressured to show allegiance to Israel, it is characterized as anti-Semitism—unfairly, I believe.

Yet how to deal with the Qur'an's harsh criticism of the Jews and the Christians for rejecting the Prophet Muhammad and with the complicated role played by the Jewish tribes of Arabia during the early days of Islam? I personally favor the explanation put forward by Firestone, who essentially argues that a clash was inevitable once the Jews of Arabia rejected the dynamic new faith of Muhammad. According to Firestone:

The Jews could not validate Muhammad's prophethood because they observed him reciting revelation that, while certainly reminiscent of and even parallel in many cases to their own scriptures, did not conform to the revelations of the Hebrew Bible. . . . From the honest and authentic standpoint of the Jews, therefore, Muhammad was a false prophet who could not be accepted or even trusted. But from the honest and authentic perspectives of Muhammad and his followers, who absolutely believed in his status as Prophet, the Jewish rejection was tantamount to the rejection of God. . . . Given the stature of the Jews, rejection was serious, endangering the success of the whole emerging religious movement.[48]

Firestone adds:

The Jews did not simply oppose Muhammad, but seem to have campaigned against him actively. This notion is very upsetting to Muslims, who see no reason for even a passive rejection of the truth of Muhammad's mission. Jews however became incensed at the accusation that their Jewish brethren might have tried to destroy Muhammad and his new community. . . . Both communities engaged in behaviors that would be unacceptable in an enlightened democratically governed society that supported equal rights and privileges for all religious communities. But the seventh century Medina was not such a place.[49]

In short, while various Jewish tribes got involved in pagan efforts to crush the dynamic new Islamic movement, at heart it was a battle of two monotheisms with overlapping source stories and shared beliefs, of which only one could emerge victorious.

In that respect, the situation in Mecca and Medina in the seventh century bears striking parallels to the other "elephant" Sabeeha and I discussed in the preceding chapter: the struggle for Palestine in the modern era, an existential battle between two rights, two just claims to the same small piece of land which, once it got underway, was bound to lead to bloodshed. Muhammad's seventh-century followers could not divine why the Jews did not simply accept what to them was the self-evident truth of his prophecies and merge with the new faith community, which, after all, upheld the Torah and the Hebrew prophets. Similarly, many Zionist pioneers could not divine why the Palestinian Arabs did not

---

48 Reuven Firestone, *An Introduction to Islam for Jews*, 35.
49 Reuven Firestone, *An Introduction to Islam for Jews*, 36.

accept as just and proper what the Jews believe was the preordained return to *their* ancestral homeland after two millennia of persecution in exile and simply move over to accommodate them. In both cases, each side was responding to its own powerful narrative and was not willing to listen to the considerable truth on the other side. Both situations evolved into zero-sum games where one side had to win and the other lose. This largely explains the mainly negative Jewish response to the Prophet Muhammad and the emergence of Islam.

Is the Torah Genocidal?

The fact is that the Torah contains a shocking number of parables that clearly appear to condone—even encourage—mass murder. I am hardly alone in being troubled by this. For two thousand years, rabbis and scholars have sought to temper and explain these passages in ways that make them morally palatable.

Each week, synagogues across the world read a specific section from the Torah (the Five Books of Moses). In Hebrew, this is called *Parashat HaShavua*, which means "portion of the week." When my son, Gene, had his bar mitzvah in 1999, the Torah portion assigned to him to recite and interpret for those assembled was a particularly disturbing one. The story of Pinchas, which is told in Numbers: 25–26, specifies that God was angry with the Children of Israel, then in the middle of their forty-year journey from slavery to freedom across the Sinai Desert and the plains of Edom to the Promised Land. The Israelites settled for a time in Moab, the land of the Midianites, in what is today southern Jordan, where an evil prophet named Balaam convinced Balak, the Midianite king, to influence the Israelites to forget their Covenant with God and to commit sin by enticing them with sexual immorality. Indeed, Israelite men soon began having sexual relations with Midianite women as well as prostrating themselves before the Midianites' pagan gods. Both of these acts deeply pained Moses, then aging and nearing the end of his strength, but he did nothing to stop it, perhaps feeling constrained to punish his fellow Jewish men for consorting with *shiksas* (non-Jewish women) when he himself had earlier married a Midianite woman named Zipporah. So Hashem, a famously jealous God, stepped in to restore order, unleashing a plague against the Israelites that the Torah tells us took 24,000 lives.

God might have continued this wanton punishment until he had killed off his entire Chosen People and perhaps started anew by anointing another one if a Jewish zealot named Pinchas hadn't stepped in and taken matters into his own hands. Incensed after seeing a Jew named Zimri of the tribe of Simeon bring his Midianite lover, Cozbi, to a conclave of the Children of Israel led by Moses himself and then retire to his tent to have sex with her, Pinchas followed the couple into the tent and pierced them with his spear, killing both. After this act, the blatant cohabitating of Jew with gentile ended abruptly and God halted his plague as well.

According to the account, some among the Hebrews accused Pinchas of committing murder and wanted to punish him, but God put a quick stop to such efforts, telling Moses to inform the populace that "Pinchas, son of Elazar, son of Aaron the Priest, turned my wrath from upon the Children of Israel, when He zealously avenged Me among them, so I did not consume the Children of Israel in my vengeance. Therefore, I say, 'Behold! I give Him my covenant of Peace. And it shall be for him and his offspring after him a covenant of eternal priesthood, because he took vengeance for his God and he atoned for the Children of Israel.'"

Gene was flummoxed by this parable, stunned that a righteous and almighty God would have rewarded Pinchas for murdering two people. Rabbi Avi Weiss, who tutored my son, explained that Pinchas had actually saved countless lives by tempering God's wrath. Indeed, the rabbi said, through his violent act, Pinchas had helped to save the Jewish people, awakening them to the error of their ways in failing to maintain themselves as a people apart, which God had commanded them to be.

Gene respectfully heard Rabbi Weiss out but told me later that Pinchas's behavior seemed crazy to him, a child on the cusp of adolescence growing up in Queens, New York, with friends from a wide assortment of religious and ethnic backgrounds. In his commentary at the bar mitzvah, Gene said he couldn't understand or justify how God could have praised Pinchas for his act or blessed him and his descendants. For thirteen-year-old Gene Ruby, maintaining Jewish peoplehood in the face of inexorable assimilation was not an issue of concern, but it has consumed the attention of Jewish scholars from Pinchas's day to our own. Even a modern-day rabbinical figure like the late Rabbi Jonathan Sacks, former chief rabbi of the United Kingdom, who is highly respected in liberal Jewish and interfaith circles, provisionally praised Pinchas's act in a 2012 essay entitled "Pinchas—The Zealot," comparing Pinchas with Elijah the Prophet, who overmatched the priests of Ba'al in a conjuring contest and then had them all killed.

According to Sacks, "There can be no doubt that Pinchas and Elijah were religious heroes. They stepped into the breach at a time when the nation was facing religious and moral crisis and palpable Divine anger. They acted while everyone else, at best, watched. They risked their lives by so doing. There can be little doubt that the mob might have turned against them and attacked them. . . . Both men acted for the sake of God and the religious welfare of the nation."[50]

Yet Sacks, like Gene Ruby, was uncomfortable with the moral implications of God's embrace of Pinchas as well as of Elijah. Sacks writes,

Their treatment in both the written and oral Torah is deeply ambivalent. God gives Pinchas "my covenant of peace," meaning that he will never again have to act the part of a zealot. Indeed, in Judaism, the shedding of human blood is incompatible with service at the Sanctuary (King David was forbidden to build the Temple for this reason: see I Chronicles 22:8, 28:3). As for Elijah, he was implicitly rebuked by God in one of the great scenes of the Bible. Standing at Horeb, God shows him a whirlwind, an earthquake, and a fire, but God is not in any of these. Then He comes to Elijah in a "still, small voice" (1 Kings 19). He then asks Elijah, for the second time, 'What are you doing here?' and Elijah replies in exactly the same words as he had used before: "I have been very zealous for the LORD God Almighty." He has not understood that God has been trying to tell him that He is not to be found in violent confrontation, but in

---

50 Jonathan Sacks. "Pinchas—The Zealot." *RabbiSacks.org.* July 9, 2012, https://rabbisacks.org/covenant-conversation-5772-pinchas-the-zealot/.

gentleness and the word softly spoken. Pinchas and Elijah are, in other words, both gently rebuked by God.[51]

Perhaps so, but in other sections of the Torah, it is God himself who commands the Children of Israel to slaughter the inhabitants of cities that have the temerity to oppose their takeover of the Land of Israel. For example, in Deuteronomy 20:16–17, He urges them to offer such cities a chance to surrender peacefully, but if they refuse, "You shall smite all the males by the blade of the sword. Only the women, the small children, the animals and all that will be in the city—all its booty—may you plunder for yourselves, you shall eat the booty of your enemies, which Hashem, your God, gave you." Faithful to Hashem, Joshua, the leader who led the Hebrews in their conquest of the Holy Land, mandated to his army before their advance on the city of Jericho in Joshua 6:17, 21 that they should execute the entire population of Jericho, stipulating that "Only Rahab shall live—she and all who are with her in her house—because she hid the emissaries we sent." After knocking down the walls of Jericho with repeated blasts of the shofar, Joshua's conquering army faithfully fulfilled that mandate and "destroyed everything that was in the city—man and woman, youth and elder, ox and sheep and ass—by the edge of the sword."

These commands to his people reached genocidal proportions in the treatment God stipulated the Children of Israel should mete out to the Amalekites, a tribe said to have treacherously attacked the Hebrews from behind as they moved along their path to the Land of Israel. In Samuel 15:2–3 it is written: "Thus said the Lord of Hosts, 'I have noted what Amalek did to Israel in opposing them on the way when they came up out of Egypt. Now go and strike Amalek and devote to destruction all that they have. Do not spare them but kill both man and woman and infant; ox and sheep, camel and donkey.'" In Deuteronomy 25:19, God commands, "You shall blot out the memory of Amalek from under heaven; you shall not forget."

So, is the Torah genocidal and is Judaism a genocidal faith? No, because while the Torah, the history of the Jewish people during the first

---

51 Jonathan Sacks, "Pinchas—The Zealot."

1,500 or so years of their existence, indeed contains genocidal moments and is characteristic, like the Qur'an, of the harsh ancient Middle Eastern world in which both were conceived, it contains many more moments of uplift and inspiration, law giving, community building, and acts of love and self-sacrifice. Even more fundamentally, the Torah is not the operating guide for how Jews are expected to behave. Later books like the Mishnah and Talmud serve that purpose.

As Rabbi Marc Schneier writes in *Sons of Abraham*, his book with Imam Shamsi Ali, "Specifically, in Judaism, we do not take the Written Law (the Torah/Old Testament) in literal fashion. Rather, in the interpretation and implementation of Jewish law, the Written Law is secondary to the Oral Law, which is fleshed out in the Mishnah, Talmud, and the works of the great rabbanim (rabbis) and Torah sages who came later. Indeed . . . it is an outright transgression, an actual sin, to read these sacred texts literally, without delving into the oral commentary that helps to explain and interpret them."[52]

In other words, while Torah, the Written Law, is the heart of Judaism during its formative period—and the only period of Jewish self-government until the advent of modern-day Israel—it is the Oral Law that is the basis of Judaism as it evolved after the defeat and dispersal of the Jews by the Romans in the first and second centuries CE. It is also the case that the whole process of interpretation and reinterpretation is the essence of the Oral Law and gives Judaism its intellectual and spiritual verve. It allows Jews today to coexist relatively comfortably with a rigorous source document that reflects the stern morality that buttressed and inspired a small tribe fighting for survival in the harsh Middle East milieu of 3,000 years ago.

The return of the Jewish people to their homeland and the reestablishment of Jewish sovereignty through the State of Israel has brought us back to a similarly harsh milieu and in the process has resuscitated some of the either-or thinking and actions that took place during the first Jewish conquest of the Land. Yet, at the same time, the international

---

52 Rabbi Marc Schneier and Imam Shamsi Ali, *Sons of Abraham* (Boston: Beacon Press, 2013), 100–101.

Judaism that developed over two thousand years persists. During that period, when the Jews were stateless and vulnerable, they also became cosmopolitan and multitextured and were influenced by various enlightenments, both internal and external. It was in the context of international Judaism that the story of the Amalekites or Amalek, as the nation is collectively referred to in the Torah and later Jewish writings, has been interpreted and reinterpreted over many centuries.

The greatest Jewish scholar and philosopher of the medieval period, Moshe ben Maimon, also known as Maimonides, left the most indelible impression in his interpretation of the Amalek story. Maimonides writes that even though God stipulated the Jewish people must fight against the descendants of Amalek until the end of time, in reality the line of Amalek and the others disappeared centuries before his own time. Therefore, Maimonides argued, it would be morally wrong to kill any people on the off chance they might be descendants of the Amalekites. Also, Maimonides notes, the Jews are not allowed to launch war on any nation—including Amalek and other Canaanite tribes proscribed as eternal enemies of the Jews—unless we first offer them the chance to accept the seven Noahide laws, which the Talmud maintains the Jews should offer all gentile nations that are ready to live according to proper ethical stipulations. Maimonides proposes what might be identified in Islam as an internal jihad: to wipe out Amalek-like behavior (i.e., the evil inclination) from the world, including in our own behavior.

Maimonides spent most of his life in the then Muslim-controlled Spanish city of Cordoba at the end of a period in which Jews and Christians were treated with great respect and contributed mightily to the culture of the Spanish Convivencia. He later moved to Cairo and became physician to the Sultan Saladin. About the Muslims of his time—whom he referred to as Ishmaelites—he wrote that they could not be considered descendants of Amalek since "The Ishmaelites are not at all idolaters. [Idolatry] has long been severed from their minds and hearts and they attribute to God a proper unity." Despite Maimonides's towering stature, there persists a Jewish tradition to identify enemies of the Jewish people as descendants of Amalek. This thinking is exhibited by modern day zealots among Jewish settlers, who often identify the Palestinians as descendants of Amalek. One settler widely believed to have been moved by this false identification to carry out an act of mass murder was Baruch Goldstein. In 1994, Goldstein, a doctor born in Brooklyn and living in Kiryat Arba, a settlement adjoining Hebron, gunned down twenty-nine Palestinian Muslims in prayer in the Cave of the Patriarchs, sacred to Jews and Muslims alike, shortly after hearing the recitation of the portion of the Torah calling for the obliteration of Amalek.[53]

Goldstein was killed by Muslim worshippers in a desperate struggle that ensued after he had opened fire and shot dead many of their compatriots. He is venerated by many in the settler community today, who celebrate his murderous act as a *kiddush hashem* (sanctification of the divine name). The legend on his tombstone in Kiryat Arba "Here lies the saint Dr. Baruch Kappel Goldstein, blessed be the memory of the righteous and holy man, may the Lord avenge his blood, who devoted his soul to the Jews, Jewish religion, and Jewish land. His hands are innocent, and his heart is pure. He was killed as a martyr of God on the 14th of Adar, Purim, in the year 5754."[54]

To be honest, there are mixed messages and recriminations between our peoples even in the precept *If you save one life*, which, despite our presentation in chapter 3, is actually far from being all hearts and flowers. On the Jewish side, there has been an internal debate since the days of the Talmud as to whether the injunction about the sacredness of every life applies to the life of every human being regardless of background or only to *Jewish* lives. Depending on the source, the precept can be read as written above or in the following form: *Whoever destroys a soul [of Israel], it is considered as if he destroyed an entire world. And whoever saves a life of Israel, it is considered as if he saved an entire world.*

53 Avram Mlotek and Jon Leener, *Amalek, Kahanism, and the Fight for the Jewish Soul*, 2019. https://jewishweek.timesofisrael.com/amalek-kahanism-and-the-fight-for-the-jewish-soul/.

54 Martin Jaffee, *The Return of Amalek: The Politics of Apocalypse and Contemporary Orthodox Jewry.* 2011. https://www.researchgate.net/publication/236787670_The_Return_of_Amalek_The_Politics_of_Apocalypse_and_Contemporary_Orthodox_Jewry.

On the other hand, the full text of the Qur'anic sura appears to accuse the biblical Children of Israel of having violated this very precept to protect every human life. "Because of that, We decreed upon the Children of Israel that whoever kills a soul unless for a soul or for corruption [done] in the land—it is as if he had slain mankind entirely. And whoever saves one—it is as if he had saved mankind entirely. And our messengers had certainly come to them with clear proofs. Then indeed many of them, [even] after that, throughout the land, were transgressors" (Qur'an 5:32).

Is Judaism Anti-Islamic?

How does the Amalek story pertain to the relationship of modern-day Jews to Islam? Is Judaism anti-Islamic? Islam did not exist during the long biblical period of Judaism. The new religion came into being when the Jews were already dispersed around the ancient world, including in Arabia. Yet many modern-day Jews still resent the treatment of the Jews of Mecca and Medina by Muhammad and believe the Qur'an is anti-Jewish. And as we saw, some in the modern-day settler community view Palestinians (Muslims and Christians alike) as present-day descendants of Amalek so as to justify persecution and murder. I consider my fellow Jews who think this way to be morally wrong, cruel, and sadistic in their treatment of Palestinians. Yet I recognize that they believe themselves to be acting out of love for the land of Israel and continuing the holy work of Pinchas and Joshua. They are the modern-day zealots, very much the Jewish equivalent of the Muslim extremists who eschew mainstream Islamic fatwas forbidding the use of violence and terrorism against innocent civilians to attain political goals.

Clearly, zealots among both Jews and Muslims can cite, and twist, difficult passages in our core texts in such a way as to justify their murderous behavior toward the Other. They are part of a wide spectrum of extremists including Christians, Hindus, and Buddhists and all manner of ultranationalists whose fear and loathing of the Other allows them to commit acts of mass murder visited on Jews at prayer in Pittsburgh in October 2018, Muslims at prayer in Christchurch, New Zealand, in March 2019, and Christians in prayer in Sri Lanka in April 2019.

The good news is that centuries of Jewish and Muslim commentary on the difficult passages have created mainstream perspectives in both faith traditions that abjure the use of violence against innocent civilians to achieve political or religious goals. Thankfully, we live in a very different world today than twelfth-century BCE Palestine or seventh-century CE Arabia. Today, in an interdependent world, all of the great religions acknowledge the legitimacy of the others and foster dialogue.

Sabeeha and Walter:

Not Guilty

Our opinion: Islam and Judaism—not guilty of the charges.

Having affirmed that, we believe we have many years of struggle ahead of us to overcome the not-insubstantial forces in both communities who believe and act otherwise. These extremists believe they are receiving affirmation for their behavior from mainstream figures like Israel prime minister Benjamin Netanyahu, who affirmed recently, "Israel is not a state of all its citizens. . . . According to the basic nationality law we passed, Israel is the nation-state of the Jewish people—and only it." It is widely reported that Saudi Arabia continues to export a radical brand of Islam filled with anti-Jewish and anti-Christian calumnies to Muslim communities around the world, making the adherents vulnerable to recruitment by extremist groups.

Jewish and Muslim zealots may anchor their behaviors in our sacred texts, but they do so in a stunted and reactionary manner that does not take into account the many centuries of subsequent interpretation or the millenarian beliefs expressed in both the Torah and the Qur'an for a world of justice and peace, of *islah* and *tikkun olam*, in which the full dignity of every human being is respected and cherished. We believe that in the battle of ideas, Jews and Muslims will ultimately embrace the humane and loving aspects of our respective faiths and leave extremists, who claim that their faith has a monopoly on truth and morality, behind in the distant past. Ultimately, as millennia of history bear out, Jews and Muslims are better than that.

Can we overcome the two elephants in the room—the Israeli-Palestinian conflict, and the religious conflicts created during our entwined beginnings? Can we build a sustainable modern-day alliance in which Muslim–Jewish and interfaith relations cease to be a zero-sum game in which one religion or the other must submit to the will of the other? *Yes, we can.* We believe Jews and Muslims can keep our footing amid tricky undercurrents created by ancient and modern conflicts while embracing each other as friends and allies.

Sabeeha:

An Anecdote of Hope

We close with an anecdote of hope. At an interfaith panel discussion at the Marble Collegiate Church in New York City, a gentleman approached me. He candidly said that he had serious issues with Islam when it came to the negative portrayal of Jews in the Qur'an. Khalid and I invited him and his wife for a cup of coffee in our apartment, and we talked. This gentleman had studied the Qur'an, the Hadith (sayings of the Prophet Muhammad), the biography of Muhammad, and other writings. Seeing how learned he was, his yearning to study and explore, we offered him our favorite translation of the Qur'an, *Message of the Quran* by Mohammad Asad. I could tell that he was touched, particularly when he told me that he would study the Qur'an "through your eyes." He kept his word. The Qur'an opened itself to him, revealing to his inquiring and sincere mind the answers to his thoughtful questions. Every week we get an update—the equivalent of a book report—on the jewels he has discovered in his readings. We continue to meet and allow ourselves to be challenged by his curiosity, expanding our horizons. He opened his mind and his heart with a quest to search for answers. That is what it takes—an open and inquiring mind.

Part 4

HEALING OUR PAST
AND CLAIMING
OUR FUTURE

CHAPTER 14

PUTTING SARAH AND HAGAR'S CONFLICT TO REST

Is that really where it all started?

Walter: The Torah makes clear that Sarah became jealous of Hagar and concerned that Ishmael, the first-born son, would inherit, not Isaac, and pressured Abraham to send her away. The account in Genesis 21:14 says, "Abraham awoke early in the morning, took bread and a skin of water and gave them to Hagar. He placed them on her shoulder along with the boy and sent her off. She departed and strayed in the desert of Beersheba." However, God steps in and ensures that Hagar and Ishmael survive and that Ishmael ultimately becomes the father of a great nation. God promises Isaac the land of Israel, and at least in the short term, Ishmael is pushed off to the side—to the desert of Paran on the border of Egypt. If I were a Muslim reading all of this, it would make me mad.

Sabeeha: We have a different narrative. The stories we were told growing up in Pakistan did not include the Sarah/Hagar conflict. We knew that Abraham had two wives, Sarah and Hagar. Hagar bore the first child, Ishmael, and Sarah later gave birth to Isaac. One day, when Hagar was in the desert with baby Ishmael, the baby started crying with thirst. Hagar went looking for water, running in between *Safa* and *Marwa*—two hills—and as the baby kicked in the sand, a spring of water suddenly gushed forth. That spring, called *Zam Zam*, flows to this day. Over time a city flourished around the spring, the city where Ishmael grew up, the city of Mecca in Saudi Arabia. Years later, Abraham came to visit Ishmael, now a young man. Together they built a cubic structure—the Kaaba—and dedicated it to the one God. It was here that God called upon Abraham to sacrifice his son Ishmael—a command later rescinded. God promised to make Isaac and Ishmael leaders of great nations. Prophet Muhammad is a descendant of Ishmael. That is our narrative.

We were not told about the jealousy between Sarah and Hagar, or that Sarah pressured Abraham to send Hagar away. I started hearing this version only years after I came to the US, when I got involved in interfaith discussions. Now that you have asked the question, I did some research and found in the Hadith that God had commanded Abraham to take Hagar and Ishmael into the desert and leave them there, and Hagar accepted that circumstance as God's will. I have always believed that Sarah, Hagar, and Abraham are to be revered. In our five daily prayers, Muslims pray for the progeny of Abraham, which includes Jews and Christians. We don't see a Sarah/Hagar conflict. In fact, Khalid and I offered the *Fatiha* prayer for Sarah when we visited the Tomb of the Patriarchs in Hebron. Our friend Dr. Faroque Khan reminded me that Sarah is a popular name in the Muslim world; his niece is named Sarah, as is Khalid's grandniece.

Walter: The Torah states that Abraham sent Hagar and Ishmael out into the desert of Beersheba. How then did Hagar end up in Mecca, a thousand miles away, according to Muslim tradition? I respect the right of Muslims to believe that, but I feel strongly about this seemingly esoteric point because I am a Jew who lived in Beersheba for six months back in 1976. The name of the town means "seven wells" in Hebrew. Often, I would go for hikes in the nearby desert and visit with Bedouin in their tents in the very area where Abraham and his family were said to have pitched their own tents, the very desert into which Hagar and Ishmael were cast out.

So for me, the historiography of this incident and most of the Torah taking place in the Land of Israel is important, is actually part and parcel of my core identity. Notice that I say historiography, not faith. I believe Abraham existed, even if parts of the story are apocryphal; that he wandered from Ur to Canaan, and that he and his family pitched their tents in the Negev Desert near Beersheba. The geographic details fortify me in that belief. Even more concretely, I believe that the First and Second Temples stood on Mount Moriah (the Temple Mount) in Jerusalem, where the Dome of the Rock stands today. I believe the latter point in the same way I believe the Declaration of Independence was signed in Philadelphia in 1776 or that Barack Obama was born in Hawaii, not Kenya—based on the preponderance of historical evidence, including, in the case of the two temples, plenty of archaeological evidence.

I respect the right of Muslims to believe Hagar and Ishmael found the well *Zam Zam* in Mecca, not in Beersheba, but honesty compels me to say that I find that belief disruptive of my historical narrative. I object more deeply to claims by some Palestinian religious and political leaders that the Jewish temples never stood on Mount Moriah at all, and therefore modern-day Jews have no claim of direct connection to the Land of Israel. As you know, Sabeeha, I am ready to share Israel-Palestine between Jews and Palestinians—I believe both peoples have strong claims to the Land. But I get uptight when folks invalidate my Jewish, historical connection.

Coming back to the question at hand, why do you believe that Hagar and Ishmael wandered all the way from Beersheba to Mecca before getting terribly thirsty, or that Mecca is the place where Abraham later came to visit Hagar and Ishmael?

Sabeeha: I never questioned that: how they ended up in Mecca. It's an integral part of our faith. But now that you ask, I went back to the scripture. Muhammad Asad, translator of the Qur'an, notes in his commentary, "[A] journey from Canaan to Mecca was by no means improbable if one bears in mind that for a camel-riding Bedouin (and Abraham was certainly one), a journey of twenty or even thirty days has never been anything out of the ordinary. At first glance . . . it appears to conflict with the Biblical statement (Genesis 21:14) that it was 'in the wilderness of Beersheba' (i.e., the southernmost tip of Palestine) that Abraham left Hagar and Ishmael. . . . However, to the ancient, town-dwelling Hebrews the term 'wilderness of Beersheba' comprised all the desert regions south of Palestine, including the Hijaz."[55] Camels can walk 120 miles a day. Mecca—in the Hijaz—is 920 miles from Jerusalem, a nine-day journey on camel.

As to your next question, the certainty of Mecca being the location is rooted in the Qur'an and the Hadith. It was Mecca where Abraham left Hagar and Ishmael, where Hagar went looking for water, running in between the hills of *Safa* and *Marwa*;[56] these two hills were located next to the Kaaba in Mecca;[57] that Abraham and Ishmael *together* built the first House of Worship in Mecca,[58] and where Abraham settled "some of his offspring."[59] In the seventh century CE, God commanded Prophet Muhammad to take this place where Abraham once stood as a place of prayer.[60] That house of worship—the Kaaba—is the direction we face in prayer; it is the place we visit when we perform the Hajj and walk in Abraham's footsteps. We walk between the two hills, paying homage

---

55 Muhammad Asad, *The Message of the Quran.* Qur'an 2:125. Commentary & Notes, 102.

56 Sahih Al-Bukhari, *The Anbiya*, vol. 4, book 55. #583.

57 Qur'an 2:158. "Hence, behold, As-Safa and Al-Marwa are among the symbol set up by God; and thus, no wrong does he who, having come to the Temple on pilgrimage or on a pious visit, strides to and fro between these two: for, if one does more good than he is bound to do—behold, God is responsive to gratitude, all-knowing."

58 Qur'an 2:127. "And when Abraham and Ishmael were raising the foundations of the Temple [They prayed:] 'O our Sustainer! Accept this from us: for You alone are The All-Hearing, The All-Knowing.'"

Qur'an 3:96. "Behold, the first Temple ever set up for mankind was indeed the one at Bakkah (Mecca)."

59 Qur'an 14:37. "O our Sustainer! Behold, I have settled some of my offspring in a valley in which there is no arable land, close to Thy sanctified Temple. . . ." Muhammad Asad's note #52: "The narrow desert valley of Mecca, which is enclosed by barren, rocky hills. By 'Some of my offspring' Abraham refers to Ishmael and his descendants who settled at Mecca."

60 Qur'an 2:125. "And Lo! We made the Temple a goal to which people might repair again and again, and a sanctuary: take, then the place whereon Abraham once stood as your place of prayer. And this did We command Abraham and Ishmael: 'Purify My Temple for those who will walk around it, and those who will bow down and prostrate themselves [in prayer].'"

to a mother's struggle, and we drink from the same spring—*Zam Zam*. Location, location, location.

I must confess, Walter, that prior to you asking, my belief rested on faith. But you compelled me to look for the evidence, and for that I thank you.

I believe we can put the Sarah/Hagar issue to rest. Muslims don't have an issue with Sarah, and we can differ about location—it was Mecca, it was Jerusalem—or who was to be sacrificed—Isaac or Ishmael—and while it is a cornerstone of my faith, it is not relevant to our relationship as cousins in faith. If there is a perceived conflict over what happened thousands of years ago, can we just leave it there and move on? Does that nearly prehistoric conflict matter? Not to me!

One more thing: Hagar was Abraham's *wife*, not his mistress. Abraham, the patriarch of monotheistic religions, God's friend,[61] would not have taken a concubine; he would have done things the right way and married her before having a child with her. That's my belief. By the way, I don't believe that Prophet David committed adultery or that Prophet Solomon had hundreds of concubines. The Qur'an holds all the Prophets in reverence: David was given the Psalms and Solomon the gift of knowing the language of the birds and having Jinns (invisible beings) in his army. Another "by the way," and this is serious: God says in the Qur'an that Prophet Abraham was a Muslim.[62] The literal definition of "Muslim" is "one who surrenders to God." Abraham submitted to the will of God, as did Moses, Jesus, Solomon, and David. They were all Muslims. Muslims are not "those who follow only Mohammad." We are not Mohammadans—and the term Muslim for the followers of Islam came into being in later years. So, in that sense, everyone who obeys God is a Muslim . . .

---

61 Qur'an: 4:125. "And who could be of better faith than he who surrenders his whole being unto God and is a doer of good withal, and follows the creed of Abraham, who turned away from all that is false—seeing that God took Abraham to Himself as a friend."

62 Qur'an: 3:67. "Abraham was neither a 'Jew' nor a 'Christian,' but was one who turned away from all that is false, having surrendered himself unto God [Muslim]; and he was not of those who ascribe divinity to aught beside Him."

Walter: . . . including the Jews.

Sabeeha: On that note, I declare the family feud to be over and done with. Shall we drink to that? Nonalcoholic for me.

Walter: A huge *shukran*, *todah*, and thank you, Sabeeha, for declaring the family feud over! I'm more than happy to join you in that declaration and in drinking said nonalcoholic toast to peace and reconciliation. First, the information and sentiment that you share above: that Muslims don't resent Sarah for sending Hagar and Ishmael out into the desert—indeed that Muslims revere Sarah, Isaac, and the whole line of Hebrew prophets emanating from Abraham and Sarah—is incredibly important for Jews to hear and process.

Allow me to share some of what your declaration and commentary evokes in me. I thank you and other Muslims for your forbearance and generosity of spirit toward Sarah, especially because I and many other Jews would consider the actions of Sarah—our matriarch—to be morally wrong, albeit all too human. Ultimately, I believe, we are understanding of Sarah's mistreatment of Hagar and her insistence that she and her son Ishmael should be cast out into the desert for the same reason Muslims are: namely, that the whole situation was orchestrated by God for his own purposes. We can show understanding of Sarah's behavior because God seems to have magnified her jealousy to the point where she could commit an act that—in the natural course of things—would soon lead to the death of two human beings. But God took care of things and didn't allow Hagar and Ishmael to die of thirst, instead blessing them and making Ishmael and his offspring a great nation, just as he did Isaac, Jacob, and their line.

Indeed, God made the Arab/Muslim nation a much larger one than He did the Jews. So, if anything, it could be said that Hagar and Ishmael got the better deal. God also makes clear in the Torah in several quotations—Genesis 18 most famously—that He is giving the Land of Israel to Jacob and his descendants "from the river of Egypt to the great River, the Euphrates." That is, to be sure, considerably larger than the Land of Israel today, but still validates the Jewish connection and sense of ownership of that Land that goes back to the very beginning.

I think most Jews are comfortable with that equation and that bargain: Muslims get half the world from Indonesia to Morocco, but Jews get to keep their beloved Land of Israel. Liberal Jews like me believe strongly that we must share the land in an ethically acceptable manner with the Palestinians. Yet, I very much share with the majority of my coreligionists the belief that the Land of Israel is truly my Land, the lodestone that constantly draws me homeward, the place to which I belong in spirit.

Just as most Jews would agree there is no point in pillorying Sarah for letting her jealousy get the better of her, most would readily acknowledge that her husband, the revered Abraham, also behaved poorly. According to Genesis 16:6, he informs Sarah, without even checking with God, that she can do to Hagar "as you see fit," sanctioning Sarah to mistreat the pregnant Hagar to the point that she can stand it no more and flees into the desert. There an Angel of God appears to her and says, "Return to your mistress and submit yourself to her domination" before promising that God would "greatly increase your offspring." Even so, the Angel of God seems to slur Hagar's son-to-be, by promising in Genesis 16:12, "He will be a wild-ass of a man; his hand against everyone, and everyone's hand against him. And over all his brothers he shall dwell." That line makes me extremely uncomfortable.

Several years thereafter, as we have seen, Abraham is morally troubled when Sarah demands that he "cast out" Hagar and her son Ishmael, after she sees the twelve-year-old Ishmael "mocking" the infant Isaac. Yet Abraham decides to comply after God reassures him that this is all in his plan. This passage at least shows that Abraham had a troubled conscience. For how long, in the natural order of things, would a woman and a boy last in the desert of Beersheba on one skin of water and a loaf of bread? Yet God had made amply clear to Abraham by that point in Genesis that He was running the show and would take care of Hagar and Ishmael.

Let us not forget that the Torah tells us that several decades later, upon the death of Abraham, his two sons came together to bury their father at the Cave of the Patriarchs (Machpelah) in Hebron-Al-Khalil. In the Torah, that coming together is treated as sort of a throwaway line, but I see the meeting of the two long-estranged half-brothers at their father's tomb as highly inspirational. In our new Muslim-Jewish movement, I believe adherents of both faiths need to look back to the Cave of the Patriarchs and put ourselves into the sandals of Ishmael and Isaac as they embraced each other.

Sabeeha, as to your other points, I'm happy to accept Hagar as Abraham's wife and not his concubine. Clearly, Abraham had strong feelings for her and for their son Ishmael. There have been important Jewish commentators over the millennia, including the medieval sage Rashi, who contend that Abraham's second wife, whom he married after the death of Sarah and who is identified as Keturah in Genesis 25:1, was actually Hagar under another name.

Yet I don't believe, as you do, that Abraham, David, and Solomon observed the moral niceties concerning sex and marriage. I believe the Torah account that David committed adultery with Bathsheba after sending her husband, Uriah the Hittite, off to war so he could be alone with her, and that he eventually had Uriah killed. It is noteworthy that David was condemned by the Prophet Nathan for his killing of Uriah, and that the subsequent death of Bathsheba's baby and the insurrection of David's son Avhalom are portrayed in the Torah as being the consequences of David's sins. I also believe Solomon had numerous concubines, as was standard operating procedure for important kings at that time.

I consider David and Solomon to be the greatest kings of Israel: leaders who made huge contributions to Jewish and world history. David created the Jewish nation-state centered in Jerusalem, and Solomon built the First Temple. Yet I also consider them to be flesh-and-blood figures who could, and did, sin. To me, they were no more "pure" than Thomas Jefferson, who wrote the Declaration of Independence but had an African American slave concubine. Some of America's greatest presidents, like Franklin D. Roosevelt, who created a more just America, took lovers, as did the modern American I most revere: Dr. Martin Luther King, one of the greatest moral leaders in human history. I would also point out that Judaism in biblical times allowed polygamy, as does Islam to this day under certain circumstances. So for me, the distinction between "wife" and "concubine" in our sacred texts becomes a little blurred.

Sabeeha, on your last point, that God says in the Qur'an that Abraham was a Muslim because the literal definition of "Muslim" is "one who surrenders to God," I am totally fine with that. The Torah makes clear that Abraham sired two nations—Jewish and Muslim—so I claim no ownership rights over him. He was truly the first Jew and the first Muslim. I am less comfortable about the concept of "submitting" to the will of a God I am not sure even exists. But I have come to know and care deeply for you and many other Muslim brothers and sisters who believe that concept deeply, and because of those personal interactions, I respect—even revere—that profound faith in God. I wish I had it.

So, if every person, living or dead, who submits themself to God is a Muslim, that would no doubt include many Jews and Christians, though perhaps not me, as I may not have enough faith and am not very good at submitting. The way I prefer to interpret that idea is that all sons and daughters of Abraham/Ibrahim are brothers and sisters, as ultimately are all human beings. We are one interdependent family; we stand or fall together, Muslims, Jews, Christians. Buddhists, Hindus, Jains, Baha'is, and Druze, people of all faiths and of no faith.

On that basis, I too declare the Sarah-Hagar family feud to be over! Let us declare a *sulha*, a reconciliation party, and drink that nonalcoholic toast to Hagar and Sarah, Abraham, Ishmael, Isaac, and everyone who came after them, including our children and ourselves. Let's remember that both Hagar and Sarah were women and human beings, manifesting both strengths and frailties while trying to fulfill their destinies as best they could under difficult circumstances. Hagar and Sarah sired our respective nations and so live on today in our flesh and bone marrow. They are our matriarchs and are part of us all. Let us cherish them together.

CHAPTER 15

THE ROAD FORWARD

Where does this leave us? Where does it take us?

Here in America, it leaves Muslims and Jews with a stark choice: to come together or stay apart. We have made the case as to *why* it is critical that we stand united and have listed some of the ways in which we have succeeded. But here is how we believe we can move forward as we work together to mitigate the impact of the Israeli-Palestinian conflict on our relationship.

Above all, we are Americans first. While the Israeli-Palestinian issue remains important and deeply emotional for both communities, it is now overshadowed by current events in America and globally: the crisis of democracy, climate change, the pandemic, and the rise of religious extremism in Islam, Judaism, and all major faiths. We have long related to the Israel-Palestine conflict as one that threatens the very survival of one or both of these two peoples, yet now, the whole world faces an existential threat. So, yes, Israel-Palestine still matters, but we live here, not there, and our common homeland of America and homelands all over the world are at risk unless we unite to save democracy and pluralism.

Second, American Muslims and Jews should acknowledge that Middle East policies are evolving rapidly and becoming more scrambled in ways that challenge our preconceptions. Since 2016, Saudi Arabia and the other states of the Gulf that are longtime enemies of Israel are drawing closer together in common enmity to Iran. We should also understand that the current leaders of Israel and Saudi Arabia, Benjamin Netanyahu and Prince Mohammed bin Salman, were not only ardent supporters of Trump but often mirrored his contempt for human rights and democracy and echoed his disinformation about "fake news." American Jews and Muslims who are uniting to protect democracy and pluralism in the United States should speak out when Israel violates the human rights of Palestinians or when the Saudi regime locks up advocates of human rights or murders its critics. The present Israeli government and dictatorships throughout the Arab world do not manifest the values that a majority of our two communities believe in, and we should call them out on it.

Third, Muslims and Jews should work together on humanitarian projects operated by nongovernmental organizations (NGOs) in Israel-Palestine, such as Project Rozana. When Walter organized a fundraising dinner for Project Rozana recently at the home of Dr. Maqsood Chaudhry in Virginia, more than one hundred people, an equal number of Muslims and Jews, came together and raised thousands of dollars. People of conscience may disagree on the parameters of an eventual political settlement, but we can and must come together to save lives and improve conditions on the ground. Undertaking this cause together will contribute to Muslim-Jewish cooperation and reconciliation in the United States as well as in Israel-Palestine. Instead of feeling angry, frustrated and helpless, we must take the initiative together to bring about a diminution in the suffering and loss of life among people impacted by the conflict. We must stand up for each other in America and around the world. What an inspiring and uplifting achievement that would be!

Fourth, Jews and Muslims should allow each other to speak up and say their piece, even when it makes some of us uncomfortable. The 2018 elections showed a growth in Muslim political power in the United States with the election of two American Muslim women in Congress, Palestinian American Rashida Tlaib of Michigan and Somali American Ilhan Omar of Minnesota. Their emergence dovetails with the rise of Linda Sarsour, one of the top leaders of the Women's March until resigning in 2019. While Tlaib, Omar, and Sarsour have said provocative and wounding things from the American Jewish perspective, Jews should not demonize them, but instead reach out and dialogue with them, explaining why many Jews found their comments hurtful while showing them the personal respect to which they are entitled. Just as Senators Chuck Schumer and Jacky Rosen and Representatives Lee Zeldin and Adam Schiff and many other Jewish Americans advocate in Congress on behalf of Israel without their loyalty to America being questioned, so Palestinian Americans and Muslim American congresspeople like Tlaib and Omar must be accorded the same right to speak up for Palestine and the Muslim world.

Fifth, we must work together to prevent the Israel-Palestine conflict from being weaponized—as it has been recently by introducing it into the American political debate in ways calculated to drive our two communities apart and thereby blunt the effectiveness of our newfound alliance. President Trump's outrageous statement that Jews are "disloyal" to both Israel and himself when they support the Democratic Party is just one blatant example of that bullying approach.

We believe that Jews and Muslims should together denounce the effort to criminalize support for the Boycott, Divestment, and Sanctions movement. Many do not support BDS—Walter is an example—but *do* uphold the right of Americans to advocate for any cause, including BDS, as an exercise of our right to freedom of speech. In that context, we oppose the campaign to delegitimize BDS as hate speech against Jews. That campaign has been making use of a new and expanded definition of anti-Semitism developed by the International Holocaust Remembrance Alliance (IHRA), which labels as anti-Semitic "denying the Jewish people their right to self-determination e.g. by claiming that the existence of a State of Israel is a racist endeavor" and "applying double standards by requiring of [Israel] a behavior not expected or demanded of any other democratic state." According to the ACLU, the IHRA definition of anti-Semitism "risks chilling the free speech of students on college campuses and is unnecessary to enforce federal law's prohibition on harassment in education." As with the anti-BDS push, criminalizing anti-Israel protest by promulgating a definition that conflates it with anti-Semitism may well lead to a situation where young Muslims, Jews, and other Americans risk imprisonment if they exercise their right to free expression. We cannot build a healthy Muslim-Jewish alliance while attempting to coerce advocates of either Palestine or Israel into silence.

Sixth, we shouldn't denigrate or demonize people on either side. Linda Sarsour correctly demands that she be able to speak freely as a proud Palestinian American, but we disagree with her demonization of Zionists, such as her statement that it is impossible to be both a Zionist and a feminist. There are plenty of Zionist feminists in Israel and in America. Indeed, many of the founding mothers of feminism were Jews who were supportive of Israel. A broad range of American Jews from left to right identify as Zionists; they support the right of Israel to exist as a Jewish state.

Seventh, just as Jews should engage with Muslims like Tlaib, Omar, and Sarsour, Muslims should engage with mainstream American Jews who consider themselves Zionists rather than allying exclusively with anti-Zionist fringe groups like Jewish Voices for Peace. If Jews talk only to a small coterie of pro-Israel Muslims and Muslims connect only with anti-Zionist Jews, no effective dialogue will take place, and our two communities will grow further apart. We need to dialogue with people with whom we may disagree on Israel-Palestine but agree on many others, including advocating for diversity, freedom of speech, and democracy here at home.

Eighth, let's be cautious about labeling one another as anti-Semitic or Islamophobic. We acknowledge the sensitivities of both communities. Jews have a painful history of suffering from anti-Semitism, and Muslims are facing the pain of carrying the burden of terrorist acts committed by extremist militants. Criticizing Israeli policies or political leaders is just that: a criticism of policies and policy makers, not a declaration against Jews. Likewise, being critical of the leaders or of policies carried out by a Muslim country does not translate into Islamophobia. At the same time, Muslims and Jews both need to be keenly aware of heightened sensitivities on the other side, and to formulate public statements in a way that they are not construed as anti-Semitic or Islamophobic, particularly if not meant as such. Respecting each other's sensitivities is simply being respectful.

We can build a mutually beneficial and uplifting relationship despite the elephant in the room. *InshAllah*. United we thrive, divided we wither. We have learned that building a positive Muslim-Jewish relationship in America has and will continue to benefit both communities and America as a whole. The goal of improving relations between our communities is too important to sacrifice for one more arid discussion on who is right and wrong in the Middle East. That debate leads nowhere.

So let's keep our eye on the prize and move forward together in America and around the world to build a vibrant network of Muslim-Jewish communication and cooperation, replete with enhanced relationships of friendship and trust between untold thousands of individual Jews and Muslims.

Kefaya. Nimas. Enough already with the conflict! We belong together and hereby resolve to refuse to be enemies.

ACKNOWLEDGMENTS

Our Joint Acknowledgments

Cal Barksdale, executive editor, Arcade Publishing for his invaluable direction, critique, and editorial guidance. Despite the demands on his time, Cal has always responded promptly to all our inquiries and calls for help, anytime and every time. Before accepting our manuscript for publication, he pressed us to ensure that our personal narratives stitched seamlessly together so as to convey that, despite our considerable differences in background and early life experiences, the two of us were on similar quests long before we ever met each other. We believe that our response to Cal's exacting advice served to make our book far more compelling and impactful than it might otherwise have been. Thank you, Cal, you are the best.

Mary von Aue for her editorial review of our first draft and helping us shape the direction and focus of the narrative. Dawn Raffel for developmental editing and devoting her summer to giving this book the attention it yearned for. Laila Al-Askari and Faroque Khan, MD, for reviewing the entire manuscript and offering their valuable input. Ambassador Akbar Ahmed, Ibn Khaldun, chair of Islamic Studies at American University, for advising us on the content and giving us the encouragement for taking on a sensitive subject. Others who gave generously of their time and offered us sage advice on streamlining the manuscript included Walter's brother, writer, editor, and genealogist Dan Ruby; lifelong friends of Walter and journalists extraordinaire Larry Cohler-Esses and Margaret Gillerman; Rabbi Nancy Fuchs-Kreimer of the Reconstructionist

Rabbinical College; Dr. Sam Freedman of Columbia Journalism School; and philosopher and social entrepreneur Peter Temes.

Sabeeha Rehman

My uncle, Khalid Javed a.k.a. Jedi Mamoon, who provided me with some of the most tantalizing and horrific stories about Partition of India and Pakistan, most notably the train ride; and for illuminating me on some of the nuances of the history of Partition. Dr. Junaid Ahmad, notable Pakistani author and academician, who devoted over an hour of his time to educate me on the history of Pakistan and the war of 1971.

My son Asim Rehman, niece Komal Kazim, and Khalid's niece Irsa Shoukat, for reviewing and providing feedback on sections of the manuscript; Fizza Sultan, Khalid's niece, for spending hours crafting the first concept of the book cover.

Members of my writers group who critiqued, deliberated over, and instructed me on my entire narrative. Thank you, Michele Duffy, Alice Cody, Caryn Schlesinger, Guirlaine Belizdire, Maureen Griffo, Maryann Giarratano, Andrea King, Toby Levine, Joanne Lyman, Peter Neumann, Chris Richter, Jackie Schechter, and Ron Trenkler-Thomson, and the Yorkville Writers Circle for their feedback and input under the steady leadership of Ron Trenkler-Thomson.

Daisy Khan, executive director, Women's Islamic Initiative in Spirituality and Equality (WISE), who introduced me to the vibrant life of interfaith bridge building in post-9/11 New York City. Maureen Rovegno, director of religion, Chautauqua Institution, who opened the doors to the interfaith community, enabling my husband and me to take our message to people across the United States. Imam Khalid Latif, Islamic Center of NYU, and Imam Feisal Abdul Rauf, Cordoba House, whose spiritual leadership enabled me to embrace a pluralistic vision of the faith. Fred Zirm and Janay Cosner, Friends of Chautauqua Writers' Center, for introducing me to the community of writers.

Rabbi Frank A. Tamburello, spiritual leader of The MAKOR Center for Spiritual Judaism, for educating me in Judaism and its history.

Michelle Koch, Executive Director, Muslim-Jewish Solidarity Committee, for including me in her relentless efforts to make interfaith engagement a joyous and culturally rich experience.

My nearest and dearest: our sons, Saqib Rehman and Asim Rehman, for humoring and encouraging Mom; and my husband, Khalid, my self-appointed agent, manager, promoter, publicist, facilitator, supporter-in-chief, and the love of my life, thank you for taking over all my responsibilities to help me focus on writing.

Walter Ruby

To my loving and deeply supportive sister and brother, Joanne and Dan Ruby; Joanne's husband, Bill Rehm, and their children, Zach and Lani; Dan's ex-wife, Kate Eilertsen, and daughter Twyla, and Tanya's daughter Hannah and her husband, Robby Bolcar. To my wonderful ex-wives Gloria Ruby and Mila Ruby; also my Israeli cousins, including Raya and Amiram Finkel, their son Achikam, Ruti Sharon, her daughter Dalit, and to the memory of Raya's parents and my aunt and uncle Penina and Ze'ev Sharon and their son Avinoam, lost in the Yom Kippur War.

To a few of the many wonderful people who contributed to my journalistic career, including my late editors at the *Jerusalem Post*, Ari Rath, Erwin Frenkel, and David Landau, and to then Washington correspondent Wolf Blitzer. To Jerry and Naomi Lippman, coeditor-publishers of the *Long Island Jewish World*, Robert Goldblum, ex-managing editor at the *New York Jewish Week*, and fellow practitioners of the esoteric art of Jewish journalism Larry Cohler-Esses, Winston Pickett, Ezra Goldstein, Larry Yudelson, and Andrew Silow-Carroll.

To dear friends from my time in Moscow and beyond: Marina Labonville, Leonid and Yelena Denisova.

To the memory of Maria Espinosa and to friends and colleagues from the Jewish-Palestinian Encounter: Chahine Hamila, Ira Weiss, Avi Katz, Efraim Perlmutter, and Aref Dajani, my coauthor of *Two States, One Common Land*.

To Khalid Lateef, a friend and brother with whom I hit the road in the 1990s to hold *A Candid Conversation between a White Jew and a Black Muslim*.

To Rabbi Marc Schneier, president of the Foundation for Ethnic Understanding (FFEU), who gave me the life-transforming opportunity to immerse myself in the field of Muslim-Jewish relations. To wonderful FFEU colleagues Samia Hathroubi, Will Eastman, Chris Sacarabany, Marie Banzon-Prince, and Ali Naqvi.

Here are a few of the people in Muslim-Jewish and Israeli-Palestinian relations in America and around the world with whom I have worked fruitfully and who moved me to enhanced understanding and inspiration:

In North America

Washington, DC: Andra Baylus, Dr. Maqsood Chaudhry, Rizwan Jaka, Hurunnessa Fariad, Imam Mohammed Magid, Dr. Sayyid Syeed, Professor Akhbar Ahmad, Dr. Mohammed Elsanousi, Gary Sampliner, Ibrahim Anli, Rashid Telbisoglu, Sahar Khamis, Susan Weiss, Symi Rom-Rymer, Rabbi Gerry Serotta, Dan Spiro, Andrea Barron, Catherine Orsborn, Ovais Sheikh, Parvez Khan, Dalia Mogahed, Meira Neggaz, Maggie Siddiqi, Nazli Chaudhry, Sabir Rahman, Rabbi Jeff Saxe, Qadir Abdus-Salaam, Imam Talib Shareef

New York and Long Island: Dr. Faroque Khan, Rabbi Yehuda Sarna, Imam Khalid Latif, Daisy Khan, Rabbi Bob Kaplan, Sheikh Moussa Drammeh, Rachmiel Harris, Afshan Haque, Peggy Kurtz, Kenneth Bob, Imam Shamsi Ali

New Jersey: Dr. Ali Chaudhry, Zamir Hassan, Mehdi Elififi, Rabbi Deb Smith, Mashal Anjun, Imam Alfred Muhammad, Jacob Toporek, Sheryl Olitzsky

Philadelphia: Dr. Racelle Weiman, Rabbi Nancy Fuchs-Kreimer

Los Angeles: Dr. Muzammil Siddiqi, Shepha Vainstein, Noor-Malika Chishti, Tasneem Noor, Aziza Hassan, Jihad Turk

Chicago and Minneapolis: Brian Zakem, Imam Wallace Muhammad, Rabbi Amy Eilberg

Detroit: Victor Begg, Rabbi Dorit Edut, Siham Jaafer, Arif Husic, Tareq Beydoun

Dallas: Azhar Azeez

San Francisco Bay Area: Rabbi Melanie Aron, Maha Elgenaidi

Atlanta: Soumaya Khalifa

Denver: Rabbi Stephen Booth-Nadav

Toronto: Karen Mock, Barbara Landau, Shahid Akhtar, Samira Kanji

In Europe and around the World

France: Rabbi Michel Serfaty, Rabbi Joseph Abittan, Mufti Dalil Boubakeur, Samia Hathroubi

Italy: Rabbi Joseph Levi, Imam Izzeddin Elzir

Austria: Ilja Sichrovsky

United Kingdom: Heather Fletcher, Qaisra Shahraz, Mohammed Amin, Jonny Wineberg, Esmond Rosen, Fiyaz Mughal, Dr. Muhammad Alhussaini, Rabbi Reuben Livingstone, Rabbi Jackie Tabick

Israel: Rabbi Bob Carroll, Yehuda Stolov, Rafaela Barkay

Belgium: Rabbi Albert Guigui, Phillip Carmel, John Malkinson, Robin Sciafani

Scandinavia: Tali Padan, Rebecca Lillian, Imam Senaid Kobilica

Australia: Jeremy Jones

New Zealand: Paul Morris

South Africa: David Jacobson

Morocco: Aicha Haddou, Andre Azoulay

Tunisia: Yamina Thabet

Ukraine: Iosif Zissels, Eduard Dolinsky, and my dear friends among the Crimean Tatars

ABOUT THE AUTHORS

Sabeeha Rehman

Sabeeha Rehman is a blogger, public speaker, and the author of the memoir *Threading My Prayer Rug. One Woman's Journey from Pakistani Muslim to American Muslim*. Her memoir was a finalist for the 2018 William Saroyan International Prize for Writing, received honorable mention in the Spirituality category from the San Francisco Book Festival Awards 2017, and was listed as a Top 10 Religion and Spirituality Book in 2016 and a Top 10 Diverse Nonfiction Book in 2017 by *Booklist*. The forum Wiki Ezvid selected Ms. Rehman and her memoir for inclusion in "5 Non-Fiction Writers Telling Captivating Stories." Ms. Rehman is an op-ed contributor to the "Houses of Worship" column of the *Wall Street Journal*. Her pieces have been published in the *New York Daily News, Forward, Salon.com, Tiferet*, and *Patheos.com*.

Ms. Rehman emigrated from Pakistan to the United States in 1971 after her marriage to a Pakistani doctor in New York. She holds a masters in healthcare administration and had a twenty-five-year career as a hospital executive that spanned hospitals in New York, New Jersey, and Saudi Arabia.

When her grandson Omar was diagnosed with autism, she left her career as a healthcare executive and devoted herself to serving families affected by autism. In 2008, she cofounded the National Autism Association New York Metro chapter (www.nationalautismny.org) and served as its president from 2008 to 2011.

Ms. Rehman has spent several decades engaging in interfaith dialogue as a public speaker. Since the publication of her book, she has given more than 250 talks in nearly a hundred cities at houses of worship, academic institutions, libraries, and community organizations, including Chautauqua Institution. She has lectured on the art of memoir writing at academic institutions including Hunter College, New York, and is a moderator for the Yorkville Writing Circle of the New York Public Library.

Sabeeha serves as a board member of the Muslim-Jewish Solidarity Committee and the National Autism Association New York Metro chapter. She has served as a judge in the nonfiction writing contest for *Tiferet*. She blogs on topics related to American Muslim experience and current events on her website at www.sabeeharehman.com.

She lives in New York City with her husband, Khalid, a retired hematologist/oncologist. They have two sons and four grandchildren.

Walter Ruby

Walter Ruby had a life-changing experience as a reporter covering the World Congress of Imams and Rabbis for Peace in Seville, Spain in 2006 and decided to dedicate himself going forward to the mission of nurturing ties of communication, reconciliation, and cooperation between Jews and Muslims.

From 2008 to 2017, as Muslim-Jewish relations director at the New York–based Foundation for Ethnic Understanding, Ruby acted as a new kind of *shadchan* (Yiddish for "matchmaker"), bringing together grassroots Muslims and Jews across the United States and around the world for dialogue, friendship building, and joint community service actions. He also worked to build lasting bonds between synagogues and mosques and Muslim and Jewish organizations. Walter presently serves as executive director of Jews, Muslims and Allies Acting Together (JAMAAT), an eclectic community of Muslim, Jewish, and Interfaith activists in Greater Washington, and as coordinator of the Washington area chapter of Project Rozana, which works to strengthen ties between Israelis and Palestinians through health care.

Ruby worked as a journalist for more than thirty years, writing for the *Jerusalem Post, Ma'ariv*, the *Forward, New York Jewish Week, London Jewish Chronicle, Washington Jewish Week, Long Island Jewish World*, and other publications. During his career, he had postings in Haifa, New York, and Moscow and covered stories of Jewish interest or related to the Israeli-Palestinian peace process in various locales including Algiers, Geneva, Berlin, Cairo, Mumbai, Reykjavik, Bogota, and Asuncion. Walter is a coauthor, together with his brother Dan Ruby, of the recently published memoir of Holocaust survivor Michael Edelstein entitled *Live Another Day: How I Survived the Holocaust and Realized the American Dream*. Ruby presently writes a blog focused primarily on politics entitled Walter Ruby: Keeping Hope Alive, https://bywalterruby.blogspot.com/.

A passionate traveler with a penchant for long-distance rambles on foot, Walter lives with his wife, Tanya, in Frederick, Maryland.